AMON CARTER

AMON CARTER

A LONE STAR LIFE

BRIAN A. CERVANTEZ
FOREWORD BY BOB RAY SANDERS

UNIVERSITY OF OKLAHOMA PRESS : NORMAN

This book is published with the generous assistance of the
McCasland Foundation, Duncan, Oklahoma.

Photograph on title page: Amon G. Carter Sr. (1879–1955). Courtesy of Special Collections, Mary Couts Burnett Library, Texas Christian University, Fort Worth.

Library of Congress Cataloging-in-Publication Data

Names: Cervantez, Brian, author.
Title: Amon Carter : A Lone Star Life / Brian A. Cervantez ; foreword by Bob Ray Sanders
Description: Norman : University of Oklahoma Press, 2019. | Includes bibliographical references and index.
Identifiers: LCCN 2018032839 | ISBN 978-0-8061-6198-3 (hardcover) ISBN 978-0-8061-9321-2 (paper) Subjects: LCSH: Carter, Amon Giles, 1879–1955. | Journalists—Texas—Biography. | Publishers and publishing—Texas—Biography. | Civic leaders—Texas—Biography. | Texas—Biography.
Classification: LCC PN4874.C26 C47 2019 | DDC 070.5092 [B] —dc23
LC record available at https://lccn.loc.gov/2018032839

The paper in this book meets the guidelines for permanence and durability of the Committee on Production Guidelines for Book Longevity of the Council on Library Resources, Inc. ∞

Copyright © 2019 by the University of Oklahoma Press, Norman, Publishing Division of the University. Paperback published 2023. Manufactured in the U.S.A.

All rights reserved. No part of this publication may be reproduced, stored in a retrieval system, or transmitted, in any form or by any means, electronic, mechanical, photocopying, recording, or otherwise—except as permitted under Section 107 or 108 of the United States Copyright Act—without the prior written permission of the University of Oklahoma Press. To request permission to reproduce selections from this book, write to Permissions, University of Oklahoma Press, 2800 Venture Drive, Norman OK 73069, or email rights.oupress@ou.edu.

For Stacey, whose love and support made this book possible

CONTENTS

List of Illustrations • ix
Foreword, by Bob Ray Sanders • xi
Acknowledgments • xv

CHAPTER 1 Last of the Empire Builders • 3
CHAPTER 2 The Formative Years • 12
CHAPTER 3 Building a Media Empire • 27
CHAPTER 4 Laying the Foundations for Political Success • 54
CHAPTER 5 For the Exclusive Benefit of Fort Worth • 91
CHAPTER 6 Waterways, Airways, Oil Production, and the Home Front • 119
CHAPTER 7 Triumphs and Trials in Peace and War • 149
CHAPTER 8 The Final Decade • 177

Notes • 211
Bibliography • 233
Index • 241

ILLUSTRATIONS

Amon Carter at three years • 79

William H. Carter and Ella Patterson Carter in 1895 • 80

William H., Addie, and Amon Carter, 1895 • 80

Amon Carter and a companion, 1896 • 81

Amon Carter, late 1890s • 81

Amon Carter and H. E. Finney, seated in aviator Cal Rodgers's airplane, 1911 • 82

Amon Carter golfing at the Grand Canyon, 1915 • 82

Amon and Nenetta at their Rivercrest home, 1922 • 83

Carter and Texas Christian University quarterback Davey O'Brien, 1938 • 84

Carter at a publishers' convention in New York, 1938 • 85

Carter and W. G. Chandler, 1937 • 86

Carter and Helen Rogers Reid, 1939 • 87

Invitation to an event at Carter's Shady Oak Farm • 88

Shady Oak farmhouse • 88

Shady Oak living room • 89

Carter with President Harry Truman at the dedication of Big Bend National Park, 1950 • 90

Carter, Dwight Eisenhower, Sid Richardson, and Katrine Deakins, 1950 • 90

FOREWORD

AS A NATIVE OF FORT WORTH whose roots in Tarrant County, Texas, go back more than 150 years, I could hardly have escaped the shadow and the dominating influence of the iconic Amon G. Carter Sr. And, as one who was eventually hired as a journalist by Carter's newspaper, the *Fort Worth Star-Telegram,* inevitably I came to know him as an almost mythical character.

In this book about the life of "Mr. Fort Worth," author Brian Cervantez does an outstanding job of demystifying the man without diminishing those traits and qualities that many in Fort Worth and Texas have come to admire in this heroic business, civic, and political leader. Carter's is an incredible story that Cervantez tells well, interweaving his struggles, dogged determination, and accomplishments with his faults and failures.

Simply put, the author presents Carter as human (with noticeable flaws), from his birth in 1879 to a West Texas farm family to his final days, when, despite suffering from heart disease, he was still wheeling and dealing.

Amon Carter: A Lone Star Life is a well-researched book, as evidenced by the hundreds of endnotes provided. However, it does not read like an academic thesis in which the scholarship gets in the way of an amazing story about a most remarkable man. There is no difficulty in following one man's incredible journey from a traveling salesman to a media mogul; from an oil baron to a beloved philanthropist; from civic cheerleader to political power broker.

Anyone as powerful and influential as Carter was obviously complex, and Cervantez documents those complexities in a way that allows the reader to better understand his subject's thinking, actions, and sheer drive as his city's and West Texas's foremost booster.

While gaining a more thorough view of Carter's life, the reader also gets a clearer picture of Fort Worth in the first half of the twentieth century, as well as an understanding of the concept of "western vs. southern." Carter's fascination with "the West" and his infatuation with western art only add to the curiosity surrounding a man with so many diverse interests.

Through research of Carter's abundant papers at the Texas Christian University Mary Couts Burnett Library, personal correspondence with some of the most powerful people in business and politics, and press coverage from around the country, Cervantez is able to paint a picture of a man who had numerous conflicts with business associates and whose family life suffered as a result of his devotion to business and empire building.

The book provides more details about Carter's maneuvers to attract major industries—railroads, packing companies, aviation and defense plants—to his city "Where the West Begins," and how he was able to persuade Washington to allocate money for some of his pet projects. New insight is also provided as to how hard he worked unsuccessfully on a dream to channelize the Trinity River, creating a commercial waterway between North Texas and Houston.

Of course, Carter's often-documented rivalry with Dallas and its leaders is discussed, but this book covers that subject beyond the myths and deals intricately with some of the nuances that sometimes pitted him against rivals to the east and other times led him to join forces with them if he thought it was good for Fort Worth and Tarrant County.

Cervantez also gives us an up close look at the less-than-ideal relationship between Carter and his family—his wives and children. As with most things in this millionaire's life, those interactions are complicated, but the author is able to convey that part of the story in an unbiased way, leaving judgment to the reader. How the family deals with Carter's son, Amon Carter Jr., being captured and imprisoned by the Germans in World War II is quite revealing.

Nor is the issue of race relations in Fort Worth and North Texas avoided in this new work. Some examples of harsh bigotry are given, as well as one instance in which Carter put on his entrepreneurial hat to capitalize on a cruel incident in Dallas. Still, it is left to the reader to decide Carter's own racial views.

Cervantez provides students of history, business, politics, the arts, and philanthropy a fresh look at a man who had an enormous impact in all those areas and an everlasting impact on the city he loved and helped shape.

Even those who consider themselves experts on Carter or Fort Worth are bound to learn something new about both after reading this book.

—Bob Ray Sanders

ACKNOWLEDGMENTS

THIS BOOK WOULD NOT have come about without the help and contributions of a number of scholars and researchers whose work made possible a scholarly analysis of the life of Amon G. Carter. More specifically, I am grateful for the assistance of Elizabeth Hayes Turner and Ronald Marcello, both at the University of North Texas, who were of great help to me when this manuscript was in its earliest stages as my master's thesis. Richard McCaslin, also at the University of North Texas, agreed to take me on as one of his doctoral students and guided my dissertation to completion. His patience, editorial suggestions, scholarly commentary, and joviality proved to be invaluable to this project in both its dissertation and manuscript forms.

I am, of course, grateful to those who were willing to read this manuscript and provide useful critiques of my writing and content. Carl Abbott at the University of Portland, whose work on the urban West provided me with a useful framework within which to analyze Carter, and Ron Tyler, former director of the Amon Carter Museum of American Art, were both essential to this project's completion. No work of this magnitude would be possible without the assistance of those laboring in archives and manuscript collections. In this regard, I would like to thank Lisa Pena, specialist at the Texas Christian University Special Collections, where the Amon G. Carter Papers are housed, for her contributions. She patiently brought me hundreds of boxes of Carter-related materials, made copies, and scanned images—all while maintaining an interest in my work. I am also grateful to Jon Frembling, archivist at the Amon Carter Museum, for his assistance, especially for enlightening me as to the ins and outs of researching an individual's art collection.

This book was, in many ways, the result of a lifetime of interest in the life of Amon G. Carter. Growing up in Fort Worth in a family full of Fort Worthians meant being reminded constantly of his contributions to the city. I am grateful to my parents, Tony and Rhonda Cervantez, for encouraging my interest in history from a young age. Their stories of growing up in Fort Worth first sparked in me an interest in Mr. Carter.

Last, but definitely not least, I would like to thank my wife, Stacey. Her unceasing love, support, patience, and encouragement were essential to my completion of this book. For that I will always be grateful.

—Brian A. Cervantez

AMON CARTER

CHAPTER 1

LAST OF THE EMPIRE BUILDERS

ON JUNE 24, 1955, Majority Leader Lyndon Baines Johnson, Democrat from Texas, delivered a special address on the floor of the U.S. Senate. In this address, Johnson eulogized the recently deceased Amon G. Carter Sr. of Fort Worth, calling him "one of the great moving forces of our time . . . a towering figure in the daily life of our citizens." Back in Fort Worth, the day after Carter's burial, fifteen thousand people paid tribute at his grave in the city's Greenwood Cemetery. Widely recognized across the nation as "Mr. Fort Worth," Carter left behind a city and state that in numerous ways reflected his influence. Evidence of the seeming infinitude of personal and business contacts he had amassed came in the form of condolences that poured into the Fort *Worth Star-Telegram*'s offices upon the announcement of his death. President Dwight D. Eisenhower, a close acquaintance of Carter's since their meeting during the Second World War, remarked that he was "terribly shocked and distressed to hear" of his death. Comedian Edgar Bergen lamented that "the people of Fort Worth have lost a great man . . . I have lost a valuable friend." Former vice president and fellow Texan John Nance Garner shed some of his characteristic prickliness to say, "I have lost a dear friend." Entertainer and Broadway producer Billy Rose observed,

"He was the last of the empire builders and Fort Worth is his monument." These telegrams and memorials illustrate the reach and breadth of Carter's professional and personal relationships, associations cultivated in his quest to be the foremost civic booster for Fort Worth and West Texas.[1]

Carter was born into a poor rural family on December 10, 1879, and his early surroundings and childhood made it difficult to believe he was destined to become one of the most influential Texans of the mid-twentieth century. Despite the obvious shortcomings of his upbringing, he quickly demonstrated an ambitious, enterprising nature, first as a "chicken and bread boy" selling sandwiches to train passengers in his hometown of Bowie, Texas, at the age of thirteen. After spending his late teens and early twenties as a traveling picture frame salesman throughout the Great Plains, he settled briefly in San Francisco to work in advertising. Despite a promising future in California, Carter moved back to Texas, where he connected with Fort Worth investors looking to start a newspaper. By 1909, this daily had become the *Fort Worth Star-Telegram*. Much of Carter's widespread influence emanated from his position as the founder and publisher of the *Star-Telegram*, turning it into the most widely circulated newspaper in Texas by the mid-twentieth century. Ever watchful of technological trends, in 1922 he established WBAP as the *Star-Telegram*'s radio arm, and in 1948 added its television counterpart WBAP-TV. Due in part to Carter's presence and influence, Fort Worth and Tarrant County attracted many major businesses, such as General Motors and Bell Helicopter, and government-funded projects, including the Will Rogers Memorial Complex and the Frontier Centennial, that attested not only to the city's dynamism but also to Carter's innate ambition.[2]

Carter diversified his contributions to the city of Fort Worth and the state of Texas during his time as *Star-Telegram* publisher. He is perhaps most remembered today for the western American art museum in Fort Worth that bears his name (he collected the art of Frederic Remington and Charles Russell—at the turn of the twentieth century, two of the most prominent artists of the American West)—but he made many other contributions to Texas and Fort Worth. Ever cognizant of the need for higher education, Carter lobbied for a state university for West Texas and was rewarded for his efforts when Texas Technological College opened in Lubbock in 1925. As early as 1911, he saw aviation's potential and promoted air transport whenever possible; within two decades he became one of the founding board members and investors of American Airways, later American Airlines. During the Great Depression and World War II, Carter leveraged his rising influence with the Roosevelt administration to gain New Deal dollars for construction projects in the city, as well as a Consolidated Aircraft plant that churned out thousands of B-24 Liberator bombers for the war effort. And, by striking oil in the 1930s, he became a millionaire and was thus able to contribute even more to his philanthropic efforts through the Amon Carter Foundation and to his personal collection of western American art.[3]

While it is relatively easy to list Carter's numerous achievements, it is much more difficult to explain the man's rise from obscure, humble origins to become a builder of a regional media empire with widespread political and economic influence. At first glance, Carter's career embodies the "Texas Myth" described by historian Randolph Campbell, a legend that "depends on a generalized belief in the Lone Star State as an exceptional place in the world, the home of self-reliant individuals who take advantage of the bountiful opportunities provided by a new American Eden." This Texas myth complements Carl Abbott's argument that for many people, the idea of the frontier West (of which Fort Worth was unquestionably, if not wholly, a part) "emphasized personal success rather than community achievement." After all, Abbott continues, "the frontier has long been viewed as the true home of the expectant capitalist, the ambitious individual for whom enterprise is a calling to be tirelessly pursued." Carter certainly pursued enterprise not only for himself but also on behalf of what he believed was his city, demonstrating his belief that his success and the success of Fort Worth were inextricably intertwined. Yet, as much as Carter might have believed in the Texas myth, his actions confirm a certain acceptance of community values and government intervention. He needed Fort Worth as much as Fort Worth needed him. Never one to wax philosophical, he rarely, if ever, articulated his motives for his persistent promotion of the city. His communications with friends and colleagues persistently lauded Fort Worth and showed a man who developed an emotional attachment to his new home, but he never explained why he chose to lavish his attention, energy, and fortune on that particular city. This leaves scholars the task of analyzing the existing archival material to assess what his motives might have been. Carter's correspondence reveals an ambitious man possessing a large ego, an insatiable appetite for success, and dogged perseverance. A cynic might argue that this was purely exploitative on Carter's part, who realized that if Fort Worth expanded, so would the reach of his newspaper and, thus, his profit margins. While self-interest was certainly part of Carter's inspiration, the consistent enthusiasm with which he promoted his city's interests (as he interpreted them) and the close bond he developed with Fort Worth complicate the matter.[4]

The image Carter developed as "Mr. Fort Worth" reflects what historian Blaine Brownell calls the "urban ethos," defined as "a general overarching concept of the city which stressed the desirability—indeed the necessity—of both urban growth and social order in such a way that they would be mutually reinforcing." The urban boosterism that Carter was so famous for (in 1952, *Time* magazine called him "a civic monument, which unlike San Antonio's Alamo, Houston's Shamrock, and Dallas' Cotton Bowl, can walk and talk at incredible speed") was "actually an expression of the urban ethos . . . a rhetorical effort to achieve the realization of the corporate-expansive city by promoting urban unity, growth, and commercial-civic opportunities." Carter devoted much of his time and a good portion of newspaper space promoting these goals for Fort Worth, a reflection of his role as one of the "first Texas news barons," as historian Patrick Cox argues. Like other contemporary Texas media moguls, Carter influenced "public opinion and policy making" while maintaining "ties with the growing commercial concerns of the state and its dominant political class."[5]

Careful study of Carter's actions within their historical context reveal that he synthesized the western urban booster ethic emphasizing aggressive urban growth, commercial development, and technological prowess with the New South business progressive philosophy. This message of business progressivism was very much in the tradition of New South boosterism begun by earlier newspaper publishers prominent in the New South movement in the 1880s, such as Henry Grady of the *Atlanta Journal Constitution* and Richard Hathaway Edmonds of the *Baltimore Manufacturers' Record*. Like-minded individuals promoted this vision for decades throughout Texas and other southern states. Carter was part of a wave of urban southern boosters, "newcomers on the make . . . willing to take financial risks and to embrace modern technologies and economic associations." Like other civic-minded southerners, Carter "merged with national elites" in "believ[ing] that progressive reforms were good for business." By the latter part of his life, he had become a member of what historian George Green called the Texas "establishment," a "loosely-knit plutocracy of the Anglo upper classes" that regularly involved themselves in state and national politics.[6]

Yet, as much as Carter embodied the twentieth-century New South booster ethos, he simultaneously reflected a quintessentially western urban ethos. Carter's and Fort Worth's orientation and identity ultimately faced the American West in both its real and mythological forms. Under his watchful eye, the *Star-Telegram* evolved into the primary newspaper for many West Texans, and their many intersecting interests were quintessentially western, according to historians of the

Urban West. Carl Abbott proposes that western cities have "been distinguished by a special relationship with wide open spaces," even though "they hold all the region's population and economic power." Fort Worth fits Abbott's model in that, like his typical western city, it developed relationships with government and industry to help transform itself into a hub for defense and aviation because of its available space. Such connections are more often cultivated by aggressive, articulate, and ambitious boosters such as Carter than they are by faceless Chamber of Commerce members.[7]

Just as Dallas, Fort Worth's rival city thirty miles to the east, served as the commercial hub for Northeast Texas, Fort Worth emerged as the de facto capital of West Texas, a "gateway city" to the arid yet increasingly fertile plains of the region. This western orientation so heavily promoted by Carter, whose public appearances were often punctuated by the cry "Hurray for West Texas and Fort Worth!" was mirrored by traditionally southern attitudes regarding Jim Crowism and the deep chasm between white and black citizens of the city as well as by the region's affinity for a one-party political system dominated by the Democratic Party. The city's population, like many others in Texas, was heavily southern in origin and in its perspectives on race and politics. And Carter, to be sure, never appeared to question this sociopolitical milieu. That said, Fort Worth's rapid growth in the twentieth century, with Carter serving as a catalyst, echoes that of western cities more than southern cities. In sum, it appears that the symbiotic relationship between the city and the man thrived in a context of a western economy developed in a southern social setting.

No discussion of Carter is complete without referring to the fierce rivalry he developed with Dallas. Enmity between the two cities was not something Carter created, but his aggressive boosting and rowdy persona provided nourishment for the rivalry—at least when he deemed it necessary. Whether the issue was an airport or the Texas Centennial celebration, he found ways to draw attention to what had once been a more traditional competition so common between cities in the late nineteenth and early twentieth centuries. As will be seen, this rivalry had much to do with outsiders viewing Carter as the primary power broker and spokesman for Fort Worth. Since their respective births, both cities featured enterprising male citizens who took it upon themselves to promote what they saw as their community's interests. But while Dallas had its Citizens Council, a select group of businessmen who dominated the city's politics from the 1930s until the 1970s, and Houston had its "Suite 8F" clique—a group that included Jesse Jones, owner of the *Houston Chronicle*, and William Hobby, owner of the *Houston*

Post—Fort Worth in the first decades of the twentieth century had neither an organized coterie like the Citizens Council nor an elite clique like Houston's.[8]

Loose organizations calling themselves the "Citizen Committee" or the "Good Government League" pushed for progressive business initiatives such as the adoption of a council/manager government in Fort Worth to replace the commission system, but none of these functioned in the same way as the Citizens Council or even San Antonio's Good Government League. By the 1940s, there were whispers of what Fort Worth critics called the "Seventh Street Gang," an informal group of businessmen such as retailers Marvin Leonard and W. K. Stripling, H. B. "Babe" Fuqua of the Fort Worth National Bank, and Carter's closest friend late in life, wealthy oilman Sid Richardson. These individuals, among others, met regularly in Carter's suite at the Fort Worth Club to discuss local politics and business initiatives. Such an informal group kept no records and had no fixed membership, but it seems safe to say that Carter dominated the group, such as it was. He was the only one, Sid Richardson excepted, who had national prominence and he controlled local media; Carter's unique position allowed him to exploit this power, and it just so happened that he had the personality and ambition to encourage such exploitation. Ironically, it was arguably his ability to dominate the city that contributed to Fort Worth's failure to match its eastern neighbor's success; "one-man rule" certainly had its drawbacks. In *Urban Texas: Politics and Development,* Char Miller and Heywood Sanders contend that at the turn of the century, Fort Worth was in a position to seriously challenge Dallas for supremacy in the region, as it was experiencing a faster rate of growth and possessed boosters just as aggressive as those of the larger city. However, they argue, "it appears that Dallas's businesspeople won this race by adopting a more sophisticated approach to economic development." Where Fort Worth focused on meatpacking and, later, oil, Dallas developed a much more diversified economy that reflected business leadership from across the spectrum of enterprises. When Fort Worth (and Tarrant County) was able to secure prominent manufacturing facilities during Carter's life, they were those of larger outside firms such as Consolidated Aircraft and General Motors. Though arguably the most famous individual in Fort Worth or Dallas by the end of his life, Carter left behind a city remarkably different yet still second to its eastern rival.[9]

Carter's exceptional qualities make it difficult to find a comparable figure in the South or the West. Most urban boosters operated collectively, not individually, and those boosters who emerge as more forceful figures, such as Jesse Jones in Houston or George Dealey in Dallas, did not enjoy the ability to implement "one-man rule" or speak singularly as Carter was able to in Fort Worth, nor did they possess Carter's ebullient, yet petulant, personality that attracted attention nationwide. In addition, Carter's formative business experiences as an adult were in sales, a fitting beginning for someone who took it upon himself to sell not just newspapers but a whole city. Layered on top of these qualities was a mind enamored with a plethora of interests ranging from art to osteopathy, canals to universities, yet always somehow in a way that reflected steely resolve (or stubbornness), not peripheral, momentary amusement.

Somehow, even with Carter's clear influence on Texas and Fort Worth in the first half of the twentieth century, very little scholarly material has been written about his life and legacy. The first academic work about Carter was a thesis written by Samuel Kinch Jr. in 1965 entitled "Amon Carter: Publisher-Salesman." The focus of the thesis is Carter's work in running the *Star-Telegram*, so while it does cover essential features of Carter's background, its purpose is not biographical. Jerry Flemmons, formerly a reporter for the *Star-Telegram*, wrote the first of two books on Carter: *Amon: The Life of Amon Carter, Sr., of Texas* in 1978, followed twenty years later by *Amon: The Texan Who Played Cowboy for America*. While these two books have a good narrative and humorous anecdotes, they also suffer from some glaring weaknesses, such as a lack of citations, poor organization, and little analysis of Carter's character. In addition, the biographies have a dearth of historical context and fail to place Carter within the framework of urban boosters so prominent in southern and western cities in the first half of the twentieth century, or within the broader context of American history. While Flemmons admits that the cowboy character that Carter loved to play in public was primarily an act, he contributes to this image by regaling the reader with numerous stories that reinforce this representation. The Carter caricature that leaps off these pages makes the reader wonder how such a cartoonish figure was able to wield the influence he did. Unfortunately, any modern scholarship that addresses Carter in a cursory manner is in the unfortunate position of having to rely on these flawed works. Oliver Knight's *Fort Worth: Outpost on the Trinity*, published in 1953, includes a several-page overview of Carter's life that was constructed in large part by the subject himself. Two newer works that have done some deeper analysis of aspects of Carter's career are Patrick Cox's *First Texas News Barons*, which ably looks at Carter as one of a select few prominent Texas newspaper publishers in the early twentieth century, and Mary L. Kelley's *Foundations of Texan Philanthropy*, which examines Carter's well-noted benevolence within the broader context of early Texas philanthropy.[10]

The relative scarcity of secondary sources about Carter, his life, and his influence belies the wealth of primary source material either left behind by Carter or available through contemporary newspapers, magazines, and trade journals. Fortunately for historians, his collection of papers (416 boxes containing thousands of pieces of correspondence, newspaper clippings, and photographs), evidence of his long reach and breadth of interests, resides at the Mary Couts Burnett Library at Texas Christian University in Fort Worth. His eponymous museum houses material pertaining to his art collection, and some of his letters can be found among the papers and letter collections of individuals such as Lyndon Johnson, Sam Rayburn, and Will Rogers. Because he was such an active individual, with political and business connections across the country, it is relatively easy to find articles and biographical sketches in publications as varied as the *New York Times, Time,* the *Fourth Estate* (a trade journal for the newspaper industry), and, of course, local newspapers like the *Dallas Morning News* and his own *Star-Telegram*. And during the 1930s and 1940s, he made a number of appearances in the *March of Time* newsreel series, usually, though not always, promoting Fort Worth in some way. An embarrassment of riches truly exists for those willing to explore his life further.

Because Carter was not a modest man, but rather someone who obviously relished being at the center of his own growing legend, one must be careful not to get too distracted by the anecdotes that inevitably appear. Even in his own lifetime, what one could call the Carter "mythos," a set of stories that circulated about this figure who single-handedly not only ruled his own city but also embodied what it meant (or what was thought by many to mean) to be a Texan, grew up around him. Here, after all, was a man whose hatred of Dallas was so entrenched that he always took a sack lunch to that city if he ever had to conduct business there so he could avoid enriching his arch nemesis—or so the legend said. Carter denied ever doing this, and, more often than he let on in public, found ways to cooperate with Fort Worth's neighbor. In other stories, he can be found firing his six-shooter in public, whooping and hollering at publishers' banquets, driving a stagecoach down Wall Street, or cajoling businessmen until they moved their enterprise (or a portion of it at least) to Fort Worth. While these kinds of episodes did occur and are entertaining, they risk being seen as the whole of Carter as opposed to merely facets of his occasionally rambunctious, but always pugnacious, personality.

It should also be remembered that while contemporary and scholarly assessments of Carter often focus on his civic activities, this very public figure had a private life as well. No scholarly analysis of Carter would be complete without an examination of his relationship with his family. Not surprisingly, this ambitious man struggled to balance his familial and business commitments, experiencing strained relationships with his father, stepmother, and siblings as well as being divorced from his first two wives, Zetta Thomas and Nenetta Burton. Yet this same man could, and often did, express deep paternal and domestic instincts, especially toward his two youngest children, Amon Jr. and Ruth, and was always ready to help out struggling relatives, especially those who reminded him of the impoverished rural past he had escaped as a young man. One thing that is especially evident over the last three decades of his life—when he had clearly reached the pinnacle of success—is his willingness to regale others with stories of his rural roots. And though he did not usually explain his motivations for doing so, evidence for these is found in an unlikely source: *The Life of P. T. Barnum*. In 1937, he was given an 1855 edition of Barnum's autobiography, and though Carter was not usually a voracious reader, his copy has pencil markings in the margins in his hand that suggest he read at least portions of it and took it to heart. Next to one particular paragraph, Carter marked seven X's: "I wish *them* and all the world," Barnum writes, "to know that my father was a tailor, and that I am 'a showman' by profession, and all *the gilding* shall make nothing else of me. When a man is ashamed of his origins, or gets above his business, he is a poor devil, who merits the detestation of all who know him."

CHAPTER 2

THE FORMATIVE YEARS

AS A BLIZZARD SWEPT ACROSS the North Texas plains near the tiny Wise County community of Crafton on December 10, 1879, nineteen-year-old Josephine Ream Carter gave birth to a healthy baby boy she named Giles Amon Carter, after her husband William's younger brother. To avoid confusion, he went simply by Amon and, at some point in his life, switched his first and middle names. At the time of Carter's birth, his parents lived with Giles in a poorly insulated log cabin some sixty miles northwest of the city that would someday bear his indelible mark. Because of the pitiable condition of the cabin, mother and child were forced to temporarily move in with a neighbor for warmth. The twenty-six-year-old William and his young wife Josephine were recent settlers in the area, as were most whites who lived in Wise County at that time. Drawn by the Western Cross Timbers' bounteous game and well-watered, gently wooded land, whites first arrived in the area in 1854 after the previous residents, the Kichai Indians, a Caddoan tribe, were defeated by the United States Army and removed to the Brazos Indian Reservation. Over the next several years, the county's population quickly grew to over 3,000, mainly through immigration from southern states, but the onset of the Civil War reversed that trend. When federal troops withdrew from the frontier upon Texas's secession, Comanche and Kiowa Indians renewed their attacks on Wise County settlements, and the number of residents dropped dramatically to 1,450 by 1870. The construction of Fort Richardson just west of Wise County in neighboring Jack County encouraged whites to move back in, and this renewed surge of settlers into the area included the Carters, who settled near the new community of Crafton, named after George Craft, upon whose land the town was laid out.[1]

William Carter was a nondescript farmer with a personality reportedly as hard and unforgiving as the soil that he farmed. On the other hand, the Arkansas-born Josephine was a relatively cultured woman who was rumored (falsely as it turns out) to have spent some time as a child living at La Reunion, a French utopian commune near Dallas. The young couple married in Bell County on November 24, 1876, when William was twenty-three and Josephine three months shy of seventeen. William and his brother Giles, born and raised in Central Texas by a father and a mother from Tennessee and Mississippi respectively, were farm laborers at the time of Amon's birth; William remained in agriculture for the rest of his life. In the census records, he first appears as a farm laborer (apparently working for someone else), but by 1900, he owned his own farm. Yet, in a 1952 *Time* magazine interview, Amon claimed that his father worked as a blacksmith, a statement substantiated in Amon's obituary and by Nenetta Burton, Amon Carter's second wife. Presumably this was something he did while working as a laborer, as the existing records do not list him as a blacksmith. William Carter also turned to raising chickens, as mentioned in *The State of Texas Book: One Hundred Years of Progress*. The chapter on the Texas poultry industry mentions William Carter as one of the few poultry men in Bowie, Texas, where he raised Plymouth Rock chickens and won prizes in Texas and Oklahoma. Needless to say, toward the end of his life, William could lay claim to some success, though nothing remotely like the success of his son.[2]

While William Carter toiled to make a living, Josephine devoted herself to raising Amon. In letters to her cousin Mary Bondred, Josephine bragged about her baby boy, Amon, saying, "I have the finest boy you ever saw." His relentless curiosity and restlessness were apparent from the beginning, as Josephine had problems keeping him "on'na palet nor hardly in the house. He is the worst rouda I ever saw." Still, she boasted, "Amon is the sweetest boy you ever saw."[3]

Despite spending only a few years of his life in Crafton, Amon fondly remembered his days there and even returned during the 1930s for a town reunion. While visiting, Amon observed that his deceased mother's Presbyterian church was in shambles and that the church bell she had loved listening to was lying in disrepair in the churchyard. Sentimental though not particularly religious, he remarked, "See that bell lying in the Presbyterian churchyard? My mother used to hear that bell in the 1870s and 1880s when she went to church. I'd like to have that bell." Will Warren, a friend of Amon's and a longtime Crafton resident, approached the church's deacons soon after to request the bell for Carter and was told: "We're not giving him that bell." Despite Warren's pleas, he was unsuccessful, so he decided to send Amon the unused bell from the Baptist church next door, saying, "It was just as old as the Presbyterian bell. And Mrs. Carter heard it too, when she went to church on Sunday."[4]

The Carters did not stay long in Crafton; sometime after their daughter, Addie, was born in 1887, William moved his family to a farm in Nocona, Texas, in adjacent Montague County just south of the Red River. Nocona was a fairly new settlement when Amon and his family arrived in the late 1880s. White settlers had moved into the area in the 1870s, but the town was not incorporated until 1887. Named after the Comanche chief Peta Nocona, the town grew steadily over the next few years largely because of the presence of a line of the Missouri and Pacific Railroad as well as Herman J. Justin's boot factory. The hustle and bustle of the town proved to be the perfect place for young Amon to begin sharpening his skills as a salesman.[5]

Sometime after William moved his family to Montague County, he began blacksmithing, a craft he unsuccessfully tried to teach Amon. During one training session, Carter was kicked unconscious by a horse and suffered three broken ribs. Disenchanted with blacksmithing, young Amon found other ways to make a little money, including gathering empty half-pint flasks from outside saloons and selling them back to the saloonkeepers for twenty cents a dozen. It is not clear if Carter began his enterprising career due to financial pressure from his family or because he simply enjoyed the thrill of making money, though one suspects that with his family struggling financially, this may have been something he was required to do. Whatever the reason, it is clear that life would have been much different for Amon if he had found blacksmithing to be more rewarding.[6]

Disaster struck the Carter family on March 7, 1892, when, for unknown reasons, Josephine died. The Ream family Bible merely reads, "Josie Carter departed this life," with no explanation for the cause of death. Soon after her death, William married a much younger woman, Ella Patterson, and moved to the town of Sunset in southern Montague County. Amon did not approve of this new marriage, possibly because of the close attachment he had with his mother, a woman he continued to remember fondly throughout his life. So, at the age of thirteen, Amon left his father's house and moved in with his grandmother, who lived nearby. After living with his grandmother for some time, he decided to strike out for Montana, though by his own account, he was unaware of where exactly that might be located. He boarded a Missouri, Kansas, and Texas train with only forty cents in his pocket, earned by the enterprising youngster in his whiskey bottle collection efforts, but he never made it out of the county. After the conductor escorted him off the train near Belcherville, Texas, Amon walked the twenty miles south to Bowie, Texas, where, without a family to support him, he was forced to earn his living in a variety of ways with varying degrees of honesty.[7]

Finding himself in a town with no relatives, thirteen-year-old Carter made his way to the Jarrott Hotel, a place he was familiar with, since the owner, Millie Jarrott, bought peaches from his father. Carter asked her for work, expressing his willingness to do whatever chores she might have for him. She replied in the affirmative, and that was the beginning of his first steady job. The kindly Jarrott paid him $1.50 a week plus room and board to wash dishes, wait tables, clean rooms, and carry luggage for customers. Carter had pleasant memories from his days working for Jarrott, and when he had the money to do so, he bought the hotel from her and ran it on her behalf. When she died, he also paid for her funeral expenses.[8]

Although Carter already had a semblance of security from working for Jarrott, he also sold peaches, ice cream, and bottled soda pop for a local bottling plant. The ever-resourceful Carter discovered that there was money to be made during the summers by traveling seven or eight miles away to Queen's Peak, the highest point in Montague County, where locals watched and bet on horse races. Desperate for a rider for his horse, Baldy, Bowie resident Horace Woods persuaded Carter to be his rider, despite the youth's lack of racing experience. Carter worried he would fall, so Woods tied him onto the horse's back; nevertheless, he slid off near the end as his horse was galloping to victory. Though his opponent argued that Carter had lost the race, since he had fallen off his horse, Woods settled the issue by brandishing his .45 Colt revolver. Carter received five dollars for his pains, as well as a reputation for hardiness.[9]

While still a relative newcomer to Bowie, and hoping to pay his way through the eighth grade, he briefly worked for Z. T. Lowry's Grocery Store, hauling buckets of drinking water into the store. These trips through the store took him down the snuff aisle, where Levi P. Garrett's Scotch Snuff was sold next to that of its prime competitor, Railroad Snuff. In a marketing gimmick, Levi Garrett Snuff began inserting nickels under the cork as a rebate. When Lowry's Grocery burned, Carter remembered those rebates and asked Lowry if he could keep whatever items he found in the ruins of the store. Lowry agreed, and the barefoot Carter promptly strode to the back of S. Daube and Company, a local general store, to pick out some old shoes so his feet would not be burned. Customers buying new shoes typically left their old shoes in a discard pile at the back, so Carter found a pair (much too large) and tied them onto his feet. Armed with "new" shoes, and a small iron rod to poke through the ashes, Amon went through the rubble and dug out six dollars in nickels before other boys showed up as competition.[10]

The most enduring image from Carter's time in Bowie is his reputation as the "chicken and bread boy" who sold fried chicken and biscuits to hungry train passengers as they stopped in the town. While working as a roustabout in a wagon yard, he killed a chicken (apparently by accident). He persuaded a widow named Brodie, whom he worked for and sometimes stayed with, to cut it up and fry it for him to sell. Soon after, he struck a deal with Brodie in which he would pay $2.50 weekly for room and board and she would cook him a chicken daily. He was able to buy chickens for twenty-five cents apiece and sell the resulting meals for ten cents each. Before long, he was making two dollars a day. If Carter was short of money or there were no chickens available to buy, he apparently either raided local henhouses or substituted rabbit meat. It really did not matter what kind of meat it was, for, as Carter later admitted, "We fried the chickens in a thick batter and you couldn't tell the drumstick from the gizzard." During the 1930s, President Roosevelt heard stories of Carter's days as a "chicken and bread boy," and when his train stopped in Bowie on a cross-country journey, Carter boarded the train to sell the president one of his famous "chicken and bread" sandwiches.[11]

Once he reached his midteens, Carter began branching out into other job ventures that were even less reputable. Having quit school after completing the eighth grade, he had more time to devote to various business enterprises. One of his more notorious money-making schemes involved the purchase of a knife-board game he operated out of a Bowie saloon owned by John and Tam Lindsay, boarders at the Jarrott Hotel where Amon was employed. With his partner, M. M. Hurdleston, a Fort Worth and Denver Railroad yardmaster currently on strike, Carter rented out the space for ten dollars a month, a price they quickly recovered as their knife-board game grew in popularity. Carter covered a board in black alpaca cloth and glued corks of various sizes (borrowed from the saloon owners) onto it along with a knife. Coins of different values were added to the corks, and customers would pay Carter and Hurdleston for the chance to toss wooden rings on the corks to win the money attached to them or onto the handle of the knife in order to win the knife. Early on, Carter developed an idea to encourage more people to play the game: he placed a five-dollar bill through the knife handle as a prize and tilted the knife in such a way as to make it easier to ring. Bowie farmer Adolph Fincher was the first to win the five dollars, and word spread of his amazing luck. The wily Amon's next move was to push the knife back into its original position so that future players would spend countless dollars attempting to replicate Fincher's good fortune.[12]

Business went so well for Carter that he moved out of his previous quarters and rented a room with Hurdleston (ten years his senior) just off the gambling hall above the saloon. Around this time, Carter encountered a lanky painter known by the nickname of "Shadow," a man who turned out to be an excellent player of the knife-board game (as well as something of a pool shark). Ever resourceful, young Amon decided to pay Shadow five dollars a week to show up a few times a week to show other customers how to beat the game, thus enticing more to keep playing. He found other ways to capitalize on Shadow's skillfulness, such as going with him to Dallas during the Texas State Fair and placing bets on pool games played with Dallas pool sharks who assumed they could beat the rural visitors.[13]

In 1897, searching for greater business opportunities and eager to see more of the world (after all, he had missed out on making it to Montana), Carter left Texas for Indian Territory, where his cousin's husband, Michael McGinley, owned a grocery store in Norman. For a while, he worked for $30 a month at the Davis Confectionery, making ice cream and selling candy. Long hours, high rent at the Grand Central Hotel, and restlessness soon got the better of Carter. Hearing of an opportunity to be a travelling salesman with the Chicago-based American Copying Company (ACC), an organization that sold enlarged portraits and frames, he quit his job at the confectionery. While not quite as blatantly fraudulent as the knife-board game, the selling practices of the ACC did go beyond what can be considered ethical business practices. Salesmen would go door to door selling pictures in small towns and cities through the West and Midwest. More specifically, the salesman sold a process by which an oversized oil painting could be made of an existing photograph. While this was oftentimes an attractive offer to customers, the problem was that the new portrait did not fit any frames but those sold by the ACC.[14]

Carter's travels took him throughout the United States, particularly the Great Plains states. In a conversation with Lou Hoover, then the first lady, he recounted selling frames just outside of Tulsa, where in one day's journey outside the city he only encountered six homes. Ms. Hoover remarked that this kind of isolation must have made it remarkably difficult for sales numbers, but he responded that, on the contrary, their loneliness made it much more likely that they would purchase whatever it was he was selling. He seemed to relish the success his travels through relatively desolate places brought him: he bought a flashy diamond ring, boots, spurs, and a six-shooter; he finally made it to Montana (where he reportedly broke up a light opera performance); and he wrote to a friend that he was "having a time with an old girl" during a brief stay in Galena, Kansas. While one can only speculate, these travels across the wide open spaces of the West at the turn of the century must have awakened in him some yearning for the mythical Old West, for the frontier that had only just been declared closed a decade before. Some of his trips were brief, but on occasion he stayed in one city and made it his base of operations for weeks on end. For example, in 1901 he stayed in Salt Lake City for the month of September and, according to his own records, sold over $2,400 worth of frames in the surrounding region. With this kind of success, it is no surprise that Carter rose swiftly through the ranks of the company; by 1901, he was promoted to a sales manager position, from which he imparted much of his knowledge of sales to his underlings. In a typed document titled "Carter's Talk," Carter laid out his philosophy of salesmanship. "To do business with a man," he states, "you must first win his confidence . . . It is not what you say to a man that impresses him, but how you say it." He continued by saying, "Never get discouraged. Do not expect to sell [to] everybody."[15]

Much of his talk centered on recruiting storeowners into the business with a shrewd blend of advertising and sales. One method the ACC used in selling frames door to door was to deliver merchant directories to homes in the area. Inside the directory was room for tickets denoting the cash spent at each merchant. If a customer purchased twenty-five dollars from local merchants that signed up with the ACC, then he/she would get a free portrait as long as the tickets inside the directory were redeemed. Unfortunately for the customer, the frames were stocked at the stores of merchants who had signed on with the ACC; they were available for purchase for $2.98. So on top of the money made for each frame sold, the merchant would pay the ACC a half cent for each ticket inside a customer's book.[16]

Carter expected that a business deal of this nature would arouse suspicion, especially on the part of the merchant. Knowing that rejection could cause further failures for his young salesmen, Carter told his employees, "If you go into a store and a man calls you down good and proper, never leave the store until you have repaid the compliment, if you have to stay there an hour. Tell him what you think of him with a smile on your face, and walk out saying, 'Well, I had the last word, and he didn't get the best of me.'" Carter proved throughout the rest of his life that this statement was more than a word of advice for young salesmen; rarely would he ever let others have the last word with him in any dispute.[17]

In the midst of his cross-country travels, Carter found the time to woo and marry Zetta Thomas, daughter of Bowie rancher Giles D. Thomas, in 1902. Little is known about their relationship due to the dearth of existing correspondence between the couple or discussions of their marriage in letters to and from friends and family. In one letter to his colleague and friend William Ince, Amon hints that Zetta accompanied him when he was temporarily headquartered in Salt Lake City, Utah; otherwise, it appears Zetta remained in Bowie while he traveled and managed lower-ranking salesmen within the company. Undoubtedly, Zetta had a hard time dealing with her husband's frequent absences from home, and the extant letters reveal a woman who desired a more present husband or at least one who stayed in contact with his family when gone. Over the years, this would cause an irreparable rift in their relationship. Three years into their marriage, Zetta gave birth to a daughter, Bertice; she would be their only offspring. Though often busy and away from home during her childhood, Amon tried to instill in Bertice the same industrious, hard-working spirit that he had shown in his life. The few letters that exist from her childhood are full of exhortations to hard work and thriftiness. Despite his best efforts to be available for his wife and daughter, Carter would find that his devotion to his work for the next decade and a half would undermine the home that he had established; sadly, this story of sacrificing domestic bliss for public success would be all too common throughout his life.[18]

In 1903, after over five years with the ACC, Carter left the company for a new career in advertising. In his travels as a salesman, he had met Edgar Swasey of Barnhart and Swasey Advertising Company in San Francisco. Armed with a strong letter of recommendation from W. J. Graham and A. L. Utz of the ACC, Carter traveled to San Francisco to a new position with Barnhart and Swasey. Evidently his work at the ACC was considered priceless, for by the next year, Graham and Utz sent him a letter in San Francisco begging him to come back for a salary of one hundred dollars a week plus expenses. While little is known about Carter's time at Barnhart and Swasey, it is clear that he must have continued to make a good impression on Swasey. In May 1905, Carter resigned his position, having been offered a two-hundred-dollar monthly salary by F. J. Cooper, a rival advertising agency, as well as possible business prospects in Fort Worth. Though initially agreeing to work for Cooper, Carter decided instead to leave California for the much more familiar North Texas region to open up an advertising agency of his own. By the end of the year, the Texas Advertising and Manufacturing Company, with Amon Carter as president, was open for business in Fort Worth.[19]

Carter's adolescence and early adulthood may have lacked stability, but his experiences provided him with training in survival, salesmanship, and networking, skills that enabled him to quickly become one of Fort Worth's elite. Why Carter chose Fort Worth as his new home is not certain from the extant documents. It could have been his desire (or Zetta's) to be in a city closer to his boyhood home and Zetta's family. It is also quite possible that he desired to make his way in a city that offered greater upward mobility and independence for a young man. By locating himself in Fort Worth, he had an easier path to becoming a prominent publisher and booster, not that there is anything to suggest that he knew that is what he would become. Whatever the motivation, there is nothing in his letters that reveals his line of thinking as he moved his family from the bustling port city of San Francisco, with 300,000 people, to Fort Worth, whose packing plants, stockyards, and railyards were the only symbols of prosperity in the large town of not even 30,000.[20]

Turn-of-the century Fort Worth was neither a completely southern nor a completely western town. Populated largely by southerners, the town possessed the reactionary Jim Crow attitude toward race prevalent across the region. Though the city had scarcely been touched by the Civil War, a monument to Confederate soldiers stood guard near the courthouse just as in other Texas county seats. David Goldfield's description of New South urban economies applies to Fort Worth as much as it does to Atlanta or Dallas: "Cities in the New South performed the same agricultural functions as they had in the Old South: they were primarily agricultural marketplaces." But while its neighbor Dallas capitalized on its position near the cotton-growing regions of Texas, Fort Worth was perched on the edge of the frontier cattle kingdom, a place Carter later described as "Where the West Begins." Carl Abbott describes Fort Worth as a "gateway city," one that, like Omaha, and Kansas City to the north, took advantage of its proximity to the vast areas of cattle and grain production in West Texas to become a center of flour milling, wholesaling, and cattle processing.[21]

Though possessing great potential for explosive economic growth, Fort Worth at the turn of the century offered few hints of what the city would become over the next half century with Carter as the leading booster. It had certainly grown since the Texas and Pacific Railroad had arrived in 1876, but the city was still firmly attached to its cattle town heritage. The city was named for the fort that had been established on some high bluffs overlooking the West Fork of the Trinity River on June 6, 1849, by Major Ripley Arnold after his recently deceased commanding officer, Major General William Worth. Its original purpose was to protect the settlers of the nearby settlements of Dallas and Peters Colony from Comanche attacks. Civilians quickly moved to the protection of the fort, but the fort was abandoned after four years as the settlement line moved westward.[22]

Fort Worth struggled, arguably surviving only by stealing the county seat from the nearby community of Birdville through apparent voter fraud. Fortunately for Fort Worth, the post–Civil War United States had a great appetite for beef, and cowboys began driving thousands of cattle from South Texas to Kansas through Fort Worth, which had several good Trinity River crossings. Regardless of the business that the cattle brought to Fort Worth, however, the town still had a sleepy reputation, which was only aggravated by a Dallas newspaper editor's accusation that once a panther was found asleep in the street. By 1876, however, the town fathers had persuaded the Texas and Pacific Railroads to build through Fort Worth.[23]

During the 1880s and 1890s, local boosters (soon organized into the Board of Trade and later renamed the Chamber of Commerce) successfully persuaded several more railroads, such as the Fort Worth and Denver City, the Fort Worth and New Orleans, and the Rock Island, to either begin in Fort Worth or pass through the town, giving the growing community connections to port cities such as Galveston and New Orleans and interior metropolises such as Kansas City and Chicago. Spurred on by critics who argued that railroads alone would not make Fort Worth into a great city, local boosters capitalized on their success as well as the presence of lively stockyards by pressing for the construction of meatpacking plants in the town. At the time, Fort Worth may have lacked a singular individual like Carter who could galvanize that effort, but promises by citizens and the stockyards to put up money for construction and other costs was enough to lure industry giants Armour and Company and Swift and Company to the city; they opened to great fanfare in 1903 and immediately began to shape the economic development of the town.[24]

The 1900 census reported that Fort Worth had a population of just under 27,000 residents, which, to be sure, represented growth over the last census's 23,076, but it was much slower than the previous decade's rate of increase thanks in large part to the fallout from the Panic of 1893 and the ensuing depression. Yet the presence of Armour and Swift quickly began to transform the local economy, and its influence was felt even into Fort Worth's hinterlands stretching to the north and west. Fort Worth historian Harold Rich makes a strong case that the two packing plants "fueled significant population and commercial increases that pushed Fort Worth beyond regional status, making it a city of national importance." By the end of the decade, the town had become the fourth-largest city in Texas with over 73,000 people, much of the growth in some way connected to the arrival of the packing plants and the ripple effect their presence had on the region. Bank clearings increased, railroad traffic grew, and the once heavily southern city began to attract a number of immigrants from places as far away as Central and Eastern Europe. Suburbs to the north and west of the central city, such as Rosen Heights and Arlington Heights, expanded, a Carnegie Library was constructed, two newspaper dailies flourished, and a commission system of city government was adopted. And, as much of the growth was contingent on the success of West Texas, this ensured that Fort Worth would, unlike Dallas, be a city with a decidedly western orientation.

Unfortunately, this western orientation did nothing to prevent the implementation of a very southern approach to race relations in Fort Worth. In the first decade of the twentieth century, while black Americans hovered between 15 and 18 percent of the city's population, they were relegated to the socioeconomic fringes. Municipal ordinances encouraged the promotion of segregationist policies, and Fort Worth whites generally did little to upset this established social order. Residential developments on the outskirts of town promised buyers "purity" in their housing: "We do not sell to Negroes," proclaimed the West Fort Worth Land Company in 1907. Less than a decade later, the developers behind the Oakhurst Land Company constructing housing northeast of the central business district promised a "sensibly restricted suburban residential district." That meant black Fort Worthians were generally to be found living east of downtown or on the Trinity River bottoms in poorly constructed housing in underserved communities. As was the case across Texas and the South at the time, the community was served by just six shoddily built schools, including one "colored" high school. And while Fort Worth had two dailies, the *Record* and the *Telegram*, like most newspapers across the South, they overlooked the black community. By the time Carter arrived in the city in 1905, the weekly *Item* had been catering to black readers for just over a decade, though with little prospect of a successful future. Clearly, as long as black citizens of the city lived directly in the grip of Jim Crow and white supremacy attitudes, economic success would remain mostly out of reach.[25]

So when the Carter family arrived in Fort Worth, the city they arrived in reflected a truly southwestern image as a place where two similar yet distinct economic and cultural regions met. It was a city on the rise that seemed to offer all a man of Carter's talent and ambition needed for success: a growing population, an emerging industrial base, and a developing social networking scene for businessmen as evidenced by the presence of business clubs and fraternal societies as disparate as the elite Fort Worth Club, the Benevolent Order of Elks, and the Fort Worth–specific Mystic Knights of Bovinia (an apparent nod to the city's kine connection). Once in Fort Worth, Carter quickly established his business, the Texas Advertising and Manufacturing Company; he was its only employee. He hoped to publish an indexing telephone directory that he had acquired the patent to in San Francisco, but to supplement his efforts, he also sold advertising cards on local streetcars. It was not long before he was distracted from his directory mission by a typewriter salesman who told him he had just heard of a method of creating fuel bricks by combining crude oil with the cow manure abundant in the Fort Worth stockyards. His interest piqued, Carter went to the stockyards for a demonstration, and there he met two young men, A. G. Record and D. C. McCaleb, who were interested in starting a newspaper to rival the recently established *Telegram*. He traded his rights to the telephone directory for a peach orchard in Arlington, Texas, then a tiny community halfway between Fort Worth and Dallas, and joined the staff of the brand-new *Fort Worth Star* as the advertising manager (and in reality, the whole advertising department).[26]

Truth be told, the Fort Worth newspaper industry did not at the moment have a record of unmitigated success. The first newspaper published in the city was the ill-fated *Chief,* published by Anthony Norton. Unfortunately for Norton, his anti-secession views ran afoul of the increasingly secessionist leanings of the town's readership, and he left the city in 1860. It was over a decade before Khleber Van Zandt, one of the foremost Fort Worth boosters of the late nineteenth century, cobbled together a group of investors to open the *Democrat* in 1871. It was common at the time for newspapermen to organize boosting activities, and Van Zandt recognized this when he later said, "Having a newspaper was imperative as a means of letting our light shine and publicizing to Texas, as well as the rest of the world, that Fort Worth was on the map." By 1876, however, he sold the weekly to another leading booster, B. B. Paddock, who turned it into a daily that he used to promote the city as the major city of North Texas as well as to encourage city leaders to improve the community's quality of life.[27]

Under Paddock's leadership, the *Democrat* became the *Gazette,* a name it retained even after he sold the controlling interest to the publisher of the *Texas Livestock Journal,* George Loving. Walter Malone, formerly part owner of the *Dallas Herald,* who was hired by Paddock as editor some years before, stayed on as editor and continued to emphasize the paper as a boosting tool. These efforts did not go unrecognized, as exemplified by the 1889 statement by the *Austin Gazette* that the paper "had done more than any other instrumentality in building Fort Worth into a trade center with a firm grip on the wholesale trade for northern and western Texas."

The *Fort Worth Star,* with Carter at the head of the advertising department, set its sights on overtaking the largest newspaper in Fort Worth, the *Telegram,* though its first edition came in at a rather modest sixteen pages. The *Star* used the much smaller United Press wire services as opposed to the Associated Press wire used by the *Telegram.* This put the fledgling newspaper at a serious disadvantage. The *Star* momentarily overcame this handicap just six weeks after its opening, however, when the San Francisco earthquake occurred. While visiting a stockbroker's office, Carter read over a business wire about the earthquake before news of the tragedy came over either the United Press or Associated Press wires. Carter remembered the map of San Francisco that he had in his office and used it to locate destroyed buildings for insertion in an extra edition of the *Star.* Before the *Telegram* was able to react, Carter had already sold numerous copies in Fort Worth and had boarded the interurban to Dallas to sell even more. This scoop boosted the newspaper's circulation but was not enough to bring the publication out of the red.[28]

Funding for the newspaper came from selling shares in the newly formed Star Publishing Company, with investment coming from prominent local businessmen such as Colonel Paul Waples, wholesale grocer, and Willard Burton, owner of a dry goods establishment, but this was not nearly enough for the *Star*'s daily expenses. Carter's business expertise, or rather, a $3^{31}/_{32}$ carat diamond he had purchased sometime before, were often needed to keep the newspaper running. In his more prosperous years, Carter remembered hocking the diamond several times just to meet payroll. And even though he came on board with a negotiated salary of thirty-five dollars a week, he soon realized that "it was much easier to cash a check on the *Star* for $20 than $35," so he worked for the much lower rate. Desperate for money, Carter took peach orders from local grocers during peach harvest season while selling advertising for the paper, then after his day's work was done, he boarded the interurban to take him to his newly acquired Arlington farm and picked peaches for their orders. He would then be up at five A.M. to deliver the orders for the day and arrive at the *Star*'s offices by eight. Another source of income came from selling advertising on a number of Fort Worth streetcar lines on which he had purchased advertising space. As the newspaper continued to bleed money and faced the same fate that so many other Fort Worth publications had experienced, Carter began to weigh competing offers; the rival *Telegram* offered him seventy-five dollars a week, while the advertising behemoth Barron Collier in New York City offered him an enormous ten-thousand-a-year salary. The extant correspondence is silent regarding his motivations in turning down these superior outside offers. It does not appear that remaining close to extended family was the prevailing issue; after all, Dallas was a short train ride away from Fort Worth. Leasing advertising space and picking peaches late into the evening speaks to the dire financial straits he was in, so why reject a tantalizing offer such as Collier was dangling in front of him? Alva Johnston's biographical sketch in a 1937 issue of the *Saturday Evening Post* posits a hypothesis that possibly contains a kernel of truth: "He was sure Fort Worth had a future; uncertain about New York." In one sense, Johnston was correct. For Carter, Fort Worth had a future. A move to New York would mean a move into management, into a society in which he would become just one of many in a growing upper middle class. Staying in Fort Worth, uncertain though the present might be, possibly might have a larger payoff, considering the relatively small size of both the city and its elites. He was already establishing connections with business leaders such as Waples, Stripling, Meacham, and others. Why not remain where the potential for personal growth and increased influence was larger? That said, trying to keep the floundering *Star* afloat was too troublesome in Carter's eyes, so he pursued a riskier course of action: buying the rival *Fort Worth Telegram*.[29]

Purchasing the successful *Telegram* in 1908 appeared to be a preposterous solution to the *Star*'s problems, but even at this early stage in life, Carter had learned the value of exercising his network of acquaintances and friends. Working through his friend O. P. Thomas, secretary of the Abilene Chamber of Commerce, Carter offered to buy the newspaper for $100,000, with $2,500 due at signing and the balance within ten days. To acquire the $2,500, Carter left three diamond rings and a diamond and pearl scarf pin as collateral with the Fort Worth National Bank. With the offer from Barron Collier of New York still waiting for him, Carter knew that if he failed to secure the balance within ten days, he would be leaving his newly adopted home of Fort Worth for the stability of an advertising career. With Waples's backing and substantial help from *Star* publisher Louis Wortham, Carter obtained enough money to purchase the *Telegram*. Both newspapers subsequently shut down operations and emerged as the *Fort Worth Star-Telegram* as 1909 dawned. Though unforeseen at the time, Amon Carter had just set himself on a course to be one of the most successful newspaper magnates in the United States.[30]

CHAPTER 3

BUILDING A MEDIA EMPIRE

BY THE TIME he reached middle age, Amon Carter had emerged as one of the leading citizens of Fort Worth by demonstrating his commitment to boosting the growth and development of the city as well as expanding his media empire by growing the *Star-Telegram* and establishing radio station WBAP. The increasingly civic-minded Carter believed that the interests of the *Star-Telegram*, Fort Worth, and West Texas were inextricably intertwined with, and thus best served by, a newspaper that promoted the interests of all three. Though not yet involved in state or national politics, as he would be by the mid-1920s, Carter used the newspaper to endorse projects that encouraged economic growth in the region. In this way, Carter established himself as someone who reflected the business-oriented progressive booster ethic of both the South and the West.

Historian C. Vann Woodward writes that "southern progressivism was essentially urban and middle class in nature, and the typical leader was a city professional man or businessman, rather than a farmer." Carter, with a position on Fort Worth's Board of Trade, membership in organizations like the Elks Club and the prestigious Fort Worth Club, and involvement in causes such as public parks and highway construction, exemplified southern progressivism and the urban ethos. This type of civic involvement could be seen across the South during the early twentieth century: "The activities of the civic-commercial elite were evident on every hand, but perhaps the most notable was the impressive array of voluntary civic organizations that cropped up throughout the urban South, the type of association which Oscar Handlin termed, 'the characteristic social unit of the modern city.'" Patrick Cox puts it well in his *First Texas News Barons,* stating that "individual newspaper publishers knew that their publications would rise or fall in part to the degree their home cities grew or declined. Like many southern progressives of their time, Texas' metropolitan publishers believed the key to their state's economic future lay with expanded industrialization and urbanization—developments that would, fortuitously, directly benefit newspapers by providing an increased readership and advertising base." Carter's tenure at the helm of the *Star-Telegram* reflects these key beliefs and practices of Texas publishers. Though increasingly of an urban and industrial mindset, these business progressives typically supported the strict system of Jim Crow implemented across the region in the late nineteenth century. Rarely of a mind to fight segregation, they often treated the black community paternalistically; black citizens who dared challenge white supremacy (or were deemed to be challenging it) could not expect that same paternalism.[1]

Events through the 1920s (and beyond) also established Fort Worth as a burgeoning western gateway city. The city's rivalry with Dallas, which Carter would ultimately do so much to encourage, as well as its location on the edge of the western prairie, positioned it to take advantage of the oil discoveries of the 1910s and 1920s. In addition, the United States' entry into the First World War marked the beginning of Fort Worth's long affiliation with the military, a markedly western aspect to the city's identity. The burgeoning population of West Texas, bolstered by agricultural production, proved to be a large market that Carter, ever the wily salesman, could penetrate with the right marketing techniques.

Carter also began to indulge his philanthropic desires during this time, though in much smaller doses than he did later and usually under the auspices of the *Star-Telegram.* While Carter's penchant for giving stemmed from his genuine willingness to help others in need, it also reflected his recognition that Fort Worth citizens would be more willing to subscribe to a newspaper that cared for the city's citizens. During the 1910s and early 1920s, the evening *Star-Telegram* battled with the *Fort Worth Record,* the city's morning newspaper since 1903, for supremacy and the loyalty of Fort Worth's newspaper readers. This battle would ultimately pit Carter against none other than William Randolph Hearst, with the result that Carter dominated the Fort Worth news market by 1925. Armed with an expanded readership and a foothold in the new technology of radio, Carter was well equipped to begin asserting more influence on a state and national level by the mid-1920s. As a civic booster with an "urban ethos," he was able to use this wider influence to leverage the expansion of his adopted city.

Despite a slow rate of growth during the first part of the 1910s, Fort Worth continued to develop during Carter's first decade and a half at the helm of the *Star-Telegram*. City leaders worked to modernize Fort Worth as well as to attract industry to the city through organizations like the Board of Trade (which became the Chamber of Commerce in 1912). Oil companies and wildcatters were attracted to the city after the discovery of oil fields west of Fort Worth in places like Desdemona and Ranger, and the military found the climate to be suitable for their operations, beginning with America's entry into World War I. Bolstered by these changes to the city's structure and economy, and reflecting a general urbanizing trend in Texas, Fort Worth's population grew from 73,312 in 1910 to a respectable 106,482 by 1920.[2]

Reflecting the progressive attitudes of the day, Fort Worth officials reformed their city's political structure and infrastructure while simultaneously using civic organizations to promote industrial growth. Politically, Fort Worth underwent two transformations in fewer than twenty years. In 1907, with the commission form of government rising in popularity after Galveston adopted it in the wake of the devastating hurricane of 1900, Fort Worth voters voted to replace their ward-based aldermen with four commissioners and a ceremonial mayoral position. Progressive views on efficient, businesslike city government influenced Fort Worth in 1925 to eliminate its commissioners and replace them with a council/manager form of government. The city's services and infrastructure were greatly improved as well. By the beginning of World War I in 1914, the city was served by natural gas pipelines and electricity, better sewage treatment, a more reliable water supply, a thriving streetcar operation, and an interurban line to Dallas. Though industrial growth was limited for the first half of the 1910s, the onset of World War I and the discovery of oil in West Texas ushered in a new period of growth for Fort Worth.[3]

Fort Worth began as a military outpost in 1849, but it had had no military presence since the United States Army left in 1853. The United States' entry into World War I in 1917 brought great changes to the city, but not yet a permanent military presence. Fort Worth already had a small attachment to the Allied war effort before 1917, as the Canadian Royal Flying Corps trained its pilots at three airfields near the city from 1915 to 1917: Hicks, Barron, and Carruthers. The same clear weather and mild climate that attracted the Canadians influenced the U.S. Army's choice in 1917 to locate Camp Bowie in western Fort Worth, where the Thirty-Sixth Infantry Division trained before going to France in June 1918. Camp Bowie closed officially in 1920, but not before military engineers improved the roads and sewage system. It would be another two decades before the military and related industries made it back to Fort Worth, and when that happened, it was with the assistance of Amon Carter's national influence.[4]

The oil boom in North Central Texas did even more for Fort Worth than the temporary location of Camp Bowie within the city limits. It had been known for some time that there was oil in the region, but few efforts were made to exploit this resource until World War I drove oil prices higher. W. T. Waggoner, a wealthy rancher and later oilman who made his home in Fort Worth, expressed disgust when, in 1902, oil was discovered while drilling a water well on his Wichita County ranch: "I wanted water, and they got me oil. I tell you, I was mad, mad clean through. We needed water for ourselves and for our cattle to drink. I said damn the oil, I want water." Though he was a reluctant convert to the oil gospel, others hoped that North Texas would yield gushers similar to those that had been discovered along the Texas Gulf Coast or in Oklahoma. Until 1917, wildcatters in North Texas struck oil in limited quantities in places like Petrolia in Clay County and Burkburnett in Wichita County.[5]

For Fort Worth and the North Texas region, this changed on October 25, 1917, when workers drilling for the Texas Pacific Coal Company struck oil while searching for coal near Ranger in Eastland County. This gusher sparked an oil boom when thousands rushed to the area hoping to replicate the success of the Texas Pacific. Oil was soon found on cotton farmer S. K. Fowler's land near Burkburnett, where previous strikes had failed to produce much, and in Electra near the famed Waggoner Ranch. The Ranger strike in particular positively influenced Fort Worth's developing economy, since the city was a railroad hub for four railroads as well as the regional capital for West Texas banking and cattle. Soon, oil companies such as Gulf, Marland, Texas Pacific Coal and Oil, and Phillips established offices in the city to oversee their numerous operations in the nearby oil fields. Inevitably, smaller independent companies were attracted to the city as well.[6]

While the city experienced rapid economic and demographic change, what did not change was the poor treatment and socioeconomic position of Fort Worth's black population. By 1920, black citizens made up around 14.9 percent of the city's population, but they were still typically shoved aside by the rigid system of Jim Crow that showed no signs of abating. Although signs emerged during the 1910s and 1920s of a growing black middle class, personified by the likes of educator Isaiah Terrell, writer Lillian Horace, and banker/Republican power broker William McDonald, the vast majority of the city's African Americans struggled as laborers and domestics. Housing, education, churches, medical care, the criminal justice system—all these were strictly segregated in Fort Worth, serving as a major marker of the city's "southernness." And while Fort Worth did not gain a national reputation for being extraordinarily violent in its enforcement of the racial barriers, that did not mean violence was not a part of Jim Crow Fort Worth.

Two cases serve as horrifying examples of the violent enforcement of Fort Worth's segregation in the 1910s. In February 1911, the struggling Dixie Theater on Eleventh and Main, in the notorious "Hell's Half-Acre" district at the south end of downtown, opened for business one day with a "For Colored Only" sign on the ticket booth—which just so happened to be staffed by a black female. Before long, a mob reportedly one thousand strong formed in the street, chasing out the black theater employees. Unsure of what to do next, the mob began smashing windows and doors of black businesses in the neighborhood, and even attacked a number of individuals on their way to attend evening services at Allen Chapel African Methodist Episcopal Church. Meanwhile, law enforcement refused to intervene in any meaningful way. Two years later, in May 1913, another riot broke out upon the arrest of Tom Lee, a black male, for murdering two policemen, John Ogletree and Walter Moore, while on a shooting spree with a 12-gauge shotgun. While law enforcement stood aside, a white mob pulled several black passengers from a nearby streetcar and brutally assaulted them. Afterward, the mob rampaged through the black business district at the south end of downtown, leaving behind damage reminiscent of "a Kansas town the day after being struck by a cyclone." The black Masonic Temple had many of its windows smashed, while small businesses had their goods completely destroyed. Leading Fort Worth boosters, including partial *Star-Telegram* owner Paul Waples, attended a meeting at the Chamber of Commerce where many roundly condemned the mob as the work of "hoodlums" and "a small, vicious minority," perpetrated against "innocent victims." Thus was Jim Crow enforced; and while the white community quickly forgot (or at least chose not to remember these horrific scenes), for black Fort Worthians, the riots served as not-so-subtle reminders of their tenuous status in a southern city on the western frontier.[7]

Carter left behind no record of his own feelings about the 1911 or 1913 riots, but a prior event in Dallas does provide some insight into how he reacted to a similar situation. On March 3, 1910, a lynch mob stormed the Dallas County courthouse where Allan Brooks, an elderly black man, was about to stand trial for molesting a three-year-old white girl. Having broken into the courthouse, the mob grabbed Brooks and hurled him out of a second-story window into the street below, where he was subsequently kicked, stomped, and dragged behind a car. The crowd then took his body and hanged him from a telephone pole underneath the Elks Arch, a Dallas landmark. By 12:30 that afternoon, the *Star-Telegram* had printed a special edition covering the horrifying episode, and Carter and two newsboys, armed with one thousand copies of the extra, took the interurban to Dallas, where they sold out within thirty minutes. At the end of the day, Carter and his two newsboys had sold over five thousand copies in Dallas, with another one thousand sent north to the cities of Sherman and Denison, where they were quickly snapped up by an eager public. His exploits were even recorded as far away as Memphis, where the *Commercial Appeal* reported not on the horrors of the lynching but on Carter's salesmanship.[8]

Against this backdrop of an evolving Fort Worth, Carter's entrepreneurial talent continued to flourish, with the primary beneficiary being the rapidly growing *Star-Telegram*. The purchase of the *Telegram* did wonders for the dying *Star*, in part because the *Star* now had access to a much larger, more modern facility, located in the heart of the Fort Worth business district on 8th and Throckmorton. In the earliest days of the *Star-Telegram,* Carter was not the sole power within the newspaper but rather served as the secretary and business manager as well as a member of the board of directors. Paul Waples, whose backing had largely made the merger possible, was the president, and Louis Wortham, already the publisher of the *Star,* retained that title and served as editor. It was not long before the newly established paper began showing signs of success. In its first year, 1909, the *Star-Telegram* recorded an average daily circulation of just over 15,000, and by the end of 1911 that number had risen to well over 20,000. The fledgling publication celebrated with a special 204-page Sunday edition on December 10, 1911, as well as a banquet at the Westbrook Hotel in which employees dined on roast turkey, mashed potatoes, and French peas followed by Neapolitan ice cream and assorted cakes. Just four years later, the *Star-Telegram* leadership hosted a marketing dinner at the recently opened Rivercrest Country Club just west of Fort Worth that celebrated an average daily circulation of 36,000 as well as a Sunday circulation of 42,000 by the last three months of the year. These stellar numbers meant that within six years, the Star-Telegram had grown to the second-largest circulation in the state, even though the Fort Worth population ranked fourth behind San Antonio, Dallas, and Houston. The menu reflected the increasing success of the newspaper: diners noshed on tenderloin steaks (provided by Swift), sweetbreads (from Armour), and oyster cocktails, washed down with glasses of wine and lager beer (Prohibition's dark, dry shadow had yet to descend on Texas or the nation). Afterward, attendees smoked cigars and cigarettes, then, for those who needed to camouflage the signs of indulging their vices, chewing gum was provided. For years after, for reasons not altogether altruistic, Carter would work to ensure that employees remained on good terms with management, and such events celebrating the contributions of the newspaper's rank-and-file became the norm.

Success, of course, was not an accident, but was the result of deliberate marketing strategies by Carter and Wortham. The *Star-Telegram* positioned itself as *the* newspaper for West Texas. Though Carter had not yet placed the famous slogan calling Fort Worth "Where the West Begins" on the newspaper's masthead, the *Star-Telegram,* "with one eye on the economy of West Texas and the other on its own image, advocated diversified farming and agricultural research." In 1912, the paper published a special 250-page edition that "promoted business and commerce in Fort Worth and the region." When it became clear that the oil boom that began in 1917 was going to positively shape Fort Worth's economy, Carter insisted that the newspaper develop its own oil and gas department with full-time writers to cover related events throughout West Texas, coverage that undoubtedly boosted sales. An undated *Star-Telegram* memo (presumably from 1920) lists the newspaper's daily circulation in Texas and Oklahoma oil towns at almost 14,700, with 13,902 coming from Texas alone. Boom towns such as Breckenridge, Desdemona, and Ranger led the way—all with over 1,000 in daily circulation. A similar document from 1920 comparing the *Star-Telegram*'s West Texas (defined in the document as Texas and Oklahoma towns west of Fort Worth) circulation with that of the *Record* and the *Dallas Morning News* reveals that the newspaper nearly doubled the combined circulation of its two rivals.[9]

Meanwhile, as the paper's circulation increased, changes that reflected Carter's ambition continued to be made in the *Star-Telegram*'s leadership. In 1913, Paul Waples resigned as president of the newspaper and was replaced by Louis Wortham. Carter became vice president and general manager, demonstrating his role as the driving force in the company and his rising stature in the Fort Worth community. The national newspaper industry was beginning to take note of Carter's contribution to the success of the *Star-Telegram*. The trade magazine *Editor and Publisher* told of how Carter had played an excellent host (a sign of many things to come) to visiting delegates from the Ad Club Convention held in Dallas in 1913 and remarked that "the *Star-Telegram* is making great progress under Mr. Carter's administration and has already become one of the Southwest's strongest newspapers." That same year, the *Fourth Estate*, a trade newspaper that advertised itself as "a newspaper for the makers of newspapers," ran an issue with a large photo of a confident-looking Carter, thinning hair slicked back, on its cover. And why not, considering "during the *Star-Telegram's* greatest growth its manager has been Mr. Carter." As far as the American public was concerned, he was still an unknown, but his counterparts across the nation were fast learning who this brash newcomer was. As his standing in the industry grew, Carter, unsurprisingly, wished for greater control of the newspaper. In 1916, he officially formed a partnership with Wortham to create the Wortham-Carter Publishing Company, which became the new publisher of the *Star-Telegram*.[10]

Carter spent much of his time traveling the United States meeting with advertisers and generally drumming up support for Fort Worth from the national business community. This cultivation was instrumental to the continued growth of the newspaper, and it provided Carter with an opportunity to expand the vast network of influential friends across the United States he had begun building in his earlier days as a traveling salesman and advertiser. At times, Carter's long trips created animosity with Wortham, president of the *Star-Telegram*. Evidence indicates that despite their generally amicable partnership, which had resulted in the creation of one of the most successful Texas newspapers, the two egos did not always work well together. At one point, Wortham accused Carter of going off on too many trips to Chicago and New York and simultaneously failing to keep him informed of business developments on these trips. One of the worst explosions between the two came in 1916 when Carter authorized the running of an ad for the Reverend J. Frank Norris, the controversial fundamentalist pastor at the First Baptist Church of Fort Worth, after Carter had made an agreement with Wortham that no Norris ads would be accepted.

In a series of letters discussing this squabble, Wortham made statements that reveal his thoughts about Carter's personality. "You are not a rational man," Wortham fumed. "You haven't been for months." He also remarked that "from the very first, I have known that you were self-willed, imperious, and arbitrary. During all this time I have recognized your ability with pride in you, but your fault has been that you have recognized ability in no one else but yourself." Interestingly, these comments were similar to ones Zetta made later upon divorcing Carter. In his response to Wortham, Carter revealed his skill in avoiding outright conflict. He wrote, "If this matter has caused you any embarrassment, I naturally regret it very much, as regardless of the outcome of our business relations, I have no desire to incur your ill will, or to cause you to work yourself into an unhappy frame of mind." Despite these occasional power struggles, Wortham served the paper until 1923, just four years before his death at the age of sixty-nine.[11]

By the late 1910s, Carter was working to consolidate his paper's position within the Fort Worth market. As long as there was serious competition to the *Star-Telegram,* his role as unofficial spokesperson for Fort Worth was limited. To achieve this dominance, Carter accomplished two feats: staving off an incursion from media magnate William Randolph Hearst and launching a radio station as a partner to the newspaper. Hearst and Carter had been acquainted with one another for some time as newspaper publishers, but how well they knew one another before 1917 is unclear. At some point in their professional relationship, Carter must have made a favorable impression on Hearst because from 1917 to 1921, he desperately tried to get Carter to work for him. In 1918, Carter sent a letter to Hearst congratulating him on his new partnership with Carter's former advertising associate from San Francisco, Edgar M. Swasey. This was not long after Carter had turned down an initial proposal from Hearst's company to join forces. Discussing the possibility of running a Hearst newspaper, Carter informed Swasey in 1917 that this would be a problem for him because, "As a rule[,] a man in the Hearst organization has too many bosses. Knowing my disposition as you do[,] you can see that I would not prosper under these conditions."[12]

Still, this did not stop Carter from entertaining offers from Hearst's magazine division editor and soon-to-be chief treasurer, Joseph A. Moore. In January 1918, Moore offered Carter a position running the Hearst newspaper in Atlanta, the *Georgian.* Carter responded by saying that for him to consider this proposal, he would have to have "absolute charge of editorial and business affairs[,] including all employees and be subject only to Mr. Hearst['s] orders." Furthermore, he required a salary of at least $36,000 a year and he would have to "dispose of [his] interest in Texas." Moore refused to conduct further negotiations by correspondence and told Carter he would have to come to New York to discuss matters with Hearst. Carter was unable (or unwilling) to travel to New York, so the matter was dropped temporarily. Carter's friend Swasey met with Hearst several times over the first few months of that same year to discuss advertising management positions, and during these discussions, Swasey suggested that

Carter would be the perfect man to resurrect the languishing *Chicago Examiner*. He informed Carter, "I told him most enthusiastically with all the emphasis I could muster that you were the one man in this country that could put that paper ahead of the *Tribune* in five years and that he ought to get you no matter what he has to pay you, so he is going to try for you again." Hearst did try again, and he was about to offer Carter a position that would have propelled Carter to the top of the publishing world.[13]

In 1919, Hearst again sent out feelers to Carter through Moore to gauge Carter's interest in working for him, this time in New York City. In February 1919, Moore wrote Carter telling him that "there is a big development brewing here in New York in connection with one of the Hearst newspapers, and the opportunity, I believe, is big enough to interest you." He asked him, "Are you ever going to be in a position to cash in on your wonderful work in Fort Worth and move on into the big tent?" Moore kept quiet on what changes might be coming but encouraged Carter to come to New York to discuss the matter further.[14]

After a second letter from Moore coaxing Carter to leave Fort Worth and come to New York to work for Hearst, Carter replied by sending a sack of pecans to Hearst as a token of appreciation for his consideration. Moore responded to Carter telling him of Hearst's feelings on the matter. "While it is very sweet of you to send these nuts to him," he wrote, "he would have preferred very much to have you present yourself in full readiness to take charge of the great big proposition which he has in mind for you here in New York." Moore was more detailed in his job offer this time around, writing that Carter could "fix up a deal with Colonel Wortham whereby you could come up to New York for W.R. and take full charge in the *New York American,* leaving your interest in Fort Worth as it is." He also appealed to Carter's ego, telling him that running a newspaper with the largest morning circulation in New York required someone with Carter's talent. As further encouragement, Moore suggested that Hearst would probably "agree to let you write your own ticket" with regard to salary. Moore impressed upon Carter the magnitude of him deciding to stay in the relatively small city of Fort Worth and eschewing the limitless possibilities of New York. Moore wired Carter the next day, begging him to join Hearst's empire: "How would fifty thousand do for a starter?" he enticed. Despite the fact that Carter was not yet a wealthy man, the offer was to no avail, and Carter firmly insisted on staying in Fort Worth. Carter's response to Hearst is unknown, but his rebuttal to Hearst's final offer two years later provides some insight into why Carter turned down such a lucrative proposition.[15]

In December 1921, Moore had a new offer for Carter to consider, writing that "Mr. Hearst seems determined to get you into this organization and he brings it up several times a month." Moore proposed that Carter sell his newspaper to Hearst in exchange for "establishing a chain of papers for him in Texas and the Southwest." Carter's response was similar to his previous ones but provided more explanation for his refusal to leave Fort Worth for the Hearst empire. He detailed for Moore the recent improvements made to the *Star-Telegram*'s plant as well as the dominance the paper enjoyed not only in Fort Worth but also in Texas. Carter bragged, "There was a time in which the *Dallas News* absolutely predominated the newspaper business in Texas," yet by "providing the reading public with the kind of paper they want . . . the *Star-Telegram* has in sixteen years, without any money to start with, built up the largest circulation of any newspaper in Texas, exceeding the *Dallas News* [by] approximately 14,000 daily, notwithstanding the fact that Fort Worth is the fourth largest city in Texas." Although Carter promised that on his next trip to New York he would speak with Hearst, the issue appeared to be dead. Carter would stay in Fort Worth to preside over his own kingdom with no one to answer to but himself.[16]

On the surface, one could look at the Carter/Hearst interactions of 1917–1921 and interpret them as Carter refusing a cosmopolitan lifestyle due to some provincial connection with Texas, like a lone rugged cowboy turning his back on the bright city lights to pursue his own individualistic way of life. But what seems clear upon further review is that Carter understood that though he could become financially comfortable working for Hearst, he would not be his own boss and he would be abandoning the influence he was building up for himself within Fort Worth. Carter was too prideful and impetuous to work for someone like Hearst, and while his power and influence at the time might be limited to Texas, he enjoyed reigning over his own realm. In hindsight, it appears that Carter made the correct choice by maintaining his position in Fort Worth, because this gave him greater opportunities to wield influence on a much larger scale. If he had left to work for Hearst, his independence would have been greatly curtailed and his work as a booster for Fort Worth and Texas more limited in scope.

After having been repeatedly rebuffed by Carter, Hearst decided on a new tactic: a head-to-head showdown with the *Star-Telegram* through ownership of the *Fort Worth Record*. The *Record* was the morning paper for Fort Worth and had been since 1903 when the former *Houston Post* managing editor Clarence Ousley and a group of investors purchased the *Fort Worth Gazette* and began printing it as the *Record*. Ousley sold the newspaper in 1913 to Fort Worth attorney

William Capps, and the newspaper had changed hands two more times by 1923. The *Record* and the *Star-Telegram* competed closely until 1913, but over the next ten years, Carter's newspaper easily surpassed the *Record*'s circulation. Hearst, who had been engaged in a buying spree since the end of the post–World War I recession, added the *Record* to the long list of recently purchased newspapers, such as the *Seattle Post-Intelligencer,* the *Washington Herald,* and the *Boston Record.* Though Joseph Moore, by now Hearst's chief treasurer, warned his new employer that funds were limited, Hearst added two Baltimore newspapers and the *Fort Worth Record* to his national newspaper stable.[17]

Hearst's motivation for buying the *Record* is not explicitly stated, but it appears that the reasons are threefold. First, he was in the middle of an expansive phase in his career in which he was purchasing newspapers and producing films. Second, he owned no newspapers in Texas, and ownership of the *Record* would open the growing Texas market for him. Finally, he had just engaged in a long struggle to obtain Carter; it was possible that Carter might sell the *Star-Telegram* to Hearst or jump ship to join with Hearst if things went well for the *Record*. Carter warmly greeted the *Record,* publishing a front-page editorial welcoming Hearst and lauding Hearst columnist Arthur Brisbane as "the world's greatest journalist." This reaction caused journalist Alva Johnston to comment, "It was the only time a competitor ever smothered a Hearst newspaper with kindness."[18]

Carter may have received the *Record*'s new ownership with kindness, but *Star-Telegram* editor James Record credited Carter's ultimate victory in this publishing war to Hearst's failure to overcome local obstacles to competing with Carter in Fort Worth and West Texas. To begin with, Hearst did not enjoy a great reputation in Fort Worth and West Texas. The fact that Hearst newspapers covered national and international news rather heavily did not fulfill the needs of the region, and even though Hearst was nationally recognized, local allegiance to the Fort Worth– and West Texas–oriented *Star-Telegram* remained strong. Finally, Hearst reporters and executives were often from out-of-state and were unfamiliar with local attitudes in a variety of areas. Early biographer Samuel Kinch revealed that part of this lack of knowledge included how locals handled race relations; under Hearst, the *Record* used "Mr.," "Mrs.," and "Miss" when referring to African Americans, whereas the *Star-Telegram* used first names in accordance with Southern tradition. In any case, though its circulation increased, the *Record* ran a deficit during the Hearst years and was never able to close the gap with its competitor.[19]

By 1925, Hearst was ready to make yet another offer to Carter. Carter traveled to California in October 1925 to meet with Hearst, who immediately offered to purchase the *Star-Telegram* while allowing Carter to manage it for $100,000 a year. Carter refused this offer but was ready with his own proposal: the *Star-Telegram* would buy the *Record* and subscribe to the Hearst news service and syndicated features. The *Record* would then become the *Record-Telegram,* in effect, a morning edition of the *Star-Telegram*. Hearst agreed to sell for $300,000, thus ending his nearly decade-long effort to secure Carter's services. Despite that fact, the professional relationship between Hearst and Carter remained intact. Carter was now without a serious rival in his own city and for the next thirty years worked to ensure that his newspaper would retain its dominant position.[20]

Meanwhile, Carter led efforts to secure a physical plant worthy of the burgeoning *Star-Telegram*. In 1919, the Wortham-Carter Publishing Company purchased land in the heart of Fort Worth's central business district at the intersection of Seventh and Taylor Streets, where they planned to build an updated facility for the newspaper. Construction began in January 1920 and by December 5, the *Star-Telegram* had moved into the four-story $1,000,000 building.[21]

The new headquarters reflected Carter's two-pronged desire to modernize and to provide a comfortable environment for his employees. To ensure that the *Star-Telegram* could keep up with growing demand, three presses churned out thousands of copies a day. To make the building more fireproof, little wood was used in its construction, with steel, concrete, marble, and brick making up the bulk of the structure. Fire hoses and hydrants were placed on every floor, and unlike most publishing plants, numerous drinking fountains were scattered throughout. Even the carriers (or "newsies" as they were called) had their own facilities complete with restrooms and a congregating area; 250 windows provided natural light; employees had showers on every floor; and, reflecting the evolving nature of the workplace, women had their own restrooms. While these details may sound mundane, such features were considered somewhat revolutionary for contemporary newspaper plants. The *Editor and Publisher,* a trade magazine covering the newspaper industry, praised it on the front page of its May 28, 1921, edition, calling it the "finest newspaper plant in [the] Southwest" and praising it for "the great space that has been given to every department and the great investment that has been made in labor-saving devices." Laudatory articles from around the nation were printed in the May 31, 1921, edition of the *Star-Telegram,* and a three-day public reception was held to show off the new building.[22]

Other changes for the *Star-Telegram* were on the horizon. Always abreast of changes in technology, Carter was intrigued by the recent development of radio. The potential of radio may seem obvious in hindsight, but at the time the new medium was regarded by many as a fad, "nothing more than another craze that would, like a weak signal, eventually fade." Even the humorist Will Rogers, future radio host and friend to Amon Carter, could not refrain from criticizing radio as "bunk." Yet by 1922, radio was growing in popularity despite listeners' hardships and frustrations due to the intrinsic sporadic programming of early stations. President Warren G. Harding's Secretary of Commerce, Herbert Hoover, took the lead in standardizing and licensing the industry, and many newspapers recognized the possibilities of this new medium. As early as 1920, the *Detroit News* had launched WWJ as its on-air arm, and other urban newspapers, such as those in Atlanta and Kansas City, soon followed suit. Though Carter did not yet own his own radio set in 1922, *Star-Telegram* circulation manager Harold Hough did, and he spoke with Carter about radio's possibilities. The *Record* had also started its own station in March of that year, so Carter was motivated to explore this new technology if only to stay ahead of his competitor. At Hough's urging, Carter agreed to invest $300 in starting a radio station, saying, "If this is going to be a menace to newspapers[,] we had better own the menace." Hough went to Washington, D.C., to visit the Department of Commerce and obtain approval for the new venture. Herbert Hoover reportedly named the station himself—WBAP, meaning "We Bring a Program"—and in May 1922, WBAP began broadcasting. At first, the station was housed in the *Star-Telegram* building, but as it grew, it soon had its own headquarters in the Medical Arts Building south of Fort Worth's central business district.[23]

WBAP enabled Carter to extend his reach beyond Fort Worth and into West Texas, thus reflecting the westward orientation he had been developing for at least a decade. In 1922, the Fort Worth Cats, the local minor league baseball team, "became the first Texas team to enjoy play-by-play broadcasts," and West Texas ranchers benefited from early-warning weather reports that enabled them to protect their livestock from incoming blizzards. In a further effort to maintain the loyalty of West Texas listeners, many of whom were farmers and ranchers, the station later began broadcasting market reports from the Livestock Exchange in the Fort Worth Stockyards. Fort Worth was not just a material gateway city but, thanks to the combined influence of WBAP and the *Star-Telegram*, an information gateway as well. And as radio's popularity grew throughout the decade, along with the circulation of the *Star-Telegram*, Carter and his properties were guaranteed to play a significant role in shaping the views of citizens of Fort Worth and West Texas.[24]

One year after beginning WBAP as the broadcasting arm of the *Star-Telegram*, Carter attained full ownership of the newspaper when Louis Wortham sold his company shares to Carter. Upon retiring from the newspaper business in 1923, Wortham focused on writing his five-volume *History of Texas from Wilderness to Commonwealth*, published the next year. By all accounts, the partnership between Wortham and Carter appeared solid, notwithstanding the occasional dispute. It seems that Wortham, while the titular head of the *Star-Telegram,* was generally content to give Carter the space he needed and the freedom he desired to take the newspaper in what he believed was the right direction. Now as the sole president and publisher of the *Star-Telegram,* Carter was able to enjoy the accompanying benefits and even more freedom than he had previously. That same year, in recognition of the *Star-Telegram*'s importance to West Texas, as well as a kind of opening salvo in his rivalry with Dallas to the east, Carter had the phrase "Where the West Begins" added to the newspaper's masthead.

Running the *Star-Telegram* understandably took most of Carter's attention, but he was wise enough to direct some of his efforts toward ensuring that Fort Worth citizens would welcome the once-upstart newspaper as part of the community. His strategy included extending the helping hand of philanthropy through two long-lasting programs designed to help Fort Worth's needy: the Free Milk and Ice Fund and the Good Fellow Fund (later changed to Goodfellows Fund). The Free Milk and Ice Fund began in 1912 and provided those two products during the sweltering months of June, July, and August to Fort Worth's needy citizens. Three years later, Carter's paper reported that nearly four hundred families received free ice and milk that summer along with occasional nursing assistance. After World War I, the program went into effect year-round, and "the scope was broadened to include education in the care and use of milk and ice and to secure ice boxes for the indigent."[25]

The Goodfellows Fund collected community donations to give gifts to poor children at Christmas and has remained an integral part of the newspaper's Fort Worth outreach during the Christmas season. It began as a men-only fund designed to assist Fort Worth's needy families but was opened to women after an anonymous woman insisted on donating money in 1912. The 1912 gift basket contained coal or wood, food, and toys, but the contents changed in subsequent years. During the early years of the fund, typical gifts given by the Goodfellows generally included food, toys, and clothes for each family. Money was raised by soliciting donations from the local business community and through ad campaigns urging citizens to "kick in a penny or two." In 1915, Carter's newspaper reported that "many children know no Santa Claus but him they call Mr. Goodfellow." As Leonard Sanders observes in his history *How Fort Worth Became the Texasmost City,* Carter had learned how to combine "business promotion, civic need, and an unabashed personal empathy." That said, records do not indicate the beneficiaries' racial status; presumably, given the racial environment and the attitudes of the *Star-Telegram* leadership, white Fort Worthians were the only recipients of this largess.[26]

The Free Milk and Ice and Goodfellows Funds are the first recorded reflection of Carter's lifelong desire to help those less fortunate. While Carter was certainly motivated by what charity drives could accomplish for his newspaper, one cannot deny that a strong part of him simply enjoyed helping others. Philanthropy would become integral to his life, first undertaken in an unorganized, haphazard fashion (but helpful nonetheless), only to become transformed into the Amon Carter Foundation after Carter became wealthy through oil interests. Though the Amon Carter Foundation was not founded until 1945, well after Carter had begun his varied acts of charity and philanthropy, it marked the culmination of his efforts to maximize the giving that he had been a part of since the start of the Goodfellows Fund. The formation of benevolent trusts did not start with Carter, of course, but he was clearly part of a trend that began in the late nineteenth century with industrial giants like Andrew Carnegie and John D. Rockefeller. Until he became independently wealthy in 1937, however, Carter would be forced to indulge his philanthropic leanings by leading fund-raising drives for his adopted causes either through the pages of the *Star-Telegram* or by exploiting the network of industrialists and businessmen he had developed over the years.

An excellent example of philanthropy through fund-raising was his successful leadership in providing a large new building for the downtown Fort Worth YMCA, which required the mobilization of the business community. The original building was, by all accounts, in sore need of repair. According to a national YMCA newsletter, Rabbi George Fox of Fort Worth remarked that "before he came to Fort Worth[,] when he had the blues he went to the YMCA, but that in Fort Worth when he went to the YMCA it gave him the blues." By 1922, Carter had taken the lead by chairing a new committee to raise money for a structure to replace the "incompetent, rheumatic old building," and he decided in March of that year to begin fund-raising for a new YMCA building. Getting the building campaign running was quite a feat, as the city in 1922 had just endured some of the worst flooding of the Trinity River, which caused over two million dollars in damage.[27]

Carter not only worked to raise some $300,000 in donations for the building fund, but he also secured a plot of land formerly owned by Mrs. Winfield Scott for the building. While Mrs. Scott did not receive any money, as she was donating the land, Carter assured her that she would be given credit through a memorial tablet erected in her honor. In addition to negotiating a plot of land for the YMCA, Carter was instrumental in working with city officials for the proper permits and even pressured Southwestern Bell Telephone Company to install the proper telephone system as specified by the National Bureau of the YMCA. On April 12, 1924, a ceremony was held to celebrate the laying of the cornerstone, with Carter speaking on behalf of the building committee. By spring 1925, when the new building was opened, it reportedly had some of the finest equipment of any YMCA in the United States. Such efforts, though not officially done under the auspices of the *Star-Telegram,* involved Carter so much that the newspaper and its image reaped valuable spillover benefits.[28]

While guiding the *Star-Telegram* toward greater circulation and local dominance through community involvement, civic boosterism, and improved facilities, Carter also cultivated his role as a civic leader in his own right by getting involved in various social and business-oriented associations. In 1911, the Board of Directors of the Fort Worth Board of Trade elected him president of the organization. He also was an active member of the Elks Lodge. As an Exalted Ruler of the Elks in Fort Worth, he presided over the drive to build a $125,000 Elks Home in 1910, a building that the *Fourth Estate* called "one of the handsomest and best appointed social clubs in the South." Even more important for forging connections with the local elite was Carter's membership in the Fort Worth Club, an organization he would lead for the last thirty-five years of his life.[29]

The Fort Worth Club had its start as the Commercial Club in 1885, an organization that, in the words of the *Fort Worth Daily Gazette,* "gives promise of great usefulness in the development of Fort Worth." This club of 180 of the town's wealthiest men was "not only a social organization" but also "the medium of advancing the business interests of the city." Combining the boosterism of a chamber of commerce (or, in Fort Worth's case, a Board of Trade) with the elite fraternizing of a social club, the Commercial Club quickly became one of the most respected organizations in Fort Worth. In 1906, Commercial Club members voted to change the name to the Fort Worth Club because, some argued, the former name sounded too much like a service club or chamber of commerce. "A place was needed," members believed, "to entertain the 'high and the mighty' of the business and corporate world. A place was needed where the city's best citizens could gather in comfortable surroundings, and where their wives and children could join them in enjoying the very best in cuisine, service and décor." Such organizations were formed all across the urban west as towns and cities attempted to present a "civilizing" image that would re-create the social institutions of their older eastern counterparts. Carter's role in the merger of the *Star* and the *Telegram* earned him a position in this exclusive club; within a few years he was named to the Board of Governors and, by 1920, president of the Fort Worth Club.[30]

From 1915 to 1926, Carter consolidated his position as a leader of the prestigious Fort Worth Club. For Carter, as for many of the city's other luminaries, the club was more than just a social club where Fort Worth's elite gathered for dinner, cigars, and—during Prohibition—illegal beverages. During Carter's tenure, the club became the unofficial headquarters of Fort Worth politics and business, and for Carter, the prime place to entertain visiting celebrities, politicians, and industrialists. Throughout his leadership of both the *Star-Telegram* and the Fort Worth Club, Carter proved to be a seasoned host, a skill that was useful when persuading others to do his bidding. Under Carter's leadership, the Fort Worth Club was able to move into an extravagant new building by 1926, and using the club's Suite 10-G as his own Oval Office, he presided over even greater expansion for his newspaper and his city. As his position in Fort Worth society rose, Carter simultaneously lessened his involvement with fraternal organizations such as the Elks and the Oddfellows. A man of his stature, with increasing influence and elevated status, could not afford to devote his time to predominantly middle-class societies.

During this formative period of his life, Carter dabbled in other passions, two of which would become great boons to the local economy. One was the new technology of aviation. This obsession with flying stayed with him from the time he first saw an airplane in 1909 until his death and ultimately led him to successfully push for an international airport serving Fort Worth. In 1909, he and other Fort Worth businessmen formed the Southwestern Aviation Conference, later called the Southwestern Aero Club. In 1911, through the editorial page of the *Star-Telegram,* he persuaded Fort Worthians to raise $7,000 to bring to the city a group of French aviators called the International Aviators. That same year, he was instrumental in having the first piece of airmail delivered to Fort Worth by aviator Cal Rodgers. Rodgers was in the midst of attempting to fly across the United States in thirty days in order to claim a $50,000 prize from William Randolph Hearst. When he landed in Fort Worth on October 17, a crowd of ten thousand people was on hand to meet him. He then delivered a piece of mail from Oklahoma to Carter and *Star-Telegram* editor James North. When the United States entered World War I in 1917, Carter assisted the Fort Worth Chamber of Commerce in lobbying the government to locate airfields in the city to train pilots. As a result of his actions, the three airfields in Fort Worth formerly used by Canadian pilots were used by the army, including Carruthers Field in Benbrook and Hicks Field on the north side of Fort Worth. Carter did not view these new contraptions as toys but saw their potential in terms of transportation and their ability to transform Fort Worth into a great hub of industry and commerce. With this new technology, Carter also believed that he could reach an even wider audience in the vast expanses of West Texas with his newspaper. By the late 1920s, Carter would be a full-fledged aviation enthusiast committed to bringing an airport and airlines to Fort Worth.[31]

Carter also recognized the importance of the oil industry to Fort Worth and West Texas. The West Texas oil boom that began in earnest in Ranger in 1917 was having a profound effect on Fort Worth's economy as oil companies and prospective oilmen began using the city as their unofficial headquarters. Some of these companies located in Fort Worth at the urging of Carter. For example, during a visit to the Sinclair Oil Company's offices in New York, Carter noticed a map with pins on it denoting the locations of Sinclair's offices around the country. Carter picked up the pin marking the recently purchased Pierce Oil Company in Dallas and moved it to Fort Worth; soon after, Sinclair moved its regional offices to Fort Worth. He also persuaded the Southern Crude Oil Company to move from Shreveport, Louisiana, to Fort Worth in much the same way. In 1924, Carter convinced the American Petroleum Institute to hold its fifth annual convention in Fort Worth and then commenced to boost the city to the attendees. Never one to remain on the outside, he also began exploring for oil in his own right, though initially with little success; he was notorious in oil circles for some time as "the only big oil producer who has never produced," because he drilled ninety straight dry holes. His wells would remain relatively dry until the 1930s, yet his enthusiasm never lagged.[32]

Carter's personal life stood in stark contrast to his meteoric rise through Fort Worth society. In 1917, after fifteen years of marriage, Zetta Carter filed for divorce. Problems had begun well before, however, as the two had been separated for at least a year before she filed for divorce. Zetta cited numerous reasons for ending her marriage to Amon, maintaining that Amon had been a devoted husband and father early in the marriage, but as he became more successful he lost interest in maintaining the marriage. In her words, "With his success came his great desire for social preference, that in a large measure the effort of homebuilding was abandoned; in many respects, the home was without attraction for him." She added that Amon "has been for years past, guilty of excesses, cruel treatment, and outrages." No specifics are shared as to what the "excesses, cruel treatment, and outrages" were, leaving outsiders clueless as to what conditions were like inside the home.[33]

The next year, 1918, the forty-year-old Carter married the twenty-three-year-old Nenetta Burton, daughter of one of the earliest investors in the old *Star* and co-owner of Burton-Peel Dry Goods, Willard Burton. In addition to this older connection, they had also forged a partnership in some of Carter's first, mostly unsuccessful attempts to strike oil. Though much sought after by young men in Virginia, where she attended Sweet Briar College, Nenetta chose to marry the much older and more established Amon. It is unclear at what point Amon and Nenetta began their relationship, but two somewhat cryptic undated telegrams from 1915–16 hint at the beginnings of some more intimate connection between the two at that time. Not surprisingly, this was about the same time that Zetta remarked that her marriage to Amon began to disintegrate. Carter, frequently gone on business trips, was in Sweet Briar, Virginia, at the Carolina Hotel (ostensibly to meet Nenetta) when he received a telegram from Nenetta's sister Olive with the message: "Nenetta and I will meet you in Lynchburg Sunday." A later telegram sent to Amon, who was once again at the Carolina Hotel, stated: "Will meet you here Sunday and stay overnight." This new relationship resulted in the 1919 birth of his only son, Amon Gary Carter Jr., whom he raised as the heir to his expanding fortune. This new relationship with the much younger Nenetta did not appeal to his daughter, Bertice, who clashed with Nenetta. A rather nasty spat arose in 1920 over sixteen-year-old Bertice's attempt to spend time with Amon Carter Jr., who had just been born to Amon and Nenetta. Nenetta took offense at this effort and Bertice's request for a picture of Amon. The bond between Bertice and Nenetta must have already been frayed when Nenetta sent Bertice a long, hastily written letter. How, Nenetta inquired of her, could Bertice ask Amon "for a picture of MY baby when you are ashamed to speak to me?"[34]

Bertice's cold shoulder toward Nenetta caused Nenetta to exclaim, "I've done everything in my power to get along with you." From Bertice's point of view, she had done nothing wrong, and she immediately appealed to her father. "You know how I have to act, dear, toward her on account of mother." She complained that "I feel so dubious of your love and yet you must have some affection for me . . .

Sometimes it is unbearable and I wish I had never been born." She closed with the mournful line, "I'm pretty blue tonight over everything so had better stop before I start crying again."[35]

Understandably, Carter rushed to mend the breach between Bertice and Nenetta by attempting, somewhat unsuccessfully, to take sides in the spat. Yet it is clear in his response to Bertice that he felt some frustration toward her. "It is unfortunate," he declared, "that things have developed as they have, and I feel sure that it was started at the time you inadvertently declined to speak to Nenetta. In my position I am trying to avoid making either side unhappy." What is interesting in Carter's letter is his philosophy of dealing with life's obstacles. Much of it seems to stem from Carter's experience of rising from nothing and becoming one of the most powerful men in Fort Worth. He told Bertice, "We all have much to live for and much happiness in store if we will only take advantage of our opportunity, make the best of things, and avoid the unpleasant things which bring about dissatisfaction and unhappiness." He closed by saying, "Let's drop it and both of us try and forget it and make ourselves happy over many other things." Rug sweeping, of course, did little to mend the fraying bonds between father and daughter.[36]

Despite the split with Zetta, Carter worked hard to maintain his status as a father to Bertice. Ever the doting (yet oftentimes absent) father, he continued his practice of showering her with gifts, as he had done since she was very young. When she was as young as eight, he tried to instill in her a sense of financial responsibility, even going so far as to try to explain how the *Star-Telegram* stock he purchased for her eighth birthday would appreciate in value over time. Some of these lessons must have stuck with the young Bertice as revealed in a 1914 letter written by the then ten-year-old. "Dad," she bragged, "I got five presents for two dollars and seventy-five cents. Don't you think I'm a bargain hunter?" As a teenager, she was sent away to school like so many other children of the elite; in her case, it was Lasell Seminary in Auburndale, Massachusetts. In addition to paying her tuition, he provided her with $25 a month, though, he argued, "you should be able to get along on $15.00 a month." In 1920, he agreed to purchase the sixteen-year-old Bertice a car and ordered her a Cadillac Coupe, an act that was sure to increase her popularity among her classmates. Though generous with his money, he did not extend this generosity toward granting her wishes to be employed as a society editor for the *Star-Telegram* over the summer of 1922. "You've always thought me so useless so now give me a chance to prove I'm not," she pleaded. She assured him it would be "on a strictly business basis as if I were an outsider," apparently ignoring the fact that most eighteen-year old outsiders would not be given many chances at being a newspaper's society editor. Despite Bertice's coaxing tone, Amon remained firm, stating that he was "somewhat averse to relatives working on the paper." Averse as he might be to this idea at the moment, his attitude changed as Amon Jr. grew up and was groomed to become the heir to the Carter Publishing Company.[37]

The evidence indicates that Amon Sr. maintained a businesslike relationship with his father as he worked to develop his business in Fort Worth. The few existing letters from his father discuss the details of raising chickens, maintaining the farm, and financial matters. In an attempt to help his father's poultry business, Amon ran advertisements in the *Star-Telegram*. Though not yet independently wealthy, Amon felt obligated to support his father monetarily. In 1909, William Carter wrote his son of some expenses incurred in improving his farm, and Amon took this as a hint to send his father money, so he promptly sent him $145.00. With just a hint of pride and self-reliance, William wrote his son saying, "I did not aim to pull your leg for that $145.00. I aim to pay it back and I still intend too [sic]." Yet Amon did not hesitate to lecture his father about the best way to handle his financial struggles.[38]

In December 1911, William wrote Amon that he owed $189.00 to John Hunt of the First National Bank in Bowie but assured him, "I am not asking you to pay it. I am just telling you about it so you will not grumble." Knowing that his father had taken out the loan to help pay for his farm, Amon had settled the account without William's knowledge. Furious at the high rate of interest his father had been charged, Amon declared, "While Mr. Hunt used to be my Sunday School teacher, I should not hesitate to take the matter up with him as he certainly has no right to take advantage of you on a matter of that kind." He then urged his father "for Heaven's sake, pull yourself together and do not lose your nerve." After all, Amon claimed, "Your troubles are small compared to mine," making it rather disconcerting to him that his father had "practically given up the ghost." "That is not the spirit that wins battles," Amon scolded. "if I had displayed the same spirit in some of my past experiences, I would probably have been driving a delivery wagon for about $25.00 a month." Nevertheless, he continued to affirm his commitment to helping his father. "I have explained to you time and time again," Amon wrote, "that it is my intention to help you, and sooner or later, I will be in position to pay the place out for you." Clearly, Carter experienced frustrations with a father who seemed content to remain a poultry farmer, while he had become a well-traveled, cosmopolitan member of the elite.[39]

In 1915, Amon's father developed a case of pneumonia. Amon rushed to his side, hoping that the doctor and two nurses he had brought with him from Fort Worth could nurse William back to health. There was little the doctor could do, however, and Amon spent what time his father had left talking with him before he passed. In a letter to his cousin Hettie Scott, Amon expressed his feelings upon the loss of his father, noting that "the only consolation I have is in feeling that I tried to do everything possible for him while he was living, saw that he was well taken care of and provided for." Though Amon had not been happy with his father's marriage to Ella Patterson after his mother's death, he felt it necessary to maintain his connection with her after his father's death. Carter continued his financial support of the family and often dispensed advice to his stepmother and half brother Roy. Though the relationship between Amon and his stepmother had improved since he had left home, the two maintained a sense of restraint in their correspondence. He called her "Mrs. Carter" in his letters to her, and she avoided the sentimentality that was often found between family members at this time. Throughout the rest of the 1910s, Ella Carter continued to rely on Amon for financial support, since her sons were too young to provide for the family. In 1919, after a brief stay with family in Macon, Georgia, Ella moved back to Texas, to Bellevue between Wichita Falls and Bowie.[40]

Amon corresponded frequently with his half brother Roy, nearly twenty years his junior, generally imploring him to go to college. He was somewhat discouraged to hear that Roy had chosen a life on the road selling stereoscopes for the Keystone View Company as opposed to opting to continue his education: "I was naturally somewhat disappointed to hear this," he wrote, "and to think that you had made a change of this kind without letting me know anything about it." After all, "you know I have been through all these road propositions myself." He offered to arrange for his college education at either the University of Texas or Texas A&M University, noting that "it would be a mistake to drop your schooling, as I have gone through the same experience, and while I have been able to survive without a good education, it has been a handicap a great many times." Roy decided that it was in his best interest to go to school but chose not to attend either university for fear that it would be too much of a financial burden for Amon; instead, he attended the much cheaper Bowie Commercial College to focus on bookkeeping. When Roy had finished his work in Bowie, he obtained a job with the Fort Worth and Denver Railroad in Wichita Falls. Upon learning of this, Amon began pressuring Roy to support his mother so as to alleviate some of the financial burden that had fallen on his shoulders.[41]

Amon also continued to correspond with his younger sister, Addie, who had married a man named Pete Brooks and lived in Henrietta, Texas, with their seven children. By 1916, tensions between Addie and her in-laws had reached a boiling point. Addie's mother-in-law and two sisters-in-law accused her of having children with other men as well as having killed her recently deceased infant. Stating that she would like to die if it was not for her children, Addie reached out to Amon for help. He aired some frustration with Pete for failing to keep his family away from her, saying, "His first duty is to you and he should see that you are protected and not annoyed with a bunch of jealous people." Once their crop was brought in, he would move them away from Pete's family. He arranged for them to move to his father's vacant farm by midsummer. In 1918, Addie and Pete moved to Arlington but apparently did not leave the marital strain behind; by 1919, she had left her husband and children to live in Dallas. Throughout these moves, and despite his disagreements, Amon continued to support his sister by sending her finer clothes from time to time as well as giving her $150 to $200 a month by the 1920s.[42]

Carter's attitude toward his family at this time reveals something about his character and approach to giving. Though his letters could be gruff at times, he never failed to support his family during their times of need. None of them ever attained the level of prosperity and success that he had, yet he firmly believed that it was his duty to provide. He complained at times that he was being stretched thin: "I have Addie and her seven children to take care of," he grumbled to his stepmother, "in addition to assisting my grandmother; have Bertice away at school; have an obligation of $500 a month to Mrs. [Zetta] Carter, besides, I have to make a living for my own family so you can see what I'm up against." All grudgingness aside, he persisted in supporting his family when they demonstrated any financial need, and, when the opportunity arose, his generosity would stretch beyond his family and to the community at large.[43]

Carter's acquaintances and friendships during the 1920s extended well beyond the world of politics and Hollywood celebrities. An avid sports fan, Carter immersed himself as much as possible in the growing world of professional sports and modern fandom. Often this meant watching a sporting event, be it boxing, baseball, or bicycling. Ever the garrulous personality, he made friends in the sports world and, of course, never failed to use these connections to try to gain something for Fort Worth. Carter had loved baseball ever since playing as a young man in Nocona and Bowie, and his national travels exposed him to the greater joys of watching major league baseball. In this way, he proved to be part of a larger trend, since "Major League Baseball's attendance expanded from 3.6 million to over nine million between 1900 and 1920." Once he attained financial stability, he rarely missed a World Series and made the acquaintances of Hall of Famers like New York Giants manager John McGraw and Boston Red Sox center fielder Tris Speaker, and he counted fellow Texan Owen Wilson of the Pittsburgh Pirates as a good friend. Since there were no major league teams in Texas, Carter was forced to root for outside organizations like the Pittsburgh Pirates and the Chicago White Sox. When the short-lived Federal League began in 1914, Carter, possibly with the hope of securing a team for Fort Worth in the future, quickly moved to make himself known to James Gilmore, president of the league.[44]

Though Carter never specifically states why he became an ardent White Sox fan, it is most likely that this occurred as a result of frequent trips to Chicago, dating back to when he was working for the Chicago-based American Copy Company. At some point, he became acquainted with team owner Charles Comiskey and hoped to use this connection to his (and Fort Worth's) advantage. In October 1917, Carter attended a celebration honoring the World Series champion White Sox at Shanley's Restaurant in New York, where he entertained the rambunctious crowd with "witty sallies and good-natured raillery against the Giants and in favor of the White Sox." Interestingly, it was during this absence that Wortham and Carter exchanged a series of letters and telegrams in which Wortham voiced some displeasure over Carter's absence as well as his willingness to run the aforementioned J. Frank Norris ad. The next year, during a spring training trip through Texas, the White Sox attended a dinner hosted by Carter for five hundred White Sox boosters in Texas. When the White Sox let it be known in 1919 that they were interested in moving their spring training from Florida to Texas, Carter said that he would "guarantee one of the best diamonds in the south and the best of hotel accommodations." Despite Carter's pressure, Comiskey decided that the White Sox would do some of their spring training in nearby Mineral Wells. This did not dampen Carter's enthusiasm for the White Sox, for later that year Carter hosted a dinner to celebrate the team's American League pennant. As a token of their appreciation, the 1919 White Sox, soon tainted by the notorious "Black Sox" scandal, gave him a baseball autographed by all the team members. That year, Carter once again attended the World Series, this time leading a delegation of fellow White Sox fans from Texas. One can get a sense of Carter's tendency to let emotional devotion override all other considerations. When asked about the Sox's chances to come back from a 4–2 deficit after 6 games (the World Series was best-of-nine then), he responded enthusiastically, "We have watched the Sox for years, and they are the greatest bunch in the world to come from behind. The Sox still have a kick. Now that they are forced to the wall, they are likely to show the world everything they have." Sadly for Carter and other White Sox fans, he was proved wrong by a team that, in part, conspired to throw the series.[45]

Locally, Carter adopted as his team the Fort Worth Cats of the Texas League, one of the best minor league baseball teams in the country during the 1920s. Though a part of the Brooklyn Dodgers farm system by the 1940s, the Cats were independent during their formative years. From 1920 to 1925, led by manager Jake Atz and slugger Clarence Kraft, they won six straight Texas League Championships, and as league champions, played in six consecutive Dixie Series against the Southern Association champion, a series played between the winners of the two leagues from 1919 to 1938. Carter's affiliation with the Cats began in earnest during this time period when, in 1919, Texas League president J. Walter Morris and Cats business manager Paul LaGrave persuaded him to help them arrange the Dixie Series. Soon after, he became vice president and part owner of the Cats, though he left the day-to-day running of the organization to business partners W. C. Stripling, a boyhood friend and son of his old *Star* investor W. K. Stripling, and Paul LaGrave. From 1921 to 1925, Carter arranged for a chartered Texas and Pacific train to take the team, a band, and strong supporters to Dixie Series away games in cities such as Memphis, Atlanta, and New Orleans, all generously paid for with the *Star-Telegram*'s money on checks signed by Carter himself. After the Cats' 1924 victory in the Dixie Series, Carter accompanied some team members to the White House, where they were welcomed by President Calvin Coolidge. Carter also presented the president with a key to Fort Worth, though it must have been a rather shoddy one, for the next year, he sent Coolidge a new gold key inscribed with the president's name. Carter's experiences with the Cats and his devotion to the team demonstrated the loyalty he held for local institutions, and of course helped boost his standing in the Fort Worth community, but just as with his future avid support for the Texas Christian University football team, his generosity and support outweighed whatever gains he might have made through this positive exposure.[46]

Carter's taste in sports extended well beyond baseball. Just as millions of Americans were embracing a diverse stable of spectator sports, he found himself following events as divergent as bicycling and boxing. Reflecting the 1920s bicycling craze known as six-day races, Carter accepted an invitation to fire the starting gun at a race at Madison Square Garden in December 1922. And, of course, there was always golf, a sport he often indulged in, though never with any apparent skill. A signed scorecard from a 1914 round of golf at the Rivercrest Country Club reveals that he had a handicap of sixteen and, on this one particular day, only made par four times. But, then again, golf for someone like Carter was much less about the competition and much more about establishing relationships with other businessmen.[47]

By the mid-1920s, Carter's achievements were numerous and his influence growing. His leadership at the *Fort Worth Star-Telegram* resulted in the largest newspaper in Texas giving him not only a profitable business venture but also a position from which he could boost his adopted city of Fort Worth. While not incredibly wealthy, he was financially comfortable. In 1920, he left Nenetta a list of his assets before he went on one of his many business trips to New York; listed was over $250,000 in stock from a variety of local companies (the prime one, of course, being the *Star-Telegram*, with oil companies such as Ranger Texas and Benmo making up much of the rest). Real estate owned included part ownership of 640 acres of land at what had been Carruthers Field during World War I and the 40-acre peach farm along the interurban in Arlington. In addition, he had a total of over $26,000 in accounts at three different banks. As a further sign of growing status, the Carter family moved from a home just south of downtown Fort Worth on West Leuda to a mansion on the grounds of the newly established Rivercrest Country Club west of the city. In less than two decades, he had risen from selling picture frames around the country to become an increasingly influential media magnate. Yet it was not in his personality simply to maintain his position, comfortable as it may have been. Having established the *Star-Telegram* as the largest newspaper in Texas by the 1920s and cemented his reputation as a generous, civic-minded citizen of his adopted city, he began to widen the reach of his influence at the state level as well as pursue national acclaim by circulating among national politicians and celebrities.[48]

CHAPTER 4

LAYING THE FOUNDATIONS FOR POLITICAL SUCCESS

BY THE EARLY 1920s, Amon Carter had established himself as the premier booster for the city of Fort Worth and, by extension, West Texas. Many of his prior activities had been limited in scope, but ownership of the most widely circulated newspaper in Texas broadened his horizons. He could now exercise influence beyond the Fort Worth city limits. Though he rarely wrote the editorials for his newspaper, the ideas and politicians promoted by the *Star-Telegram* reflected his views. Now he was sought after in political circles, though, at first, generally at the state level. Along with this greater political influence and activity came greater publicity, something Carter never avoided. Hollywood celebrities and star athletes found themselves enjoying his gracious hospitality. With his publishing business expanding and his influence growing, Carter seemed to be reaching the pinnacle of his career during the 1920s. When the Great Depression began to impact Texas and Fort Worth in 1930–31, Carter discovered that though the economy may have collapsed, his fortunes had not. The 1930s and the age of Franklin D. Roosevelt would prove to be an enormous boost to his sway in Texas, and his political activity in the previous decade made this possible.

Carter's first years at the *Star-Telegram* were not full of political activism, either through the newspaper or within his correspondence. The paper's stances reflect the typical southern progressive attitudes of the day: good government, good roads, better parks, etc. Though a Democrat like the majority of Texas voters, Carter was not as politically involved as he would later become. For example, in 1912, his main political contribution appears to be one dollar donated to the Woodrow Wilson–Thomas Marshall presidential campaign. By the late 1920s, however, he was recognized as a leader within the Texas Democratic Party and remained active at national Democratic conventions. At the state level, Carter began to be more politically aware, possibly reflecting a certain level of comfort now that his newspaper consistently had one of the largest circulations in the state. At the same time, governors and senators had to be aware of the power of an endorsement or negative statement from a newspaper with the readership of the *Star-Telegram*. Since it was the newspaper of record for Fort Worth and much of West Texas, politicians could not fail to recognize the importance of winning Carter's support. The political power Carter began enjoying during the 1920s would not wane until the ascension of Carter's opponent Jim Wright to the House of Representatives in 1954.[1]

During the 1920s, "business progressives" reached the pinnacle of their power in Texas and throughout the South. Historian Randolph Campbell describes business progressives as businesspeople who were "progressive in their willingness to support administrative reorganization, better roads, and improvements in education, but they favored business on matters of labor-management relations, the protection of women and children in industry, and worker's compensation." "Efficiency and order" were the watchwords of the day for business progressives as they emphasized what historian Francis Simkins called the "trinity of Southern progress": education, industry, and good roads. Carter, like many of the politicians he supported, was a business progressive. Though he did not enjoy a warm relationship with every Texas governor or senator during the 1920s, this fact helped him maintain open communication with important figures in Austin and, later, Washington.[2]

The swirling maelstrom of Texas politics proved irresistible to Carter. Never one to hunger after his own political seat, presumably because of the limitations this would have placed on his boosting effectiveness and general influence, he nevertheless waded into the fray during the 1920s and beyond. He first used his leverage to rally support for creating a college in West Texas during Pat Neff's governorship. Having been successful at this venture, he turned his sights on the duo of James and Miriam Ferguson, better known as "Pa" and "Ma." The feud with the Fergusons that erupted in 1925 lasted well into the next decade as Carter, being a business progressive, found himself at odds with their rural values. In an attempt to keep the Ferguson faction at bay, Carter later threw his support behind business progressive candidates like Dan Moody and Ross Sterling. By the end of the decade, Carter was comfortable enough to begin getting involved at the national level of politics, such as when he served as a delegate to the 1928 Democratic Convention in Houston. The 1920s clearly illustrate Carter's growth as a person of greater political influence, mainly at the state level, providing him with experience that would enable him to take advantage of the new opportunities of Roosevelt's New Deal during the next decade.

Neff was elected governor of Texas in 1920, having staved off a challenge within his own party from former United States Senator Joseph Weldon Bailey. Since Texas was an overwhelmingly Democratic state at that time, elections were not so much between Democratic and Republican candidates as they were within the Democratic primary. While much of the rest of the nation had sworn off Wilson's style of progressivism by electing Republican Warren G. Harding over Democratic candidate James Cox, Texas continued to follow Wilsonism in choosing Neff over conservative Bailey. Bailey had served as a United States senator from Texas from 1901 to 1913, usually espousing an old-style Texas conservatism against the rising tide of progressivism. When he reentered politics in 1920, his core message of fighting against progressivism had not changed. During the 1920 campaign, he "denounced Prohibition, woman suffrage, labor unions, the League of Nations, the Woodrow Wilson administration, socialism, monopoly, class legislation, and class domination," while promising to "lead Texas back into the straight-and-narrow path of the time-honored principles of the old 'Bailey Democracy.'" Neff, on the other hand, supported Wilson's progressivism, Prohibition, and women's suffrage. He campaigned on a typically business progressive platform, supporting "a huge highway building program, a system of state parks, and water conservation policy." Neff's reelection in 1922 confirmed the continuing popularity of progressivism and Prohibition among many Texas voters who supported the ideas of efficient and good government promised by progressives.[3]

Neff did not always enjoy a smooth relationship with the Texas legislature and failed to push through many of his educational initiatives, such as a "state board of education, larger appropriations for public schools, a nine-month school year, and a fixed amount of support for colleges and universities." He was successful, however, in persuading the legislature to create a State Parks Board, and he did score a victory for higher education when, in 1923, he signed a measure that created Texas Technological College in Lubbock. Behind the push for the creation of Texas Technological College stood a variety of men, including Carter.[4]

The creation of a college for West Texas came during a time when many of that region's citizens believed they were being ignored. Some West Texas lawyers and newspapermen went so far as to invoke a clause in the 1845 congressional joint resolution annexing Texas that gave the state the option to spin off four new states. Concerned citizens formed a West Texas A&M campaign committee that proposed locating a branch of the Agriculture and Mechanical (A&M) College of Texas "west of the 98th meridian and north of the 30th parallel." Victory seemingly was achieved in 1917 when the state legislature passed a bill creating John Tarleton Agricultural College in Stephenville and setting aside $500,000 for a future West Texas A&M College. The prospective site of West Texas A&M was to be decided by a five-man committee chaired by Governor James Ferguson. As often seemed to happen when Ferguson was around, "it appeared that chicanery was involved," since the committee voted to locate the college in Abilene and not in Snyder, where a majority of members reportedly wanted the college. Before an investigation could clear up the confusion, Ferguson was impeached and convicted for mishandling public funds; the Texas Senate later voted to bar him from holding any future state office.[5]

Ferguson was replaced by his progressive lieutenant governor, William P. Hobby, former editor of the *Houston Post*. Hobby had been a member of the West Texas A&M site committee, yet he refused to pursue the matter further. Instead, he persuaded the legislature to repeal the bill, and supporters of West Texas A&M found themselves having to fight for a college once more. In spite of their best efforts, West Texans were unsuccessful in getting the Texas Democratic Convention of 1920 to include support for a West Texas college in its platform. Two West Texas legislators, Representative Richard Chitwood of Sweetwater and Senator William Bledsoe of Lubbock, crafted a bill appropriating $50,000 for a college that passed the Texas House and Senate, but Governor Neff vetoed the bill on the grounds that there was no support for this in the 1920 Texas Democratic platform, and the recent postwar recession had left Texas financially strapped. Later, Neff mentioned in a speech in Lubbock celebrating the creation of Texas Technological College that he had also felt that such an appropriation was far too small, saying that "if I had not vetoed it for any other reason, I would have vetoed it because it did not carry an adequate appropriation to build the foundations for a college that would adequately serve this great region of Texas." West Texas supporters reacted strongly, with some even raising, once again, the specter of secession.[6]

Carter and Louis Wortham, his business partner and *Star-Telegram* editor, entered the fray to dissuade secessionists with a 1921 editorial arguing that a "movement for a separate state is more likely to divide West Texas than to have any other result. But a movement to get justice for West Texas . . . will raise up friends for justice throughout the State." The secessionists failed to gain widespread support for their cause, but in 1922, Texas Democrats at the state convention succumbed to the West Texas delegation and voted to include a plank in their platform calling for a West Texas college. When the legislature convened in January 1923, several legislators from Lubbock to Dallas were ready with bills proposing some kind of college for West Texas. Neff let it be known that he would support a bill and urged lawmakers to ensure a large enough appropriation. With momentum moving in favor of a West Texas college, two hundred delegates from West Texas met on January 12 in Fort Worth with Carter and legislators R. A. Baldwin, Bledsoe, and Chitwood to resolve their conflicting proposals. Because the attending legislators failed to craft a compromise bill immediately, a more private meeting of the involved legislators was held in Austin on January 25. Present, in addition to Baldwin, Bledsoe, and Chitwood, were Representatives Lewis Carpenter of Dallas and Burke Mathes of Hale, as well as Homer Wade of the West Texas Chamber of Commerce and, with the blessing of Carter, reporter Silliman Evans of the *Star-Telegram*. Once they had all entered the Senate reception room where they were meeting, "Wade closed the doors and said: 'You have been invited into this room this morning for the purpose of reaching an agreement upon a West Texas college bill. I have the keys to the door in my pocket, and they will not be removed until such an agreement is reached." Within two hours, an agreement had been reached to craft a bill calling for a $1,000,000 appropriation for Texas Technological College. Carpenter and Chitwood guided the bill through the House of Representatives, while Bledsoe and R. A. Stuart of Tarrant County took responsibility for doing the same in the Senate. On February 10, Neff signed the bill and then set about naming members to the nine-person board of directors.[7]

On February 19, Neff wrote Carter: "Knowing full well your interest in the educational life of Texas, and appreciating your ability to render services, I am today naming you as a member of the first Board of Directors of the Texas Technological College." Carter leaped at the chance, stating that "while I have never accepted a political appointment before, I really felt not only complimented but delighted to have an opportunity to serve on the board of an institution of this character." Carter was unanimously elected chairman of the board at the first board meeting in Sweetwater and promptly declared that the board would begin meeting the next month to discuss the future of the college as well as to decide who should be its first president. Soon after, the board of directors chose Paul W. Horn, a Texas educator since 1892, as the first president of Texas Technological College. After visiting sixty proposed sites, the locating committee met in Fort Worth and voted to select Lubbock as the location of the college. Carter's task on the board also included handling construction contracts, so he announced that "all contracts were let to the lowest bidders," which, on some occasions, happened to be Fort Worth companies. The board selected Acme Brick to provide the brick for the administration building and the president's residence and the architectural firm Sanguinet, Staats, and Hedrick to design several buildings. By 1925, the new college was ready to open and Carter had helped score a victory for West Texas. In recognition of his efforts on behalf of the college, Texas Technological College awarded its first honorary Doctor of Laws degree to Carter in 1930. While in the beginning, the wider public may have been unaware of his role as chairman of the board of directors, a well-publicized clash with the Fergusons in 1925 brought Carter's presence on the board to the forefront of Texas politics.[8]

Carter hated James and Miriam Ferguson, who polarized Texas politics for twenty years. "Pa" Ferguson was elected governor in 1914 as a "Hogg Progressive Democrat" who appealed mainly to poor farmers by promising rent ceilings for tenant farmers and sharecroppers and the improvement of public schools. In his survey of Texas, *Gone to Texas,* Randolph Campbell notes that Ferguson "practiced a far more personal than principled brand of politics," and that he "abused the powers of his office to such an extent that he became the only governor of Texas to be impeached and convicted." Though he made enemies with Prohibitionists (for making liquor a nonissue) and the University of Texas (for demanding the firing of six faculty members who opposed him) during his first term, he was easily reelected in 1916. He did not fare so well during his second term, since he continued to fight the University of Texas by vetoing the 1917 university appropriations bill, saying, "I do not give a damn what becomes of the University." Sensing Ferguson's weakness, his Prohibitionist enemies joined the fray, and in July 1917, a Travis County grand jury indicted him for misusing public funds and embezzlement. His refusal to comply with the legislature's requests to disclose personal finance information only made matters worse; the House voted to impeach him, and by September 22, the Senate convicted him of ten charges mainly dealing with his financial situation. In addition to removing him from office, the Senate disqualified him from ever again holding public office. The wily Ferguson refused to stay down, however, and later found a way to reenter Texas politics.[9]

Ferguson found his way back into Texas politics in 1924 in the guise of his wife, Miriam. "Ma" was, by all accounts, an apolitical person for much of her life. Even while "Pa" was governor, she remained uninvolved. When asked about women's suffrage in 1916, she said, "Personally, I prefer that men shall attend to all public matters." Eight years later, her stance had changed. With "Pa" barred from holding public office, she rose to stand in for him. During the 1924 campaign, she began her rallies with a short speech and then gave way to "Pa" for political discourse. In a close Democratic primary in which Prohibition and the Ku Klux Klan were major issues, she emerged the winner due to the Fergusons' popularity among rural Texans as well as their strong anti-Klan stance. Because of the polarizing nature of the Fergusons, Republican gubernatorial candidate George Butte actually polled well that November. Still, it was not enough to stop the Ferguson duo, and in January 1925, Miriam Ferguson was inaugurated as the first woman governor in Texas. It must be stated, however, that "Mrs. Ferguson occupied the governor's office, but Pa, who had his own office next door, ran her administration."[10]

Up to this point, Carter had refrained from entering the political fray, but in less than a year, he found himself embroiled in a long dispute with the Fergusons. The Fergusons' administration became enmeshed in a battle with the youthful State Attorney General Dan Moody over highway contracts given to Ferguson supporters, particularly those who bought advertising in Pa's newspaper, *The Ferguson Forum*. This clash began in July 1925 when *Star-Telegram* reporter Silliman Evans informed Carter that Highway Commissioners Frank Lanham and Joe Burkett had granted contracts "without competitive bidding, without bonds, and at excessively high prices." Later it was revealed that some contracting companies were using state-owned equipment to complete private jobs. The *Star-Telegram* began running a series of articles investigating such irregularities, putting the newspaper on a path toward a clash with the Fergusons. The next month, Evans's source, Louis W. Kemp, secretary of the Texas Highway and Municipal Contractors Association, met with Moody and Assistant Attorneys General George Christian and Ernest May in Evans's Austin hotel room to inform them of his belief that the State Highway Department needed to be investigated by the attorney general's office for graft in the State Highway Department. As Moody pressed forward with investigations of state finances and various contractors, the Fergusons refused to cooperate, claiming that allegations of wrongdoing should be ignored. When Moody's findings caused him to file suit against the American Road Company for excessive profits of $650,000, Governor Ferguson ordered the State Highway Commission to resist, arguing that "the attorney general had no authority to bring suit in the name of the state unless so directed by the governor. George Calhoun, the district judge hearing the case, denied Ferguson's request, and ultimately the state was able to recover over $600,000 from the American Road Company. The anti-Ferguson crowd, already smarting from Ma's victory in the recent gubernatorial campaign, seized upon the highway scandal as a reason to pursue Ma Ferguson's impeachment. Pa Ferguson, rising to her defense, accused Moody of wanting to be governor himself and claimed that the present scandal "was caused by 'disgruntled contractors, County commissioners who had lost their clabber on highway contracts, and men with political bees in their bonnets.'"[11]

There was also the issue of Governor Ferguson's lenient clemency record. Ma had promised to follow a more lenient pardon policy, and from the beginning of her tenure in office, had made good on this campaign promise. In 1925 alone, "the number of clemency proclamations had reached 1,201, including full pardon; conditional pardons; paroles; restorations of citizenship; commutations of death sentences to life imprisonment; and reprieves." This practice aroused anger from all fronts; the Methodist Episcopal Church meeting in Dallas condemned this action as "a menace to law and order and good society." Others viewed her actions with mistrust, suspecting that Pa's alleged "wetness" on the Prohibition issue influenced his wife's pardoning of violators of this law. Allegations of bribery abounded. The *Star-Telegram* began publishing her clemency totals daily as a constant reminder to readers of the lawless path their governor was taking.[12]

The skirmishing between Carter and the Fergusons, which so far had been limited to the pages of the *Star-Telegram,* garnered national attention after the November 1925 Thanksgiving Day football game between the University of Texas and Texas A&M University in College Station. Both Carter and the Fergusons attended the game, though obviously not together. Seated in a box not far from the Fergusons, Carter could not restrain himself from yelling, "Hurrah for A&M!" "Hurrah for Dan Moody!" He was escorted from his seat by a policeman, but "no sooner had he been escorted out of the grounds than he was ceremoniously escorted back in again." In an interview soon after the incident, Carter defended himself, saying that "I was unaware that I was anywhere near the box occupied by the executive party. I had been pacing up and down the grandstand runway, following the position of the players on the gridiron and rooting for the A&M players. My enthusiasm kept mounting as the Aggies scored their first and then their second touchdowns. I was crying 'Hurrah for A&M! Hurrah for Dan Moody!'" An obvious thought was that Carter was hinting at the current highway contract investigation, but he "asserted that nothing was said about the highway contracts in the course of his cheering." As a matter of fact, it was only "by accident" that he passed the governor's box, and the only reason he mentioned Dan Moody in his cheering was because his enthusiasm over the game and over Moody's "exposure of the highway situation" was so strong. Or so he maintained. Upon being escorted out, he inquired of the policeman (whom he identified as a colonel with the Ferguson party), "Is it against the law to cheer for A&M?" "No," he answered. "Is it against the law to cheer for Dan Moody?" "No, Mr. Carter," was the reply. "Then what's all the shooting about anyway?" Carter asked. Despite the seeming frivolity of the event, the reaction from the Fergusons said otherwise.[13]

Pa Ferguson, furious at Carter's outburst, struck back at Carter, as well as at the critics of his wife's administration. Two days after the game, on November 28, the Fergusons issued a statement that included a veiled swipe at Carter for his recent public support of Attorney General Dan Moody, as well as those they accused of using their wealth to evade Prohibition laws. Governor Ferguson's proclamation offered a "reward of $500 for the arrest and conviction of any citizen of this State for violating the liquor laws, who is worth, in property or money, as much as $5,000." Though Carter was not specifically named in the statement, Ferguson did mention a "big newspaper publisher, in a North Texas city," who "can dispense pints of liquor by the dozen, and, under the influence of liquor, display himself in a public place." This unnamed millionaire was allegedly "drunk as a biled owl" at the recent football game and had, according to Pa, given a dinner for the 'Oil Men's Association,' actually the American Petroleum Institute, in 1924 where he had given away six hundred pints of liquor inside three hundred imitation Bibles and three hundred imitation canes. With an eye on their dwindling popularity, the Fergusons portrayed their actions not as revenge but as protection of the poor. Pa Ferguson compared this recent event hosted by Carter with a clemency case he had recently heard wherein a nineteen-year-old boy was imprisoned for a year for having a flask of liquor at a country dance. In the Fergusons' eyes, because of this double standard, "justice becomes a mockery, and the law becomes a stench in the nostrils of all law-abiding people."[14]

The attack from the Ferguson camp became even more public when Governor Ferguson wrote a letter to Carter, which he promptly published in the *Star-Telegram*. Though her letter contained statements he considered to be libelous, he encouraged other newspapers to publish it to show his "good faith and sportsmanship." In her letter, Ma Ferguson requested that Carter resign from his position on the board of Texas Tech for his alleged dispensing of liquor the year before and for his antics at the Thanksgiving Day game. She attributed his rigorous cheering to being under the influence of alcohol and stated that "in your state it was but natural for you to have been unable to distinguish between a Colonel on my staff, dressed in khaki yellow, and a town policeman, dressed in blue, who, under orders from the local authorities, ejected you from the grounds in the interest of public peace." His actions, she continued, did not serve as good examples for young Texans, and for that reason his resignation should be forthcoming. Her letter sparked even further fighting between Carter and the Fergusons, a battle that Carter, as a man who made a "business of writing," seemed sure to win.[15]

In his response published the next day in local newspapers, and even the *New York Times,* Carter accused the Fergusons of creating a "smoke screen to divert the mind of the public from the real issues." Responding to charges of serving liquor in hollowed-out Bibles and canes at the previous year's American Petroleum Institute convention, Carter asserted that "there was no violation of the law and there could have been no such action as is charged, because present with this party were members of the law enforcement departments of both county and city." He went on to wonder why, if this gathering was indulging in illegal beverages as Ferguson alleged, did she hold on to this information for almost a year. Could it have anything to do with trying to distract the people of Texas from the faults of the Ferguson administration? Carter denied having been drunk at the football game but asked, "Is it any more of an offense against law and morals to toss up one's hat for Dan Moody than to obstruct the Attorney General in his suit against highway contractors?" He strongly insisted on retaining his post as chairman of the board of directors at Texas Tech, arguing that the Fergusons' charges were "malicious and without justification." He could not let "sideline issues interfere" with the growth and development of the new college, he maintained. Echoing the popular sentiment that the "real" Governor Ferguson was Pa, Carter asserted that he was like "a ventriloquist behind the scenes" who "puts his words into the figure on the stage." The war of words had begun, and Carter's feud with the Fergusons was far from over.[16]

Support for Carter poured in from around the state and the nation as many were aware of the dwindling Ferguson reputation thanks to constant media coverage. Sidney Hardin of Mission, Texas, governor of the South Texas Rotary Clubs, wrote saying he was "within ten feet" of Carter at the football game and urged him to continue voicing his support for Moody. Insurance agent H. M. Marks noted that it was "peculiar that the Governor should wait nearly a whole year in which to comment on the manner in which you were supposed to have entertained the delegates of the American Petroleum Institute." Carter should not resign his position, he added, and "the people of Texas would be fortunate to have a man for Governor who at times might dissipate personally rather than one who allows state funds to be dissipated without any regards for the tax payers." Edward Jordan of Cleveland asserted, "Ma Ferguson certainly made you a greater national character, if such a thing is possible," adding, "You already are a national institution." The *Miami Tribune* reported that the son of a Miamian who was at the University of Texas–Texas A&M football game witnessed the whole affair: in his eyes, "Carter was innocent of the charges of drunkenness." Both former governor Pat Neff and Texas Tech President Paul W. Horn wrote to Carter assuring him of their support. Neff declared, "You were not appointed originally on the board of the Technological College with the thought that you would at this time tender your resignation." Having read Carter's response, Neff rallied behind him: "On with the battle!" he exhorted. President Horn thanked Carter for supporting the college through his newspaper and encouraged him to retain his position. Carter was grateful for the hundreds of letters and telegrams "insisting that I fight it out and set steady in the boat." Though he had no intention of resigning, the widespread show of support stiffened his resolve.[17]

The fight carried on through the New Year with fresh volleys from both the Ferguson and the Carter camps. James Ferguson, ever willing to raise the specter of Klan activity, charged Carter with being a Klan leader and a supporter of Republican candidate George Butte in the recent gubernatorial contest, accusations that had no grounding in truth. Carter responded by publishing an editorial in the *Star-Telegram* that dubbed January 1926 "Laugh month" for the antics of the Fergusons as they tried to maneuver their way out of the highway contract scandal. The editorial called these charges "ridiculous," pointing out that the *Star-Telegram* had never supported any Klan candidates since the recent resurgence of the organization. The editorial noted that when the 1924 Texas Democratic gubernatorial primary came down to Miriam Ferguson and Klan-supported Felix Robertson, the newspaper failed to support either candidate. Finally, Carter and the *Star-Telegram* were both unwavering in their support of Attorney General Moody, a man who had gained fame as a staunch opponent of the Klan. The Fergusons' scattershot accusations failed to persuade Carter to apologize for his outburst, admit to serving alcohol, or resign his Texas Technological College board position. Ultimately, the Ferguson attacks solidified Carter's opposition to them while showing their inability to respond to the corruption charges stemming from the State Highway Department scandal.[18]

Throughout 1926, Moody's supporters grew more vocal in urging him to run for governor that year. Though Carter refused to air Moody's campaign opening speech on his radio station WBAP, he did urge support for Moody. When Moody formally announced the opening of his gubernatorial campaign in May 1926, Carter wired him congratulations, saying that "Texas needs men such as you in public service and I sincerely believe the people of the state can render no better service for themselves than to elect you governor." Seemingly a shoo-in for the Democratic nomination that year due to the State Highway Department and clemency scandals and general Ferguson fatigue, Moody defeated Governor Ferguson twice that year: once in the initial primary in which he earned just under 50 percent of the vote, and again in the runoff, when he defeated her resoundingly 495,273 to 270,595. In the initial primary, Moody faced Houston businessman Lynch Davidson as well as Governor Ferguson. Carter took some time to gloat when Moody emerged as the front-runner over Ferguson and Davidson, even going so far as to send a mocking wire to Davidson. "For a man who has claimed credit for almost everything except building the Rocky Mountains," he scoffed, "it must be distressing to stop[,] look[,] and listen." Moody supporters wrote Carter thanking him for his support for their candidate through the pages of the *Star-Telegram,* lauding the power of the press to sway the vote of the people.

The thirty-three-year-old Moody took office as the youngest governor in Texas history in January 1927, riding a wave of reform and business progressivism reminiscent of former Governor Neff. Moody's four-year tenure as governor (he was reelected in 1928) offered "competent, business-oriented, progressive leadership," and for the most part he delivered as promised by cutting waste in the State Highway Department, increasing fuel taxes to pay for more roads, halting the indiscriminate pardons of his predecessor, and working somewhat successfully to reform the state prison system. Though Carter and Moody had been friendly since the Carter-Ferguson feud had erupted in 1925, the two men were soon at odds with one another over Moody's failure to allow Carter widespread influence within his administration. The *Star-Telegram* soon became one of the most strident anti-Moody publications in the state, and the onset of the Great Depression further exacerbated the widening rift between them.[19]

The Carter-Moody split began when Moody refused to name Carter-supported nominee Cato Sells of Fort Worth to the State Highway Commission after being advised by former attorney general Thomas Watt Gregory that such an appointment would be "deeply regretted in the future." Carter's wrath was unleashed, and Moody forever "incurred his endless enmity." The stunned governor was concerned by the sudden loss of Carter's support for both personal and political reasons. Carter and Moody had struck up a casual friendship through reporter Silliman Evans ever since the beginning of the Ferguson highway scandal, and Carter had spent much of 1926 extolling Moody's virtues. Now, however, Carter's tendency to make all political denials personal damaged his friendship and cost Moody his support. When Moody embarked on a campaign to reform Texas prisons, he encountered widespread resistance, especially from Carter and the *Star-Telegram*. Carter's paper took the position that Moody's reforms would lead to overcrowding, as prisoners would have to be relocated while new prisons were being built. This would not be the only time his prickly personality would impact politics; throughout the rest of his life he feuded with politicians who refused to become his mouthpieces. Carter's actions bothered both the governor and his wife, Mildred. Writing in her diary, Mildred observed that Carter's attempt to "dictate to Dan" by practicing tactics of "rule or ruin" weighed heavily on her husband. For the next four years, the *Star-Telegram* took the anti-Moody route and criticized the governor for everything from his attempts at prison reform to his response to the Fergusons' attempt to reenter politics in 1930. For example, part of his reform plan included opening a centralized prison complex near Austin; when the state prison board ordered that no new prisoners be allowed at the existing prison at Huntsville, the *Star-Telegram*'s editorial page excoriated the administration for the decision, claiming that it was "designed to 'force the legislature to enact Mr. Moody's Prison Monument in Austin.'" In 1929, after having easily been reelected in spite of Carter's best efforts, Moody complained that the Fort Worth newspaper unfairly and incorrectly reported on his positions by allowing editorial views to influence the news columns. Unfortunately for Moody, his second term marked the beginning of the Great Depression and the collapse of what had, in many ways, been a prosperous decade for the state. Carter, his newspaper unable to stem the Moody tide with consistently unfavorable coverage, railed from the sidelines, waiting for new opportunities for political influence.[20]

Locally, Carter continued to pursue his desire to make Fort Worth a center of aviation and industry. As mentioned previously, Carter had been entranced by flight since his first encounter with an airplane in 1911, but opportunity to begin seriously investing in the future of aviation was not possible until the late 1920s. The aviation industry was still in its fledgling years during the early 1920s, but Carter believed in its infinite potential. If at all possible, he wanted to see that Fort Worth stood to benefit from the strides made in commercial aviation. Toward this end, he remained active in promoting any effort that might give greater publicity to the industry, such as heading the Fort Worth Aviation Club's unsuccessful effort to bring the 1923 Pulitzer Air Races to Fort Worth. Much more fruitful were his exertions ensuring Fort Worth would be a stopping point for a 1929 women's air derby in which thirteen competitors raced from Santa Monica to Cleveland. After a particularly difficult leg from El Paso to Fort Worth that saw four of the fliers fail to reach their destination due to mechanical failure, nine airplanes finally touched down at the city's municipal airfield; the second pilot to touch down, Amelia Earhart, was immediately greeted by a throng twenty thousand strong that easily overwhelmed the thirty police officers securing the airfield. Upon arrival, the determined aviators were whisked away to Carter's Shady Oak Farm for a lavish banquet in their honor. Inspiring and exhilarating as these kinds of events might be, it was still a fact that the post–World War One aviation industry was overall in a poor state, so it would be a few years before conditions were right for any progress to be made. By the late 1920s, however, government legislation promoting civil aviation and allowing private carriers to carry mail combined with the general boom in financial markets to enable many investors to become serious about entering the aviation industry. As a result of these changes, "capital investment in aviation rose from $10,000,000 in 1921, to $125,000,000 in 1928, and twice that a year later." Carter, as a budding aviation enthusiast, took part in this national trend, as evidenced by his role in the formative airline companies Southern Air Transport and Aviation Corporation.[21]

Carter's first serious step toward greater interest in aviation is best demonstrated by his interactions—though somewhat limited in the 1920s compared to future decades—with regional aviation corporations that would form the core of American Airlines by the middle of the next decade. When Fort Worth brothers Chester and Temple Bowen began Texas Air Transport (T.A.T.) to provide airmail service within the state, Carter was asked to christen the original fleet and to serve as the master of ceremonies at the opening festivities in February 1928. The Bowen brothers did not retain control of the company for long; by November of that year, Fort Worth businessman A. P. Barrett had purchased the company. Barrett was already a wealthy man from his work as chairman of the board for two large utility companies operating in Texas, Louisiana, and New York. A firm believer in Fort Worth's role as an aviation center, his decision to enter the industry reportedly came at the urging of his three-year-old son, Hunter. Hunter, playing in the backyard of his Fort Worth home, spotted a plane flying over and exclaimed, "Daddy, I want that airplane." Barrett took his son to Fort Worth's Meacham Field, the recently completed air field for the city, and discovered that T.A.T. owned planes at the hangar. Instead of buying a plane, he opted to purchase the entire company from the Bowens and began pursuing his vision of transforming Fort Worth into an aviation hub.[22]

Under Barrett's leadership, T.A.T. expanded its operations to include a flight school, a passenger service, and a radio station. Its rapid success gave Barrett the opportunity to expand his aviation empire, and he and his associates purchased a controlling interest in Southern Air Transport and merged the two corporations. This regional airline, which dominated commercial aviation in the South, was targeted by Aviation Corporation (AVCO), a massive holding company worth over $200,000,000 formed in 1929. AVCO's origins were murky at best, and company historians tasked with researching its past have concluded that there was not much to discover because of the twisted nature of the company's family tree. It was to have been a subsidiary for the Fairchild Manufacturing Company, but through the numerous acquisitions made by the new corporation, their roles were soon reversed. Over the next several years, AVCO purchased numerous airlines and airline holding companies until it became a bloated behemoth with little organization or central control. Carter officially entered the aviation industry in 1929 through Southern Air Transport and its parent company, AVCO. Upon the merging of Southern Air Transport with AVCO, Carter was elected a director of the company. Over the course of the next decade, he would emerge as a leading figure within the company as it transformed into American Airlines, as well as a promoter of aviation in general around the nation.[23]

Though ostensibly devoted to profit, politics, and promotion, Carter found time to indulge his appetite for wading into the emerging celebrity culture of the 1920s. He was not alone in this endeavor but became part of a larger trend in American culture. In an article in the *Organization of American Historians Magazine of History*, Amy Henderson observes that while early Americans tended to idolize "military heroes, romantic fictional protagonists, and eminent statesmen who embodied the ideals of virtue and self-reliance . . . by mid-twentieth century, the pedestal belonged not to politicians or generals, but to baseball players and movie stars." While Carter could point to his increasing wealth and influence as signs of success, "in a culture of personality, 'celebrity' became a measure of success" as well. This meant expanding his personal network beyond the usual core group of businessmen and politicians into the burgeoning ranks of radio, movie, and sports stars. During the 1920s, Carter did not enjoy the high level of friendship and intimacy with as large a number of celebrities as he would later in life, but he did begin to cultivate relationships with a variety of nationally known personalities. He began hosting his friends at his suite at the Fort Worth Club or at his newly acquired Shady Oak Farm on the shores of Lake Worth on the outskirts of Fort Worth. Though he typically conducted business at the Fort Worth Club, Shady Oak Farm became the place where he began entertaining personalities as diverse as British newspaper mogul Harold Harmsworth (Lord Rothermere), New York City mayor Jimmy Walker, popular syndicated columnist O. O. McIntyre, and actor/columnist Will Rogers.[24]

Oscar Odd McIntyre, better known as O. O. to his readers, wrote one of the most widely read newspaper columns of the 1920s, "New York Day by Day." Like his counterpart Will Rogers, McIntyre brought a small-town sensibility to writing—in his case, a column that focused on the glitz and glamour of New York. The historical record does not reveal when Carter met McIntyre, but they struck up a relatively close friendship that helped introduce Carter to the nation through McIntyre's columns. McIntyre's columns usually consisted of a number of humorous anecdotes, and Carter seemed to possess a personality crafted for this format: a loud, confident Texan who knew how to play to type. In one 1924 piece, McIntyre relates a trip to Paris in which he heard an Amon Carter story that was "going the rounds of Paris." Asked if he wanted soufflé potatoes, he asked with some skepticism, "Are those the kind that are blown up?" Told he was correct, he responded, "Well, I won't have any until I know who blowed them up." Other McIntyre anecdotes reinforced this image of Carter as a kind of innocent abroad in the big city. At an unnamed high-society luncheon, Carter, Will Rogers, and other guests were served the restaurant's famous eggs Florentine. As Rogers dipped his fork into the rich, gooey dish that "suggested an Italian sunset," he remarked to an apparently aghast Carter, "Don't say anything. It's eggs." Sometimes Carter made an appearance as one of the many celebrity friends that seemed to matter-of-factly populate McIntyre's life and writings. "In the evening to the Lee Olwells for dinner," McIntyre remembered, "and Amon Carter, the Texas publisher, and Nanette [sic] there. And Amon told of days when he sold crayon pictures from door to door and recited his canvassing address, which would make the most hilarious movietone monologue I know." On one occasion, McIntyre recounted strolling down Broadway, thoughts running through his head: "The sickly greenish glow of quick photo shops. Mannish women with swagger sticks. Beauty parlor sign: 'Cigarette stains removed immediately.' Fulton Oursler and Bide Dudley. Amon Carter of Fort Worth. Hurrah for West Texas!" Thus, for many years, readers nationwide were regaled with tales of this blustery, larger-than-life westerner, and these stories helped make Carter and Fort Worth much more familiar.[25]

What did not make McIntyre's column was an incident on the Pennsylvania Railroad in December 1923, which provides us with a glimpse of Carter's temper and willingness to personally reinforce, with violence, the humiliations of Jim Crow. Carter, McIntyre, and McIntyre's wife, Maybelle, were headed from St. Louis to New York on December 3; Nenetta was at home with the one-month-old Ruth. McIntyre and Carter shared a table with another gentleman, and, from Carter's perspective, the black waiter failed to provide good service to McIntyre. The unnamed gentleman sharing the table with the two friends remarked that the waiter must be hard of hearing, upon which the waiter replied that he "was not hard of hearing when people talked to him." Enraged, Carter stood up and promptly slapped the waiter with enough force that he fell into McIntyre's lap. When the car steward, an older white man he interpreted as sympathetic to the waiter, rushed to the scene to see what was the matter, Carter replied that "whenever necessity compelled me to hit a negro for insolence . . . I never stopped to call a director's meeting, or ask someone else what they thought about it." This account, it must be noted, comes from Carter, since he took it upon himself to write a letter of complaint to W. W. Richardson, a manager at the Pennsylvania Railroad's St. Louis office. Carter went on to say that he refused to eat his dinner after the incident, "as I have had too many dealings with negroes to take a chance with what they might do to my food after an altercation of this kind." He complained that the waiter's attitude reflected that of the typical "northern negro" that was "naturally one-thousand per cent more impudent than a negro would dare to be in this country." Therefore, Carter suggested, the railroad should hire "a few negroes from the South that know how to treat your customers," the implication being that they "knew their place" in society. If the company would only hire the "right sort," remedy the lack of Virginia ham, and stop providing poor-looking jarred figs (he included culinary complaints in the same letter), it would be a perfect railroad to rely on for Carter's numerous trips to New York. No record exists of how the railroad responded to his complaint, but in a short note written after the assault, O. O. remarked to Carter, "Perhaps after you slap a few more niggers it will turn out a regular road."[26]

What to make of this disturbing episode? First, it must be noted that for many black males, being a porter on a Pullman car was the highest level many could hope to attain. Granted, being a porter meant a career in a subservient position, since one could expect to spend time shining shoes, pressing clothes, or, as in the case of the gentlemen accosted by Carter, waiting tables, but as Adam Fairclough writes, "Given the other alternatives for earning a living—laboring, sharecropping, and domestic service—working on the Pullman cars was relatively attractive." As a matter of fact, "along with postal workers and longshoremen, Pullman porters made up the aristocracy of black labor." But while being in the "aristocracy of black labor" might earn them standing in the black community, this did not translate to respect from white passengers, as the Carter incident so clearly reveals. This letter to the Pennsylvania Railroad is the most explicit statement on race from Carter the author encountered, so it is impossible to say with certainty whether his attitude improved or moderated over time. In his role as civic father, Carter played the part of the paternalistic caretaker of Fort Worth's black community from time to time, an action more frequent in his older years when he engaged in greater acts of philanthropy. At the same time, his remarks to the steward about "being compelled to hit a negro" and refusing to eat his dinner for fear of what the waitstaff might have done to his food imply that this kind of action was not altogether foreign to Carter; presumably he had found it necessary to "hit a negro" for presumed insolence before. McIntyre's off-handed comment in the aftermath is revealing as well, for it demonstrates that white northerners, too, could be not only complacent but supportive of how white southerners handled the issue of race. In any case, this incident reveals the many-layered nature of racism in the 1920s. Racial violence did not just come in the form of lynch mobs and Klan whippings but could also be found at the personal level. In addition, the fact that a prominent newspaper publisher could attack a black waiter and not expect any repercussions, either in the moment or afterward, provides us with clear insight into the deep-seated nature of Jim Crow as well as its long reach.[27]

Southern as his racial attitudes were, Carter deliberately honed a more western persona in large part to garner greater national attention. Boosting was never far from his heart, and he was not content to be just one of endless civic leaders carefully jostling one another for the attention of outside investors. Soon after he acquired Shady Oak Farm in 1923, he began gifting his famous Stetson hats to his guests, typically there to be wined and dined by the consummate host. A 1926 issue of the *Lowell Sun* called him the "father of the 10-gallon hat," remarking that his habit of exchanging a cowboy hat for his visitors' more urbane headwear contributed to him having "won loads of publicity for Fort Worth."

While McIntyre and Carter were developing a close friendship, Carter and Will Rogers, the prominent actor, humorist, and cultural commentator, cultivated a much deeper relationship that lasted from 1922 until Rogers's death in a plane crash in 1935. The two men met while visiting mutual friend New York Giants manager John McGraw in New York City during the 1922 World Series, and over the next few years maintained close contact with one another. By 1925, Carter, whose Fort Worth–centric character was good for plenty of humorous yarns, began to make regular appearances in Rogers's widely read syndicated columns. In one particular column, part of the series titled "The Worst Story I Heard Today," Rogers regaled readers with a story of how Carter enjoyed himself a bit too much in New York "entertaining the oil convention," and called for a doctor. Upon arriving, the unnamed doctor put his head to Carter's chest and remarked, "Your circulation is poor." Enraged, Carter turned to the doctor and roared, "Circulation poor? You are crazy. Our circulation is one of the biggest in the South. We passed the *Dallas News* and are right on the heels of the *Memphis Commercial Appeal*." A 1931 Rogers column contained the following musing about a recent visit to Fort Worth: "Was met here by Amon Carter. You can try to sneak into his city on a bicycle, but Amon Carter will meet you at the city limits and welcome you. No other city in America has anything like approaching such a public citizen as Carter. He met me by special plane 200 miles out to prevent me from going into Dallas first. He poisoned one friend just to keep him out of Dallas." Such humorous, yet insightful, anecdotes served to endear Carter among Rogers's readers as well as create a stronger bond between the two figures: one already a celebrity and the other, if not seeking, then certainly not shirking, the limelight. By the end of the decade, Rogers had become a frequent visitor to Shady Oak Farm and the suite at the Fort Worth Club, giving rise to even further accounts of their developing bond. According to Rogers's biographer Ben Yagoda, their friendship was "cemented" at the 1928 Democratic Convention in Houston, where Carter and Will Rogers shared a room and crossed paths with noted columnist H. L. Mencken. Carter's ensuing antics at the convention seemed to reflect Rogers's western image that he had so carefully honed in his movies.[28]

The 1928 Democratic Convention was a historical event: it was not only the first presidential convention held in Texas but also the first held in a southern state since 1860. On the strength of his growing influence within the Democratic Party, Jesse Jones, a prominent banker as well as the publisher of the *Houston Post,* persuaded the national party to meet in Houston for that year's Democratic National Convention. Though the perpetually controversial issue of Prohibition swirled around the convention hall, the wet governor of New York, Al Smith, was solidly entrenched as the front-runner and sacrificial lamb for the Democrats as they sought a nominee to face the popular Herbert Hoover. With little drama surrounding the convention results, Carter decided to create his own, possibly influenced by a recent Will Rogers film, *A Texas Steer.*

During the mid-1920s, Rogers was in the middle of transforming himself from a vaudeville performer into one of the most highly sought after actors of the silent era. One of his more famous roles came in the 1927 movie *A Texas Steer,* based on an 1890 play of the same name. In this film, Rogers plays brash rancher Maverick Brander from Red Dog, Texas, who is elected to Congress. Accompanied by his wife, daughter, and "three rowdy Texas cronies" named Yell, Bragg, and Blow, Brander proceeds to proselytize his fellow congressmen about Texas's greatness. One Washington lobbyist, eager to gain Brander's support for his particular project, claimed that "since Mr. Brander arrived, our eyes have been opened. We have learned to appreciate the greatness and future glory of Texas! He has taught us that Texas is the coming Empire State!" In another instance, Brander's Texas triumvirate of Yell, Bragg, and Blow start a riot at a dinner party after brandishing their pistols. Rogers received high praise for his performance, and the movie influenced future representations of the comic Texan so common in many westerns. Carter, who spent much of his later life trying to represent the archetypal Texan, could not have missed this performance by his friend, and some of his actions, especially in Houston in June 1928, appear to reflect this exposure.[29]

Before heading to Houston for the 1928 Democratic Convention, Carter waited in Fort Worth for the separate arrivals of Will Rogers and noted columnist and cultural commentator Mencken. By this time, Mencken had already gained a reputation as a severe critic of the South through the pages of magazines like *The Smart Set* and *American Mercury.* This evidently had no impact on Carter, who, as a publisher, could not have been unaware of Mencken's caustic comments about the "Sahara of the Bozarts." Mencken, unlike Rogers, had never met Carter, but accepted an invitation from him to stay at the Fort Worth Club for a night. Upon reaching Fort Worth, he was greeted by Carter, who was holding two hats as gifts: a Stetson cowboy hat and a Borsalino fedora. The Stetson had become Carter's trademark gift to celebrities and politicians and was typically inscribed inside the hatband with the words "Shady Oak Farm, Fort Worth, Texas, Where the West Begins, The Latch String Always Hangs Outside, Amon Carter." After posing for some publicity photographs for the *Star-Telegram,* Mencken and Carter spent the evening at the Fort Worth Club, where they enjoyed cigars, whiskey, gin, and T-bone steaks. The next day, they met Rogers at the airport and spent the afternoon at Shady Oak Farm. Though the acerbic Mencken appreciated Carter's gestures of hospitality, he noted later that "the Texans were not my kind of people ... Amon G. Carter's hospitality at Fort Worth, though it was earnest and lavish, was more of a nuisance than a joy." Unfortunately for Mencken, his time with Carter was not over.[30]

When Carter arrived in Houston, reportedly "with an immense stock of liquors," he booked a suite near Mencken's at the Rice Hotel. Mencken, already weary from his two days with Carter, was disturbed to discover that Carter was intent on barging into his room without invitation, "two or three times a day, usually accompanied by his friend and retainer, the sheriff of Fort Worth [Carl Smith] and the two of them wasted a great deal of my time." Carter did more at the hotel than bother Mencken; he mingled with the delegates, hoping that he could persuade them that Representative John Nance Garner of Uvalde, Texas, was the preferable presidential candidate. Though he failed at this venture, he did succeed in frightening hotel boarders when he fired a gun at a glass elevator door in frustration at waiting too long for the slow-moving, single-passenger elevator to stop for him. Fortunately, wire mesh on the door prevented the glass from shattering. Bystanders intervened, preventing him from firing more shots; local law enforcement, seeing that no one had been hurt, released him with little more than a warning. Meanwhile, on the eleventh floor of the Rice Hotel, Mencken was in his suite recovering from his own encounter with Carter and his firearm.[31]

Earlier that day, while on one of his many forays into Mencken's room, Carter pulled out his six-shooter without warning and fired three shots out of the window; the bullets hit the hotel across the street near the room where the Ku Klux Klan was meeting. The shocked Mencken was sure Carter was drunk and was even more amazed when Carter placed the weapon underneath the mattress and slipped out to avoid being found out by the Texas Rangers searching the building for the perpetrator. When the Rangers entered Mencken's room and found three bullet holes in his window, they proceeded to arrest him but were halted when Carter strode in to clear up the situation. Arresting Mencken, he argued, would make Texas look "ridiculous" to the rest of the nation; after all, the columnist was "known as a peaceable and virtuous character by millions of people." Carter explained that the shooting must have happened when Mencken was in the bathroom; some Klan enemy had clearly slipped in and fired the shots at the moment Mencken flushed the toilet. A local judge who accompanied the Rangers was unsure of his explanation and ordered a complete search of the room. The search revealed no weapon and the judge relented, convinced of Mencken's innocence. Once the judge and the Rangers were gone, Mencken "got Carter's pistol from under the mattress, handed it to him, and desired him to clear out at once." Mencken, analytical critic of southern culture, explained Carter's behavior as being driven by his desire to be seen as a "West Texan, which connoted familiarity with firearms and a willingness to use them."[32]

Such an episode makes one wonder about Carter's motives in playing to the Texan stereotype in front of Mencken. Was he having fun at Mencken's expense? Was he inebriated as Mencken alleged? Or was he intent on giving Mencken a sampling of what he seemed to expect from a Texan? It is possible that the answer can be found in the previously mentioned Rogers movie *A Texas Steer*. The boisterous maverick Brander and his trio of rowdies reveled in parading their "Texanness" in front of the urbane Washington crowd. During the 1920s, Mencken certainly represented what many Texans would have interpreted as typically snobbish eastern attitudes, and Carter's actions in his hotel room can easily be construed as an attempt to give Mencken a taste of what he clearly expected. And though Mencken was not present in the Rice Hotel lobby when Carter fired at the elevator glass door, the national press certainly was, thus cementing his reputation as the type of Texan Hollywood presented to the nation. Inebriation cannot be ruled out, however; note Carter's behavior at the 1925 Thanksgiving football game at which he taunted the Fergusons and was accused by them of being drunk. And Mencken, bitter foe of Prohibition and all its supporters that he was, surely knew what intoxicated behavior looked like. After all, just two days before, Carter had plied him with gin and whiskey in his Fort Worth Club suite, and it is highly doubtful that he was against bringing some refreshing beverages with him to Houston for the festivities.[33]

Does this mean he had an alcohol problem, or was this merely conduct "to be expected" from someone looking to maintain his image as a rugged westerner? Drink was certainly always present at Carter gatherings, Prohibition or not, and records suggest that even well after its repeal he kept a sizable stash on hand in his suite. Neither of his first two wives mentioned the negative influence of alcohol on his behavior, though clearly some of his actions toward them could very well be construed as those of someone under the influence; both wives mentioned cruel verbal treatment at his hands. At the same time, his outsized and enthusiastic personality, which occasionally tended toward the outrageous, should be taken into account as well. At the most, it seems safe to say that he might have been inebriated in public at times, but there is not enough evidence to suggest that this was a common occurrence.

One might expect that events of this nature could prematurely ruin Carter's national reputation, but the "Houston Incident," as it was commonly called, was quickly forgotten. Mencken only mentioned the episode in posthumously published memoirs, and Rogers, Carter's companion in Houston, failed to discuss the controversy in his columns covering the convention. As one might expect, Mencken and Carter failed to develop a long-lasting friendship, though they would have another encounter four years later at the next Democratic Convention. And when Al Smith emerged as the official Democratic nominee, the loyal Carter ensured that the *Star-Telegram* remained a Democratic newspaper that year, even though the majority of Texans voted for Hoover, the Republican candidate, in what was clearly an anomalous year. In the aftermath of Hoover's landslide victory over Smith, Darwin Kingsley, longtime president and chairman of New York Life Insurance Company, inquired of Carter as to his thoughts on Texas voting Republican for the first time ever. Was he correct in speculating that the three reasons for this were, in descending order of importance, Prohibition, Tammany Hall, and Smith's Catholicism? In his estimation, the first two overshadowed religion, but he wanted confirmation from a noted observer of the Texas political scene.[34]

In a letter that revealed his keen sense of politics, Carter, clearly impressed by these observations from someone who was neither a Texan nor a political figure, replied that yes, these observations were correct in his opinion. "There is no doubt, in my opinion," he remarked, "that the controlling factor was the Eighteenth Amendment." "Smith's election," he went on, "was presented to the voters by the prohibition forces, the ministers, and church lay leaders, as meaning not only the complete breakdown of the prohibition laws, but of the early return of the open saloon." Carter was quick to point out that he was not saying religion played no role in voters' decisions; on the contrary, "There is no gainsaying the fact that religion entered the overturn, to a considerable extend [sic]. But," he clarified, "I have not viewed it as a compelling factor, for the reason that most of those actuated by some degree of religious prejudice also would have been against Smith because of his prohibition views, if his religion had been different." That said, he felt that regardless of who the Democrats put forward, that candidate was bound to lose because of the prosperity of the decade. And while many Democrats in Texas and beyond worried that the election results portended the rise of the GOP in the state, Carter thought otherwise. "If Texas were a two-party state," he mused, "we should have a better type of men put forward for the high offices of government, a better character of state administrations and campaigns fought upon party lines and perhaps constructive issues rather than upon bitter personalities and the question of how some candidate voted on some matter that by the wildest flight of imagination could affect neither his fitness for office nor the administration of the office sought." Interesting words from someone who was often knee-deep in such clashes of personality. Of course, it would be quite some time before such a realignment would happen in Texas and the South. It would be more than two decades before Texas again voted for a Republican candidate in a presidential election, though in that case, the once loyal Democrat Carter would be supporting the Republican.[35]

Of course, politics was never the whole of Carter's entertainment, as has already been proven, and interest in sports increasingly took up more of his time. An avid boxing fan, he often accompanied Rogers to prizefights around the nation. Among the many friends he had in the athletic world was boxing promoter George "Tex" Rickard. The two had met while Rickard was the city marshal of Henrietta, Texas, during the 1890s. By the 1920s, Rickard had become nationally known for his role in arranging fights involving heavyweight champions such as Jack Johnson, Jack Dempsey, and Gene Tunney. In April 1926, Carter arranged for Rickard and Dempsey to meet in his suite at the Fort Worth Club to sign an agreement that ultimately pitted Dempsey against Tunney for the heavyweight title. Sadly, Rickard died in 1929 after complications from an appendectomy; Carter served as an honorary pallbearer, along with other notables such as Walter Chrysler, Jack Dempsey, and James Farley, a future campaign manager for Franklin D. Roosevelt. Clearly Carter's interest in sports was national; he continued to support local teams, but his national connections enabled him to become a well-traveled sports fan during the golden age of sports.[36]

Along with enjoying greater prestige in the business and political realms, Carter worked at settling once more into domestic life. His first wife, Zetta, no longer played any role in his life, but he devoted as much time as possible to ensuring that their daughter, Bertice, successfully transitioned from boarding school to college and into the professional world. After graduating from Lasell Seminary, the all-girls boarding school in Massachusetts she had been sent to as a teen, she began attending Northwestern University to focus on earning her degree in journalism. Northwestern already enjoyed an excellent reputation as a journalism school, and attending the university enabled Bertice to remain close to her mother, Zetta, who lived in nearby Winnetka, Illinois. While living in Chicago, Bertice met and married Harry Kay. Throughout their marriage, and for the rest of her life, Bertice often relied on her father for financial support. Through much cajoling and coaxing, she persuaded her father that he should use his influence within the oil industry to get Harry a job. Despite misgivings, Carter was able to find him a job with Sinclair Oil in Chicago. While her marriage with Harry did not last, her background in journalism enabled her to find work within the field as well as a second marriage.[37]

Closer to home, in 1923, Carter and Nenetta welcomed a new addition into their lives with the birth of Olive Ruth, named after Nenetta's sister. From the existing evidence, it appears that the Carter household was relatively calm and comfortable during the 1920s as the family settled into a routine typically expected of contemporary urban elites. While Amon busied himself expanding his network of business and political contacts, Nenetta became a Fort Worth socialite, hosting parties at their Rivercrest home and collecting what she called "pretties": fine articles such as trees made of jade. While she spent many of her later years involved in philanthropic efforts, these activities were limited until the 1940s, when she began taking a more active role in organizing Amon's burgeoning philanthropy.[38]

If Carter had remained content with his accomplishments by 1929, no one could have faulted him for lacking ambition. The *Star-Telegram* continued to have the highest circulation in the state, enabling him to bring in a substantial salary as president and publisher. By 1928, he earned $60,000 a year plus profits from his investments in stocks and bonds. His 1928 portfolio, one of the few available to researchers, reveals that he owned stocks in a broad array of companies: Durant Motors, Warner Brothers, Paramount, and Humble Oil, for example. He also invested in commodities such as wheat and cotton through Fenner and Beane, a brokerage firm in New Orleans. Though not a man of great wealth, Carter was certainly more than able to provide a life of comfort and ease for himself and his family. The next decade of his life, a time of decline and despair for many Americans, would prove to be a decade of profit and prominence for Carter as he learned to exploit Roosevelt's New Deal for the benefit of his region while also becoming independently wealthy through the discovery of oil. The urban booster was prepared for the national stage.[39]

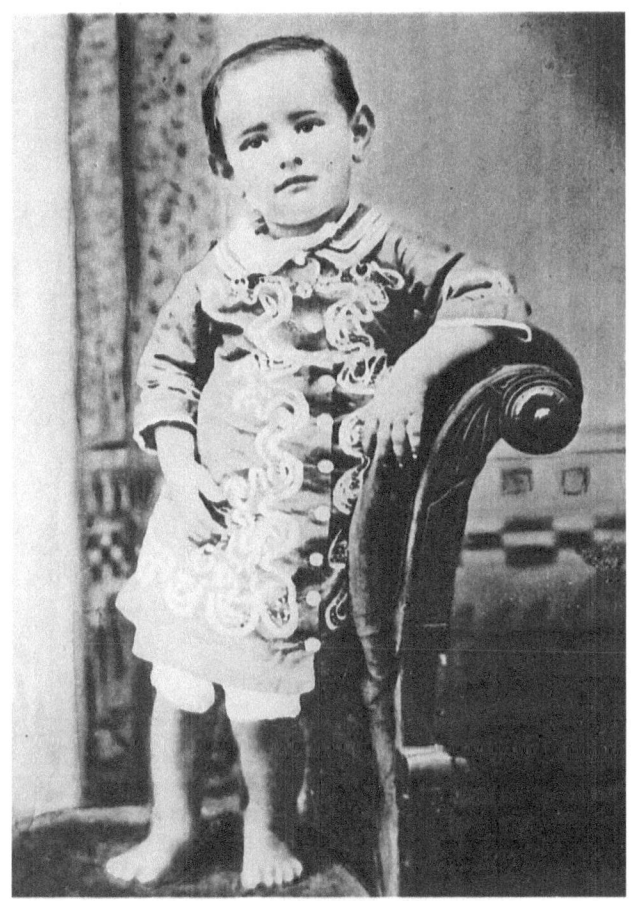

Amon Carter at three years old.
Courtesy of the Amon G. Carter Papers, Special Collections,
Mary Couts Burnett Library, Texas Christian University, Fort Worth, Texas.

William H. Carter and Ella Patterson Carter, his second wife, in 1895.
Courtesy of the Amon G. Carter Papers, Special Collections,
Mary Couts Burnett Library, Texas Christian University, Fort Worth, Texas.

William H. Carter, Addie Carter, and Amon Carter, 1895.
Courtesy of the Amon G. Carter Papers, Special Collections,
Mary Couts Burnett Library, Texas Christian University, Forth Worth, Texas.

A sharply dressed Amon Carter (right) and an unnamed companion, 1896.
Courtesy of the Amon G. Carter Papers, Special Collections, Mary Couts Burnett Library, Texas Christian University, Fort Worth, Texas.

Amon Carter, late 1890s. His solemnity in this photograph reveals little of his already rambunctious personality.
Courtesy of the Amon G. Carter Papers, Special Collections, Mary Couts Burnett Library, Texas Christian University, Fort Worth, Texas.

Amon Carter and H. E. Finney, general manager of Armour's Fort Worth meatpacking plant, seated in noted aviator Cal Rodgers's airplane, 1911.
Courtesy of the Amon G. Carter Papers, Special Collections,
Mary Couts Burnett Library, Texas Christian University, Fort Worth, Texas.

Amon and Nenetta standing outside their Rivercrest home, 1922.
Courtesy of the Amon G. Carter Papers, Special Collections,
Mary Couts Burnett Library, Texas Christian University, Fort Worth, Texas.

Opposite, bottom
Amon Carter golfing at the Grand Canyon, 1915.
Courtesy of the Amon G. Carter Papers, Special Collections,
Mary Couts Burnett Library, Texas Christian University, Fort Worth, Texas.

Amon Carter and Heisman Trophy–winning quarterback Davey O'Brien, of Texas Christian University, seated atop a stagecoach on Wall Street, 1938.
Courtesy of the Amon G. Carter Papers, Special Collections,
Mary Couts Burnett Library, Texas Christian University, Fort Worth, Texas.

Amon Carter proudly displaying his support for his adopted Horned Frogs of Texas Christian University at a publishers' convention in New York, 1938.
From the author's personal collection.

Amon Carter conferring with W. G. Chandler, general business manager of Scripps-Howard Newspapers, at the American Newspaper Publishers Association meeting in 1937. Scripps-Howard owned the *Fort Worth Press*, the *Star-Telegram*'s major intracity competitor.
From the author's personal collection.

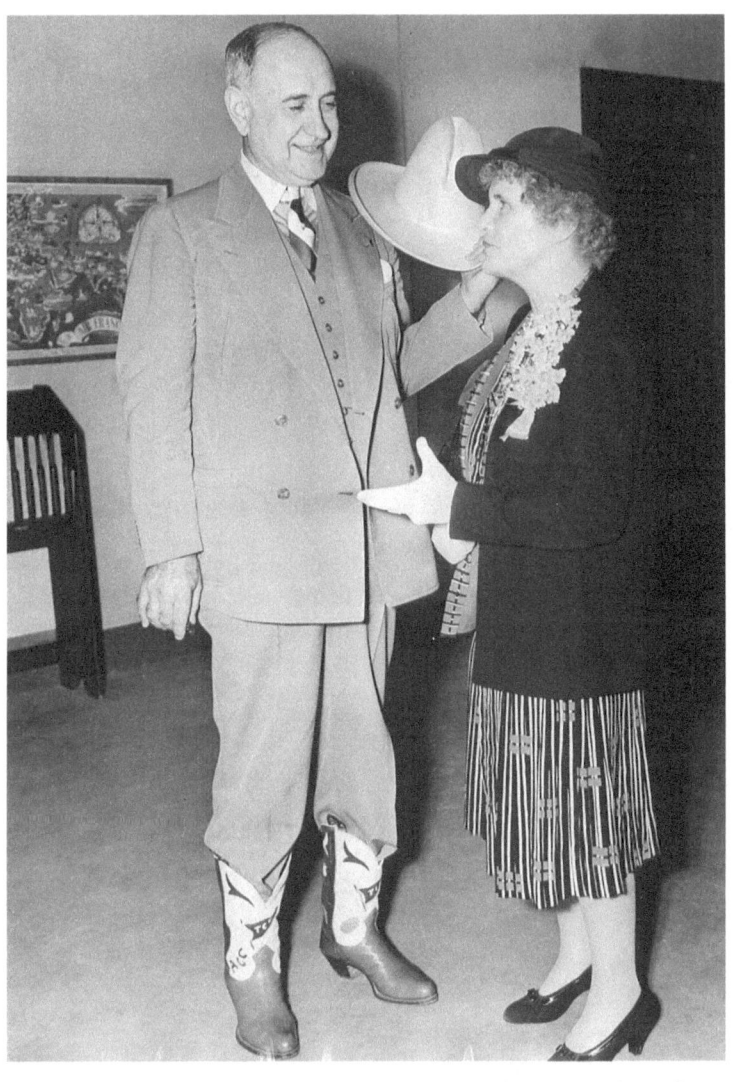

Amon Carter chatting with Helen Rogers Reid, vice president of the *New York Herald Tribune,* before a Pan Am flight to England, 1939.
From the author's personal collection.

The front page of an undated invitation to an event at Amon Carter's
Shady Oak Farm. Note the Texas flag flying above the United States flag.
From the author's personal collection.

Shady Oak living room. Clearly, the internal and external setting of Shady Oak was not meant to awe visitors but instead to remind them of Carter's humble roots and rustic sensibilities.
Courtesy of the Amon G. Carter Papers, Special Collections,
Mary Couts Burnett Library, Texas Christian University, Fort Worth, Texas.

Opposite, bottom
Shady Oak farmhouse.
Courtesy of the Amon G. Carter Papers, Special Collections,
Mary Couts Burnett Library, Texas Christian University, Fort Worth, Texas.

Amon Carter standing behind President Harry Truman
for the official dedication of Big Bend National Park, 1950.
Courtesy of the Amon G. Carter Papers, Special Collections,
Mary Couts Burnett Library, Texas Christian University, Fort Worth, Texas.

Amon Carter, Dwight Eisenhower, mutual friend oilman Sid Richardson,
and Carter's personal secretary, Katrine Deakins, 1950.
Courtesy of the Amon G. Carter Papers, Special Collections,
Mary Couts Burnett Library, Texas Christian University, Fort Worth, Texas.

CHAPTER 5

FOR THE EXCLUSIVE BENEFIT OF FORT WORTH

ON NOVEMBER 1, 1935, Jesse Jones, the head of the Reconstruction Finance Corporation (RFC), wired Amon Carter the simple statement "Your cowshed has been approved." This cryptic telegram verified that the Texas publisher's influence reached beyond the wide borders of his home state. At the height of the New Deal, Carter found ways to acquire government money for Fort Worth, even though he held no elected office and was an entrepreneur of the same class that often clashed with President Franklin D. Roosevelt over certain parts of the New Deal. Vice President John Nance Garner, a close friend of Carter, wryly commented that "[Carter] wants the whole Government of the United States to be run for the exclusive benefit of Fort Worth and to the detriment of Dallas." While something of an exaggeration, Garner's comment reflected the attitude many in the Roosevelt administration had regarding Carter's approach to the New Deal. Simultaneously, Carter opposed the leftward tendencies of the latter part of the New Deal, though he always found a way to reconcile his political disagreements with his loyalty to the national Democratic Party. Clearly, his fickle relationship with the New Deal reflected his business progressive roots as a New South urban booster.[1]

As a lifelong Democrat, Carter had understandably had limited influence with the Republican presidential administrations of the 1920s, but the coming of the Great Depression, which upset the Republican ascendancy in favor of Democratic politicians, allowed Carter greater influence in Washington. The Democratic domination of national politics for the next two decades provided fertile soil for his booster ethic. For a time, he did not view a more active, interventionist federal government as a menace, and he welcomed the possibilities for public works spending and direct relief that he and many other business progressives hoped would stimulate the national economy. Historian Roger Biles notes that the "sweeping changes engendered" by the Great Depression and the New Deal hastened the move of "traditional sources of power in local government and reoriented southern urbanites away from city halls and toward the nation's capital," and Carter quickly learned to use the *Star-Telegram*'s wide readership as leverage within Roosevelt's Washington. If the federal government was going to attempt to "prime the pump" of the economy with New Deal spending, he wanted to ensure that Fort Worth received its share of the benefits.[2]

The Great Depression did not descend on the nation with one swift stroke as is often imagined. The Stock Market Crash of 1929, while unwelcome, was not seen by many contemporaries as a harbinger of doom but rather a natural correction to the headiness of recent years. The Texas press, Carter's *Star-Telegram* included, greeted the news of the crash with words of calm and comfort for the state's citizens. On October 30, 1929, the newspaper carried articles headlined "No Major Depression Seen in Plunge by U.S. Leaders" and "Note of Optimism Is Heard Amid Market Crash Echoes." On the editorial page, it was stated that the efforts of the banks and the Federal Reserve to limit the economic damage looked to be successful. The *Star-Telegram* was not alone in voicing this sentiment. The *Dallas Morning News* surmised that "while the losses incurred will affect business to some extent, due to the intertwining of interests over the country, observations of several bankers and merchants indicate this will be slight and of no immediate consequence." The *San Antonio Express* echoed the beliefs of many Texans that somehow the state was somehow insulated from Wall Street's problems: "Here is no boom, no artificial inflation of values or fictitious prosperity based upon the shifting sands of rash speculation and unsound promotion." Sadly, for many Texans, the coming years would be all too horrible, eroding the proud sense of individualism many believed made Texas exceptional.[3]

Even during 1930, it seemed to many Texans that disaster had been averted. While the industrial Northeast was starting to feel the brunt of the Depression, the unemployment rate, though creeping upward, was still relatively low in Texas compared to other parts of the nation. As the historian Lionel Patenaude writes, "Texans were reluctant to admit that something had gone wrong with the economy." Governor Dan Moody, reelected in 1928, faced little criticism from the public, since the state's economy had not yet begun to contract. The lack of awareness of worsening conditions combined with having eleven candidates in the Democratic primary meant that the 1930 gubernatorial race would be more about personality than anything else. Moody was willing to run for an unprecedented third term, but then chose not to run against Ross Sterling, chairman of the State Highway Commission, owner of the *Houston Post,* and former president of Humble Oil Company. Former governor James Ferguson attempted to run but was unable to get his lifelong disqualification from state political office overturned. As in previous years, his wife, Miriam, ran in his stead, and James campaigned vigorously on her behalf.

Carter, having made a break with the Moody administration, did not support newspaper rival Sterling, and obviously his past with the Fergusons precluded any support for Miriam. Instead, his support (and, by extension, the *Star-Telegram*'s) went to State Senator Clint Small from the tiny Panhandle town of Wellington. Small, with his "vision of business rather than politics, a vision of a growing state with happy contented people who are made prosperous by their industry and frugality," appealed to Carter's sense of individual achievement. Texas voters, presented with a choice of Ferguson or a Moody-affiliated candidate in Sterling, voted in large numbers for these two candidates, and Small did not make the runoff. In the initial primary campaign, the *Star-Telegram*'s editorial page targeted Sterling, "realizing, as the returns later justified, that [he was] the one candidate necessary for Senator Small to eliminate." The editorials questioned Sterling's choice to remain as chairman of the State Highway Commission during the race as well as his qualifications: "We know that he is a rich man and that he favors a state highway bond issue. Neither of these things necessarily qualifies a man to be Governor."[4]

When the Democratic primary became a race between Sterling and Ferguson, Carter unsurprisingly chose to support Sterling's candidacy. Wishing to ease Sterling's mind about the recent editorial slant of the *Star-Telegram*, Carter wrote the candidate that he wanted to "assure you that we hope everything indicated in our campaign against your election in the first primary will prove to be a misconception on our part, and when you go in as Governor we want to assure you this newspaper and organization expects to accord you every cooperation possible." Texas voters, not yet feeling the worst effects of the Depression, were more concerned about the prospect of another two years of the Fergusons than about how either candidate was going to address economic issues; in the runoff, Sterling easily won with 55 percent of the vote.[5]

Unfortunately for Sterling, his term as governor was marred by Texas's continued downward slide into economic depression. Like many other political leaders, including President Hoover, Sterling continued to preach a message of optimism even in the midst of discouraging economic signs. Texas cities, less industrialized than their northern counterparts, did not feel a serious economic pinch until mid-1931, and in some cases, as late as 1932. This did not mean signs of economic distress were absent until those years. Texas farmers, a group that did not exactly share in the prosperity of the 1920s, were hit particularly hard from the beginning of the Depression just like farmers across the nation. Texas banks experienced some difficulties, reflecting the general lack of stability found in many other states of the union. The oil industry, an expanding sector of Texas's developing economy since the famous Spindletop gusher in 1901, neared a crisis due to overproduction and plummeting prices. Meanwhile, Carter and his city struggled to maintain and then restore confidence amid the crumbling economy.[6]

At the onset of the Great Depression, Fort Worth appeared insulated from impending economic doom because of a relatively stable banking sector and an extensive building program funded in large part by the oil money flooding into the city from recent discoveries west of the city in places such as Ranger, Desdemona, and the Permian Basin. But in 1930, a run on the First National Bank threatened to upset the presumed stability of Fort Worth banking. The run on First National appears to have been nothing more than a panic based on unfounded rumors, but by three o'clock on February 18, 1930, the lobby of the bank was full of depositors desperate to withdraw their money from the allegedly failing bank. Fort Worth elites, desiring to stem the panic, emerged to calm the milling crowds clamoring for their money. Wealthy oilman and rancher William T. Waggoner, a First National Bank board member, told the panicked throng, "I hereby pledge to you every cent that I own or possess in this world that you shall not lose a single dollar in this bank. I will sell every cow and every oil well if necessary to pay for any money you lose here."[7]

Never one to be outdone, Carter confronted the bank run by spending the evening at the bank. He rallied the crowd from atop a desk, urging depositors to leave their money in the bank and arguing that Fort Worth could weather any financial crisis. Carter then supplied the crowd with sandwiches and coffee and brought in two bands, who played enthusiastic songs such as "There'll Be a Hot Time in the Old Town Tonight," and "Hail, Hail, the Gang's All Here." Satisfied that their money was safe and comforted by the sight of Federal Reserve men bringing $5,000,000 from Dallas, the crowd began depositing their recently withdrawn money. As word of his successful effort to halt the panic spread, Carter received telegrams from as far away as New York, where one acquaintance of his, J. M. Davis, humorously urged him to "dispose of your newspaper interests and devote your entire time to banking."[8]

The next day, Carter addressed the bank run in the *Fort Worth Record-Telegram,* the morning edition of the *Star-Telegram.* He condemned the run as a demonstration of what "idle gossip, unfounded rumors and a state of hysterior [sic] upon the part of merely a few hundred people can do." He blamed the panic on "idle gossips, busybodies, and talkers"; by all accounts, the bank was financially stable and supported by some of the wealthiest men and companies in West Texas and Fort Worth, such as Waggoner, the Samuel Burk Burnett estate, and Carter's very own *Star-Telegram.* If the bank was so unstable, these Texas luminaries would not keep their money there. Appealing to people's civic pride, he reminded readers that "Fort Worth's good name is at stake" and finished his front-page editorial admonishing "sober-minded people" to "stop, look and listen" before jumping to any conclusions about the status of reputable Fort Worth banks. Carter and Waggoner were not alone in quashing the run; the bank issued a statement that showed the bank to "be in the best condition in its history, that it did not owe a penny to any individual or company, and that it has sufficient cash on hand to meet all possible demands." The governor of the Dallas Federal Reserve Bank, Lynne Talley, assured depositors that the bank was "one of the strongest banks in the United States and that the resources of the Federal Reserve Bank were at the disposal of the institution." Never one to keep quiet about these kinds of successes, Carter bragged to Will Rogers, "Just to show you how we do things down here, the bank stayed open until every sucker who wanted his money had received it, served sandwiches in the lobby to everybody and had two orchestras entertaining the crowd. Instead of a run it turned into an old-fashioned party."[9]

With the panic stemmed and Fort Worth banks secure, it appeared that the city had avoided the problems that were beginning to plague other American cities. Fort Worth was not the exception, though, because other Texas cities continued to show signs of strength, too. Neighboring Dallas reported an unemployment rate of only 4.7 percent in 1930, and hundreds of new businesses had opened up throughout the year. Austin's economy was slow to decline as well due to the presence of the state government and the University of Texas. Houston, more industrialized than other major Texas cities, suffered more with a staggering 23 percent unemployment rate by the beginning of 1931. Despite the positive signs through 1930, by 1931, it was clear that Texas would not escape the Depression's wrath. Fort Worth's major construction projects ended that year, and Dallas construction slowed as well. Texas farmers "faced steadily worsening conditions as the price of cotton fell from nine to ten cents a pound when the 1931 crop was planted to a little more than five cents at harvest time. Prices for corn and cattle were more than fifty percent lower than in 1929." Clearly, the state had entered the throes of depression in 1931.[10]

In January 1931, as Fort Worth and other Texas cities' public and private charitable coffers drained, Will Rogers excitedly telegrammed Carter with a proposal to do a Texas tour later that month that would be organized in part by the Texas Federation of Women's Clubs. He suggested he would pay his own expenses and sell tickets at relatively high prices and take donations to raise funds for the unemployed. Carter readily agreed that this was an excellent idea and quickly went to work to help organize the tour and ensure widespread support. Of course, Rogers being arguably the most famous, well-liked man in the United States meant that Carter had to do very little. Though originally planned as a charitable endeavor for the unemployed, plans changed after Rogers visited with Hoover about relief for drought-stricken farmers. The president, wary of Congress infringing on private charitable giving, insisted that it would be best to handle this not through congressional appropriations but via donations to the Red Cross. As Carter described it to Miriam Lindsay, president of the Texas Federation of Women's Clubs (TFWC), "The President felt in the event they should pass the appropriation it would be the end of the Red Cross as any time in the future the necessity for Red Cross aid should appear it would immediately be turned over to Congress for an appropriation." Rogers thought that if that was the case, it would be best to turn over proceeds from his Texas tour to the Red Cross for drought relief.

The change in recipients did not derail Rogers and Carter, and the two forged ahead, working with the TFWC to ensure the tour's success. Though originally slated to appear in eight towns and cities, the ever-in-demand Rogers added five more communities to his list in an attempt to raise as much money as possible within the short window of time he had available. In addition to his mandatory stop in Fort Worth, he performed in the state's larger cities of Dallas, Houston, San Antonio, and Austin, as well as smaller towns such as San Angelo, Breckinridge, and Mineral Wells. During his Fort Worth stop, a singular episode remembered by Betty Rogers, Will's wife, reveals much about the state of race relations at the time, as well as Carter's paternal attitude toward the city's black community. On Friday, January 30, Rogers had just flown in to Fort Worth from doing a show in Houston. He was on his way to a show in Wichita Falls, but insisted on a quick lunch and shave at the Fort Worth Club. Outside the club headquarters, a black porter stopped him and said that he wished there was some way black Fort Worthians could see Rogers's show. Rogers, a man whose views on race were ever evolving, insisted that he would find some way to make that happen in spite of the fact that he only had a brief window that evening in which he could do a show; Carter agreed to see what he could do. Later that evening, after returning from Wichita Falls and before his scheduled eight o'clock show in front of a whites-only Fort Worth crowd, Rogers delivered a strong performance at the imposing Mt. Gilead Baptist Church, a prominent black church perched on the eastern edge of downtown on Fifth and Grove. In many ways, Mt. Gilead served as an unofficial symbol of the resilience of Fort Worth's black community amid the horrors of segregation. In addition to serving as a church, it also offered daycare for working mothers, a gym, and a swimming pool—the only one open for the city's black residents. While willing to arrange the occasion, Carter was not going to oppose a racial barrier that he does not appear to have ever questioned in the first place. From his perspective, black residents of the city deserved some level of positive attention, but only within the well-defined limits of Jim Crow. Unlike the supposed "insolence" that brought about the Pennsylvania Railroad slapping incident, such an event did not challenge white authority but instead reinforced the image of Carter as a paternalistic figure for black Fort Worthians.[11]

Though Carter received numerous appeals from desperate cities and towns not fortunate enough to make the list of concert venues, such as Tyler and even small towns like Graham northwest of Fort Worth, he firmly but kindly rejected their requests on the grounds that Rogers was unable to visit every town that requested his presence. By the time the tour ended at the end of the month, over $80,000 had been raised via donations and ticket sales. Fort Worth alone brought in $18,350, some of it from Carter pressuring oil companies with a presence in the city, such as Sinclair and Continental, to contribute to the fund. While not enough to provide relief to every desperate, drought-stricken farmer in the state, the effort illustrates Rogers's seemingly tireless generosity as well as Carter's willingness to devote time to any worthwhile endeavor undertaken by the man who was arguably his closest friend.

As a businessman, Carter began to formulate ideas about how best to combat the Great Depression as early as 1930. He began corresponding with President Herbert Hoover in June, and through these communications, one can begin to learn about the publisher's political and economic views. Though not close friends, the two men had been acquainted since the former secretary of commerce authorized the establishment of WBAP, the radio arm of the *Star-Telegram*, in 1922. In June 1930, Congress, dominated by protectionist Republicans, passed the controversial Smoot-Hawley tariff. Though presented as a bill that would protect struggling American industry and agriculture, it encountered strong opposition in some quarters. Over one thousand economists signed a letter urging Hoover to veto the bill due to concerns about its impact on consumers and the possibility that many countries would retaliate with like-minded tariffs. Carter added his voice to the cacophony of protest, wiring Hoover that though a believer in protective tariffs, he feared the results would bring more harm than good. Concerned that other nations might engage in "direct reprisals" and noting that "some of our basic industries, among the largest employers of labor, are very fearful of its plot," he urged the president to veto the bill and thus "put an end to the disturbance to general business that it has created." President Hoover, driven by a firm belief in the merits of high tariffs, signed the bill into law in June 1930 against the outcries of the opposition. What is interesting to note in this incident is that Carter did not adopt the trade stance attributed to most southerners at the time. Though it is generally assumed that southerners still held strong antiprotectionist tendencies, as they had since the days of Jefferson and Jackson, by 1922 tariffs had started to enjoy considerable support from the region's agricultural and industrial producers. Carter was therefore no different from the rest of the southern business community in voicing support for a moderate protectionism or in criticizing what he calculated would be the tariff's baleful effects.[12]

In January of the next year, as Congress debated the aforementioned drought relief bill, Carter once again contacted President Hoover, this time urging him to support direct relief to farmers hurt by a drought in the South, not just loans that would cover supplies and seed. He wired Hoover a copy of a *Star-Telegram* editorial explaining why farm relief was essential to the survival of those affected by drought. Some argued that loans should be limited: "If aid in the form of loans is justified at all, inclusion of food loans is justified as well." Addressing those who argued that these loans were little more than federal handouts, he remarked, "To say that [the farmers'] case is mainly one of charity dispensed by way of soup kitchens is to display a lack of appreciation of the quality of these sufferers."[13]

Hoover, however, believed differently. In a letter he wrote to Carter marked "Purely Personal," signs appeared of the defensiveness he had acquired as the economy crumbled around him. "I have thought that it is about time we had a little old-fashioned Americanism and self-reliance in this country," he wrote. "I regret that you cannot support me." Detailing how he had intervened to make loans available to "rehabilitate agriculture" as well as coordinated with the Red Cross to "support the hungry," Hoover argued that he was able to "cover the whole situation." With a hint of bitterness, he predicted that "because I have disapproved government doles I shall now be a public enemy, and . . . those making politics out of human misery will score with the Southern people." With a nod to Carter's staunch Democratic credentials, he added, "You may be interested in a message of a great Democratic president upon this subject." To drive his point home, Hoover attached to his letter a selection from President Grover Cleveland's veto of an 1887 drought relief bill for Texas farmers. Though Carter's direct response to this reference is unknown, this episode demonstrates that, as a business progressive, he was open to the concept of direct relief, a position he continued to hold as the New Deal dawned. For the moment, though, he would have to be content to support Rogers's efforts to raise funds from private sources, however inadequate that might seem.[14]

Despite Governor Sterling's effort to prevent Texas from descending further into depression, the state continued its downward slide well into 1932. In 1931, East Texas oil prices plummeted as a consequence of overproduction, and the legislature refused to grant the Railroad Commission sufficient powers to restrict output. Sterling responded in August by declaring martial law and sending National Guardsmen to halt production. In February 1932, the legislature passed a law reducing cotton production. In both cases, the state Supreme Court responded in the negative, claiming in the former that Sterling had overstepped his powers, and in the latter that the legislature had violated property rights. Things had gotten no better in Fort Worth. By 1932, the city's budget deficit stood at $2.6 million, and city leaders were faced with having to provide for the city's unemployed by operating a soup kitchen and putting men to work raking leaves in local parks. As the New Deal got under way in 1933, the city council asked for federal funds to build and improve various streets and bridges in the city. By the end of the New Deal, thanks to Carter, Fort Worth would have more than improved streets and bridges for which to thank the federal government.[15]

As the nation's economy worsened, Carter continued to look for ways to increase his political influence at the national level. With the Depression virtually guaranteeing Democratic victories across the board in 1932, he was determined to enjoy greater influence within the administration of whichever Democratic candidate emerged victorious. His political activities that year caused Will Rogers to comment in his syndicated column, "I haven't heard from my good friend Amon Carter of Texas. I am afraid he is taking politics too serious, for he was awfully able and entertaining before." Carter's candidate of choice for the Democratic presidential nomination was Speaker of the House John Nance Garner of Uvalde, Texas, nicknamed "Cactus Jack" by opponents and admirers alike. First elected to Congress in 1902, Garner had toiled for thirty years, earning a reputation as a moderate Democrat with progressive tendencies and the ability to bridge the two parties. Elected House minority leader by his fellow partisans in 1928, he advocated items such as lower tariff rates and higher public works spending, two issues supported by Carter. After the Democrats swept into power in the 1930 congressional elections amid the failing economy, Garner was the first Democrat in a decade to be elected Speaker of the House, and he subsequently used this position to push across legislation, including a $1 billion public works bill and the creation of the RFC, a government agency designed to loan money to banks, corporations, states, and municipalities. With his reputation as a prominent national politician growing, Garner was often mentioned by the more conservative wing of the Democratic Party as a possible candidate for president in 1932. Publicly, he remained demure, going so far as to say that New York governor Franklin D. Roosevelt "looks like the man for us."[16]

Despite Garner's reluctance to run for president, Carter began to tout his candidacy. Clubs advocating Garner for the presidency sprang up in Texas as early as December 1931, and the next month, William Randolph Hearst gave a radio address on his behalf. The next year, Garner, supported by Hearst and many House Republicans, agreed that a sales tax on all items except food and clothing should be imposed to balance the budget, and Carter informed Garner of his strong support for the tax. Simultaneously, Carter harangued Texas's two senators, Morris Sheppard and Tom Connally, for opposing the proposal, claiming that their ideas of progressive taxation were merely schemes to "soak the rich" that would end up damaging the already fragile economy. Connally, the junior senator from Texas, worked with Robert La Follette Jr. of Wisconsin to lead the antisales tax coalition in the Senate, believing that the proper revenue could be raised through higher income tax rates on individuals and businesses. The sales tax never materialized due to Garner's mishandling of the debate as well as overwhelming opposition from many fellow Democrats, including the rest of Texas's congressional delegation. Though southern congressmen overwhelmingly voted against the sales tax, Carter's support for the plan reflected an odd reality: his views on this issue were much more in line with Republicans and urban-oriented Democrats than with fellow southerners.[17]

In February 1932, Carter publicly demonstrated support for Garner by giving him one of his famous Stetsons, but with the words "Hooray for John Garner and West Texas" inscribed on the inside, a deliberate play on Carter's trademark yell, "Hooray for Fort Worth and West Texas!" Of course, his support went well beyond gifting a hat; the *Star-Telegram* began publishing pro-Garner editorials, and Carter used his extensive network of contacts within the Democratic Party to promote his candidate. As one of the most vocal Garner supporters as well as chair of the National Garner Finance Committee, Carter was then chosen to lead the Texas delegation to Chicago for the Democratic Convention in June. In his weekly column, Will Rogers described the scene from Chicago: "The Texas deligation [sic] arrived on burros. Headed by that fearless old statesman, Amon G. Carter, the genial dirt farmer of Shady Oak Post Office, Texas. Amon is National Committeeman, deligate [sic], alternate, steering wheel, banker, receiver, and wet nurse for the Texas deligation [sic]."[18]

When Carter and the Texas delegates arrived in Chicago for the Democratic Convention, they found their favorite son placing a comfortable third behind Roosevelt and former Democratic nominee Al Smith, thanks in part to Garner's recent win in the California primary. The first round of voting showed Roosevelt was the clear front-runner with 666¼ votes, but he did not have the requisite two-thirds of the votes to win the nomination outright. Al Smith was a distant second with 201¾ votes, but Garner at 90¼ held enough sway among the anti-Roosevelt delegates to be a possible compromise candidate. Carter was determined Garner would become the Democratic nominee, causing Rogers to remark that convention noise was either "a Rube Band or just Amon Carter whispering about Jack Garner to somebody." A Garner win in what promised to be a poor year for Republicans would certainly create new political opportunities and clout for Carter. If Carter could somehow persuade Texas and California delegates to stand firm in their allegiance to Garner, his candidate could possibly emerge victorious.[19]

The convention's first day ended with Roosevelt still shy of the two-thirds vote necessary for the nomination, and the third round of balloting on the morning of the second day still left him short. Louis Howe, longtime Roosevelt confidante and political adviser, viewed Carter as a "'powerful king-maker type' who 'breaks with everyone'" and believed that his position as the head of the Texas delegation was important for the Roosevelt campaign to bear in mind. James Farley, Roosevelt's campaign manager, knew that the Texas delegation held the key to Roosevelt gaining the requisite 2/3 of the delegates; he dangled the vice presidency in front of Garner as a way of persuading him to withdraw his candidacy. Garner, learning of this offer through Representative Sam Rayburn and Senator Tom Connally, replied through Nebraska congressman Edgar Howard that "no man, situated as he is, can decline the honor of the vice-presidential nomination." Garner then authorized the California and Texas delegations to switch their support to Roosevelt. This turn of events caused the Texas delegation to be "thrown into confusion," and a fierce struggle among the delegates ensued. Senator Cordell Hull of Tennessee made an appearance among the delegates and asked Connally to make a motion to switch the state's support to Roosevelt, but he refused. Rayburn, presiding over the proceedings, handed the gavel to Carter and left the room with tears in his eyes "without expressing his wish as to how they should vote or for whom."[20]

Infuriated that Garner's chance at the presidency was fading, Carter labored stubbornly to keep the delegation together in his favor. According to Rayburn's recollections, Carter "was going to nominate Garner whether he had the votes or not." Unfortunately for his cause, however, only 105 of Texas's 180 delegates were in the room; the rest were canvassing other state delegations for Garner votes. As confusion reigned in the Texas caucus, "angry words flew thick and fast," and "there were several near altercations," with Carter in the thick of the verbal fray. Many in the delegation felt they had been betrayed for two reasons: quite a few had been under the impression Garner would not accept second place, and many were angry they had been left out of the negotiations. When one delegate, W. A. Tarver of Austin, moved that the caucus switch support from Garner to Roosevelt, "Carter urged his fellow Texans not to desert their state's top Democrat." Rayburn, who had returned, countered that this was not desertion, but a move that reflected Garner's wishes. When order was restored and a vote taken, the Roosevelt faction won 54 to 51. Yet, in the face of this crushing blow, Carter believed he had one last chance at giving victory to Garner. He would talk to William McAdoo, head of the California delegation and a longtime Carter acquaintance.[21]

California, like Texas, had been holding out in favor of Garner. McAdoo, former treasury secretary and the late Woodrow Wilson's son-in-law, was committed to supporting Garner's nomination. Once it became clear that Roosevelt's nomination was inevitable, McAdoo began listening to appeals from Farley to move California into his column. Yet, Carter pleaded with McAdoo not to release the California delegation to vote for Roosevelt, saying that if California stayed with Garner, then

Texas most certainly would remain loyal to its favorite son. McAdoo later remembered that Carter really "believed that Garner could eventually be nominated. Amon was very vigorous in stating his position[,] but I told him that the strategic move to end the threatened deadlock was for California to switch to Roosevelt on the fourth ballot." Once it became clear that Roosevelt had sealed the nomination, Carter expressed his disappointment through comments that were later carried on the radio. "We quit too soon," he grumbled. "We realized Garner's only chance for nomination lay in a deadlock . . . We had a chance of a lifetime to nominate a President from Texas, but a few of our friends were a little weak-kneed."[22]

Weak-kneed or not, Texas delegates had nothing to be ashamed of, since Garner served as vice president for the next eight years, guaranteeing that Texas politicians and boosters would have a friend and advocate in Washington, D.C. But, for the short term, Carter's emotions gained control as he expressed frustration to the noted wit H. L. Mencken. In Chicago covering the convention, Mencken found "Garner's cool desertion of his Texas lieges . . . one of the most exhilarating episodes of the convention," though Carter clearly saw otherwise. When Carter saw Garner's presidential chances slip away, he "came to the press-stand and unloaded his woe" to Mencken "with tears in his eyes." Nevertheless, Carter soon learned that it behooved him to forget his sadness. Switching his loyalties to Roosevelt proved to be a small price to pay for the federal largesse delivered to Texas during the New Deal and World War II.[23]

Carter's political attention in 1932 was not just focused on placing Garner at the head of the Democratic ticket; to his dismay, the specter of Fergusonism once again reared its head in the form of Miriam Ferguson. Due to the depressed economy, the political climate in Texas was ripe for a Ferguson victory. Sensing the desperate mood of Texas voters, Carter attempted to head off what seemed to be sure disaster for Ross Sterling. Sterling, seeking a second term as governor, had defeated Ferguson two years earlier and believed he could keep the forces of Fergusonism at bay. Carter subtly communicated to Sterling, in person and by letter, his belief that he should refrain from running for reelection. Arguing that he was "not altogether fearful of the result of the campaign," Carter did "fear its character." While Sterling was justified in seeking reelection, Carter believed that he would be better served by bowing out:

> By no stretch of the imagination could your refusal to seek re-election be termed a sign of weakness, or a desire for vindication. It would be taken by the public merely as a case of a successful businessman of large affairs,

who sacrificed his time and his means for the public good, desiring the opportunity to recoup his personal fortunes. Instead of criticizing you, I believe the public would commend you and if anything have a higher appreciation of your services and the sacrifice that you have made than is now the case.

Carter then assured Sterling that whatever his decision, he would have the support of the *Star-Telegram*. Hoping to assuage Sterling's fears that he was being nudged out in favor of another candidate, Carter declared that his suggestion came "merely because you have attained all the honor that can be attained out of the office."[24]

Sterling ignored Carter's request, causing Carter to turn to one of Sterling's former Humble Oil associates, Harry Wiess. Sterling, he complained, was in no shape to run against the Fergusons. "The campaign is going to be an extremely nasty one and it will not only be embarrassing to the Governor, but it will be humiliating," he fumed. Because the Depression had hit Sterling's fortunes and those of his supporters particularly hard, Carter worried that he would not be able to mount an effective campaign against the populist Fergusons, who, he claimed, "can operate one on a shoestring budget." Carter's pleas fell on deaf ears, and Sterling went ahead with his campaign. As promised, Carter supported Sterling, but to no avail. His defensiveness in support of Sterling during the primary was seen not only in the editorial page of the *Star-Telegram* but also in private letters written to Ferguson supporters, some of whom were complete strangers to Carter. One letter, to Mr. D. D. Grubb from the Central Texas hamlet of Ireland, reached an epic length of fifteen pages, each leaf filled with arguments for Sterling and examples of Ferguson nefariousness.[25]

The Fergusons' campaign promised little more than tax reductions and focused on the unpopularity of Sterling's declaration of martial law in the East Texas oil fields. Sterling, due to the strong current of anti-Fergusonism, forced a runoff in the first primary but fell four thousand votes shy of winning the runoff. Allegations of Ferguson vote stealing abounded, yet no investigation was ever undertaken. When it became clear that Ferguson was slated for victory, Will Rogers humorously wrote in his column, "I would like to ask a favor of my friends, no matter where they be, if they have any flowers, old wreaths, or crepe bows, to please send 'em to Amon G. Carter of Fort Worth Texas." "He always staid [sic] clear of politics," he continued, "but the summer heat got 'em and he started to actively campaign against Jim Ferguson. One hundred and twenty millions, and he picks out Jim to argue politics with! It would be like me arguing lip rouge with Greta Garbo." Carter therefore faced double political disappointment in 1932: Roosevelt, not Garner, in the White House and the Fergusons in the Governor's Mansion. Fortunately for Carter, Roosevelt proved to be a much more valuable political asset than he could have imagined. For the rest of the 1930s, Carter found that, given how much more could be gained, the lure of national political bargaining was much more enticing than despairing over who was the governor of Texas.[26]

Loyal Democrat that he was, Carter had little problem pledging allegiance to Roosevelt. As the Roosevelt campaign accelerated in the fall, Carter began fund-raising for the cause, collecting over $9,000 from fellow Fort Worthians in September and October 1932, and contributing $2,000 of his own money. After Roosevelt's election, Carter worked with the Democratic National Committee to raise money to offset the deficit it had incurred from campaign expenses. In January 1933, as Roosevelt's inauguration neared, Will Rogers reported that he had heard from the "inside" that Carter was being seriously considered as Patrick Hurley's replacement as secretary of war. The fact that he got along with all Democrats and "fifty per cent of all of the Republicans" would make him an excellent choice, he opined; from his vantage point, Carter's nomination to the position was "cinched." "Though it hasn't been generally broadcasted," he closed, "those in the know say it's 'in the bag.'" Based on Carter's recent political activities, Rogers had good reason to believe his sources, whoever they were. Carter had spent much of the last year involved in state and national politics, and had been spending an inordinate amount of time in New York and Washington. His fondness for Garner and desire to promote Texas from the seat of national power might have been enough to persuade him to leave his newspaper behind. In the end, Carter would have none of it and said as much in the *Star-Telegram* with a note added at the end of Rogers's column: "The publisher of this paper never has accepted political appointments of any character and has no intention of so doing." Though fellow Texas newspaper publishers Jesse Jones and Ross Sterling had recently entered politics, Carter had little desire to do so, preferring instead to wield influence behind the scenes. A position as a power broker held more appeal than a political position in which he would be forced to respond to the requests of boosters like himself.[27]

Rumors of Carter's political ambitions continued to swirl throughout 1933, especially after he hosted a party in October for Garner, Postmaster General (and Roosevelt campaign manager) James Farley, and Jesse Jones at his famous

Shady Oak Farm just outside of Fort Worth. *Time* covered the trip in great detail, alleging that Carter's "generosity as a contributing Democrat is only equaled by his enthusiasm for the cause and, perhaps, by his ambition to hold office." The article also mentioned Carter's 1925 clash with the Fergusons at the football game (Carter was "full of high spirits" the article said), his shooting episode at the Houston hotel in 1928, and his fondness for liquor ("Texas corn and Scotch . . . which he usually takes neat"). Carter took great offense at the magazine's coverage of the trip and promptly voiced his complaints in a five-page letter to the editor that *Time* saw fit to publish in a later issue. "I am not thin-skinned," he claimed, "but even the most callous individual would resent the untruths and false insinuations that drip from page 13 of your October 30th issue." He then went on to harangue the editor for publishing thirteen false statements. Carter found the accusations of seeking political office particularly irksome. Calling these allegations "ridiculous," he stated that "I have never held public office and have stated repeatedly . . . that I never expect to hold one." Unabashed booster that he was, it was inaccurate to portray Carter as someone who sought political office. His experiences peppering politicians and cabinet members with requests and demands could not have made holding office a desirable option. In his mind, better to be the one pestering than being pestered.[28]

With new boosting opportunities available, Carter greeted the New Deal enthusiastically. For example, in December 1933, he wired Roosevelt a Christmas greeting filled with praise for the accomplishments of the last year. "You are [the nation's] Santa Claus," he gushed, "for through your inspiring leadership and the constructive and humanitarian policies you have inaugurated, the nation this year is enjoying its happiest and best Christmas in four years." Such optimism was understandable, as Carter had ensured that he had friends and acquaintances throughout the Roosevelt Administration and in the Texas congressional delegation. In addition to his friendship with Garner, he had developed relationships with Jesse Jones at the RFC, Senators Tom Connally and Morris Sheppard, James Farley, and Elliott Roosevelt, the president's Fort Worth–residing son.[29]

Because the New Deal was in many ways ideologically incoherent beyond a general belief that government should play a larger role in the nation's economy, Carter's relationship with the Roosevelt administration oscillated throughout the 1930s. In general, he supported the idea of federal spending on public works and internal improvements as a way to provide employment and stimulate economic growth. At the same time, he remained rather skeptical of the federal government's attempts to create a more centrally planned economy, empower labor unions, and raise taxes on the wealthy. Yet, whatever doubts he had about the direction of the New Deal, Carter never flirted with anti-Roosevelt movements like the Texas Regulars or the Liberty League. Complaining about certain New Deal policies was one thing—abandoning the Democratic Party was quite another.

The passage of the National Industrial Recovery Act (NIRA) in March 1933 gave Carter two opportunities to interact with the New Deal, though in very different ways. This act created two federal agencies designed to boost industrial recovery and confidence: the National Recovery Administration (NRA) and the Public Works Administration (PWA). The NRA aspired to spur industrial recovery by creating greater cooperation between business and government through the implementation of industrial codes, setting wages, hours, and production levels, while the PWA was designed to "prime the pump of recovery" by funding the building of large-scale construction projects. Through these two agencies, Carter attempted to increase his reach beyond the borders of Texas, sometimes to great effect.[30]

General Hugh Johnson, head of the NRA, began creating committees to establish the codes of conduct for hundreds of American industries. Johnson had experience working with the government in a similar capacity during World War I when he served on the War Industries Board under Wall Street financier Bernard Baruch. During his tenure at the helm of the short-lived NRA, Johnson yearned to emulate the corporatist style of governance seen in fascist Italy.[31] Carter spent much of 1933 working to establish what is best described as the newspaper cartel. Through his active involvement with the American Newspaper Publishers Association (ANPA), Carter was tapped to join Howard Davis, president of ANPA, and John Stewart Bryan, publisher of the *Richmond Times-Dispatch*, on the newspaper publishers' code committee. The committee's job was to formulate codes that were palatable to Johnson, but naturally the men wanted to retain some semblance of control over their industry.[32]

Existing evidence does not reveal how large a role Carter played in the decision making because the committee often spoke as one voice, but due to its small size and his outspoken personality, it is fairly easy to assume that he must have been an active member. The committee's major concerns were hours, wages, labor power, and press freedom, and its members found that their views clashed with Johnson's. The publishers would accept no less than forty hours as the standard work week, a position that countered the previously proposed thirty-two hours. J. F. Young, the president of the Pacific Northwest Newspaper Association and publisher of the *Spokane Spokesman-Review,* complained to Carter that the existing code clause that called for a return to the 1929 prevailing wage (in many ways, an implementation of Hoover's earlier insistence on keeping wages high) would mean bankruptcy for numerous publishers, many of whom were already struggling with lower circulation during the Depression. It did not help Johnson's case that the newspaper publishing industry was generally antilabor; Section 7a of the NIRA guaranteed workers the right to organize and bargain collectively, and newspaper publishers like Carter were wary of granting too much leverage to labor unions within their industry.[33]

The code committee wished to keep the discussion limited to wages and hours, thus addressing the explicit requests of President Roosevelt to assist with the employment situation. However, Johnson pressed for the newspaper publishers to discuss fair competition, among other issues. Elisha Hanson, the committee's legal adviser and former counsel to former treasury secretary Andrew Mellon, expressed discontent with this request and suggested to Johnson that the "code was so drafted that its provisions deal exclusively with the problem of wages, hours and working conditions." By mid-August, the committee and Johnson had reached some compromises regarding wages, with the new code establishing a "guaranteed minimum rate of pay" based on the 1929 prevailing wage, but there was still disagreement between the two parties regarding the "open shop" the committee desired as well as their insistence on a free-speech clause.[34]

The speech clause so strongly supported by the publishers stated that they would only submit to the rules contained in the code and would not follow any regulations that might restrain their freedom of speech. Johnson believed that the freedom of the press clause the newspaper publishers insisted on was merely their way of avoiding labor standards and Section 7a, and he "contended that no act of Congress, not even an emergency measure such as the National Industrial Recovery Act, could nullify or restrict any part of the Constitution." The committee "answered that if press freedom guarantees were to be considered so axiomatic, why should they not be expressed again in their industrial "Constitution"? After some volleying between the two sides, Johnson appeased the publishers and approved phrases "guaranteeing the freedom of the press," yet he refused to budge on the "open shop" issue. President Roosevelt approved the final draft of the newspaper code in February 1934, but the code did not remain in place for long. The NRA had little life left because in 1935 the Supreme Court struck it down as unconstitutional in *A. L. A. Schechter v. United States,* ruling that it violated the interstate commerce clause of the Constitution by giving the president power to interfere in intrastate business.[35]

Carter's membership on the newspaper code committee, with its staunch support for a freedom of speech clause and approval of a code that limited labor power, revealed that his support for Roosevelt's New Deal had limits from the beginning. As long as the government limited its activism to providing relief and promoting recovery through "pump priming," Carter could support the New Deal. The business progressive ideal so prominent among the southern business community "did not embrace any comprehensive challenge to conservative ideas in the area of capital-labor relations," and as a business progressive, he could go no further.[36]

Carter's crowning achievement in his efforts to obtain New Deal largesse for Fort Worth lay in the acquisition of funds for Fort Worth's Will Rogers Complex in 1935. As Texas prepared in 1935 for the Texas Centennial to be celebrated the next year, he seized this opportunity to see if he could coax financial support for a public works project in Fort Worth. In a letter to Harold Ickes, secretary of the interior and head of the PWA, Carter outlined his plan for a PWA grant to be given to the city to build a coliseum for the annual Southwestern Exposition and Fat Stock Show in Fort Worth and an adjacent auditorium for practical use year-round. The complex would be named in honor of his recently deceased friend, Will Rogers, who had died in a plane crash in August 1935. Fort Worth had recently applied for a $300,000 grant from the Texas Centennial Commission; therefore, Carter wanted a $700,000 loan to complete the funding for what he estimated to be a $1 million project. In addition to this, Carter hoped to receive funding for his proposed Frontier Centennial, a Fort Worth event that he believed would rival the official Centennial celebration in neighboring Dallas.[37]

Ickes, ever vigilant regarding the spending of public funds, believed this grant required further scrutiny to determine if such a construction project would serve the public interest and whether the PWA had the power to administer such a loan after the initial expiration of the National Industrial Recovery Act on June 16, 1935. Furthermore, similar loan applications had been made in the past, and all had been rejected. Nevertheless, as vice president of the Southwestern Exposition and Fat Stock Show, Carter and his fellow committee members submitted a formal application to Vice President Garner, who was chair of the United States Centennial Commission for Texas. By this time, Fort Worth had received $250,000 from the state's Centennial fund and planned a $1,250,000 bond election. Therefore, the committee asked for a $250,000 allocation from the federal government to cover the remaining cost, which had been adjusted to $1.5 million.[38]

Despite couching this proposal in terms of future benefit to Fort Worth and Texas and making a trip to Washington to plead with Ickes personally, Carter was unable to win his immediate approval. Earlier, Ickes had claimed that previously approved projects in Fort Worth, consisting of a school and a sanitarium, were much more important for social welfare than livestock buildings. However, he declared, "if Fort Worth wants the livestock pavilion rather than the projects we have designated, we will make the shift." Evidently, Carter had made leeway in persuading the obstinate Ickes of the project's positive attributes. Carter then decided to travel once more to Washington to visit President Roosevelt and Farley to discuss the need for "Amon's Cowsheds," as the politicians derisively labeled the buildings. After this visit and one more official application resubmission, he received word from RFC head Jesse Jones that "your cowshed has been approved."[39]

By using his contacts in Washington, Carter was able to gather federal money for the Will Rogers Complex. It is doubtful that Fort Worth would have been granted such generous amounts of money to construct the buildings without his involvement. It is also worth noting that in the first formal application for federal funds, there was no mention of alleviating unemployment through the construction of this complex. Rather, the focus was on the benefits that Fort Worth and the local livestock industry would receive from this publicity. (The *Fort Worth Press* noted that the construction would bring 1,500 jobs.) Fittingly, in his letters regarding the applications, Carter failed to note the immediate benefits that could be reaped by the city by putting more than a thousand people back to work. At the front of his mind was the boosting of Fort Worth into a city of great renown.[40]

Carter was not finished attempting to acquire federal funds for Fort Worth. In 1936, Texas celebrated its Centennial, and many cities around the state celebrated it in different ways. Carter's rivalry with nearby Dallas flared up when that city was awarded the site for the official Texas Centennial celebration. Since "Carter viewed the naming of Dallas as the site of the centennial exposition a gross miscarriage of justice," he decided to back a different kind of celebration in Fort Worth. In a January 1936 *March of Time* newsreel, Carter is seen in what appears to be a Fort Worth hotel ballroom stirring up the local partisans with an anti-Dallas harangue. The Frontier Centennial, as it was to be called, would focus on entertainment instead of educational and industrial exhibits. To attract visitors who would be in the region at the Texas Centennial in Dallas, Carter positioned signs and billboards in Texas and in surrounding states that beckoned: "Dallas for education, Fort Worth for entertainment." Offering a dazzling program developed by noted entertainer and promoter Billy Rose, who was basking in the success of producing the dazzling show *Jumbo,* the Frontier Centennial promised to deliver a rollicking good time for visitors drawn to the western-themed grounds. As Carter remarked in a press conference at Fort Worth's annual Southwestern Exposition and Fat Stock Show (which happened to be recorded for the *March of Time* newsreel, "You'd think Dallas invented Texas just because they bid higher for the Centennial than any other city. But we're gonna put on a show of our own and teach those dudes over there where the West *really* begins!" It turned out that to make this possible, he would have to turn, in part, to the New Deal.[41]

Carter decided that the Frontier Centennial would be held at the newly constructed Will Rogers Complex. Funds for the glitzy exhibition, which featured a restaging of *Jumbo,* the Paul Whiteman orchestra, and, most famously, the dancer and actress Sally Rand, began shrinking as the original $250,000 grant from the Texas Centennial Commission was spent and the local bond sales were slower than expected. By midsummer 1936, the cost of opening the Frontier Centennial had soared to over $1 million, well over the projected amount of $911,000. Thus, Carter turned to his friend Jones of the RFC to loan additional money. President Hoover had originally formed the RFC in 1932 to provide loans for banks, railroads, and agricultural stabilization corporations. Now Carter wanted it to breathe new life into the Frontier Centennial, believing full well that his previous associations with Jesse Jones would merit support from the head of the RFC. After all, Jones actively invested in Fort Worth real estate during the 1920s, in part because of encouragement from Carter. Jones biographer Steven Fenberg notes that "Jones relied on Carter to turn up potential tenants" for his downtown Fort Worth construction efforts, forging a business partnership of sorts. Having done so much to assist Jones, Carter turned to him for help, implored him that the money was needed quickly because of the shortage of funds, and expressed confidence that Jones would "be fully justified" in waiving any restrictions on loaning the money. The publisher believed that the inevitable success of the Frontier Centennial should clear Jones's mind of any lingering doubts. Fortunately for Carter, President Roosevelt's son Elliott was also a close friend and a Fort Worth resident. Through this friendship, Carter was able to exert more pressure on Jones to grant the loan. Finally, Jones informed Carter that the RFC would cooperate in the $300,000 loan already given by local banks and would underwrite half of another $200,000 loan. Therefore, the RFC would commit $200,000 to the Frontier Centennial.[42]

Despite the pressure exerted by Elliott Roosevelt to extend an extra $75,000, the RFC would not be able to take on any more than that amount. Though he succeeded in getting $200,000, Carter was not quite satisfied with the amount. Jones told him, "Unlike thousands of others during the past few years, you want the Directors of the RFC to make a loan on terms which you prescribe, and a loan the eligibility of which is not clear, and the security not very tangible." It is clear that Jones was unsure of the practicality of the loan in the first place but approved it due to his friendship with Carter and pressure from Elliott Roosevelt. Carter's ability to exploit the presence of Texans in the Roosevelt administration had worked.[43]

With the exception of some quibbling over the NRA newspaper code, Carter generally remained supportive of the Roosevelt administration during the first term. Like other southern business progressives, it was only after Roosevelt's reelection in 1936 that he began to oppose the administration's position on issues like taxes and labor relations. Therefore, when it came time for Roosevelt to seek reelection in 1936, Carter remained staunchly Democratic and seemed excited about the prospect of another four years of President Roosevelt. After all, there was no reason for him to look elsewhere, even if he was somewhat uncomfortable with the president's excoriation of "economic royalists" during the campaign. The Republican Party clearly held no appeal for him, and his connections within the current administration were legion and too valuable to risk. Upon hearing of Roosevelt's victory, Carter wrote Marvin McIntyre, Roosevelt's assistant secretary, that the Republican campaign that year had been nothing but "squaks [sic]," and that even "investors do not seem to worry regarding the outcome of the election." Thanks to his (and the *Star-Telegram*'s) unwavering support for Roosevelt over the last four years, Carter was rewarded with a seat on the president's platform for the 1937 inauguration. Yet even a prized position behind Supreme Court Justices Benjamin Cardozo and Owen Roberts at the inauguration did little to prevent him from beginning to believe that Roosevelt's New Deal had gone too far.[44]

The 1935 passage of the National Labor Relations Act, better known as the Wagner Act after sponsor Senator Robert F. Wagner of New York, created the National Labor Relations Board and gave unions the right to organize and collectively bargain. The immediate effect was the strengthening of labor unions. American workers began joining unions in greater numbers than before; thus emboldened, many unions demonstrated greater willingness to strike. In March 1937, the United Automobile Workers (UAW), heady from a recent victory over General Motors, informed the Chrysler Corporation that it would be the sole bargaining representative for Chrysler workers. Chrysler executives were willing to negotiate with the UAW, but not on these terms, and the UAW responded with a sit-down strike in nine Chrysler plants. Though Roosevelt gave no encouragement to the strikers, his silence alarmed southern Democrats like Carter. In a confidential letter to Garner, Carter called a recent April 1937 sit-down strike in Michigan "un-American," and he condemned Governor Frank Murphy for not intervening to break the strike.[45]

In thinly veiled terms, Carter asked Garner whether the administration was afraid of John L. Lewis of the United Mine Workers because it made no effort to halt the wave of strikes currently sweeping across the country. He also brought up a recent statement by the Congress of Industrial Organizations (CIO) that Roosevelt wanted everybody to join it. Did the president really say this, and, if not, why was no denial made? Carter also used his position as president and publisher of the *Star-Telegram* to clarify his feelings on labor and the sit-down strike, congratulating Texas governor James Allred for banning sit-down strikes. If Michigan governor Murphy had reacted similarly to Allred, Carter claimed, business would not have been interrupted, and the country's recovery would remain on track. He insisted that he was prolabor, but from his perspective, the sit-down strike smacked of radical law breaking that undermined organized labor's goals.[46]

Carter also was displeased with the proposed federal Child Labor Amendment, recently ratified by the Texas state legislature, which would have given Congress regulatory power over children under the age of eighteen in the workplace. He cordially informed President Roosevelt of his displeasure and espoused the idea that this issue was best left for the states to tackle; Congress should not meddle in child-rearing, he maintained. Carter reminded the president how he had started working at age eleven and then put his own son to work at about the same age. Without child labor, he claimed, he would not have been able to become the self-made man that he was. After all, a large part of the "Carter mystique" was his experience as a "chicken and bread boy" in Bowie, selling chicken sandwiches to passengers on the Fort Worth and Denver Railway. Even Roosevelt later paid homage to this image when, on a 1938 trip that took him through Bowie, he purchased biscuits and chicken from Carter and joked, "You should have an apron on, Amon."[47]

Carter noted that the term "child labor" was often used pejoratively, but he believed a child should have the opportunity to work if the desire or necessity arose. "After all," he said, "idleness has been the cause of many youngsters falling by the wayside." On the other hand, he recognized the danger of sweatshops in which children were overworked and underpaid. However, he argued that even these problems did not require Congress to resolve them. Solving the child labor problem, he thought, "should be purely a state matter" because "the raising of our children should not be left within the province of the whims of some particular Congress." The Child Labor Amendment stalled when only twenty-eight states ratified the law, but the Fair Labor Standards Act, signed into law by Roosevelt in 1938, placed serious restrictions on the use of child labor.[48]

Carter also disagreed with increased government spending, though he appeared to exempt requests that benefited Fort Worth and Texas. He candidly expressed these sentiments to Garner on several occasions, knowing that Garner was emerging as a fierce critic of Roosevelt's second-term policies favoring labor unions, higher taxation, and increased government spending. In addition, the 1937 recession gave many conservative critics of the New Deal ample opportunity to criticize what many perceived as Roosevelt's antibusiness policies. Carter charged that such heavy government spending would lead to higher taxes, which would burden the already tired shoulders of business and industry. A 1937 *Star-Telegram* editorial chastised local governments for begging the federal government for money to spend on sidewalks, streets, and sewers. Projects like these, it claimed, should be financed by the state and local governments, not by Washington. If this spending were to continue without raising taxes, the situation could worsen if the government's credit were damaged. The editorial argued that the recovery effort should be shifted to private enterprise; for that to happen, Congress should remove what he perceived as antibusiness legislation that was passed in Congress's last session.[49]

Frustrated with the 1937 recession and with federal policies that he believed exacerbated the economic turmoil, Carter wrote Garner a lengthy letter in which he outlined his growing displeasure with the New Deal. Carter argued that the tax on undivided profits was an obstacle to recovery because it "penalizes the sound practice of plowing profits back into business, a practice which has made American business management effective." Proposed by Roosevelt in 1936 and passed in the same year, the undivided profits tax was a way for the federal government to prevent the wealthy from leaving large sums in their corporate accounts, therefore avoiding any taxation on that accumulated wealth. In addition to this, the tax also sought to prevent corporations from retaining earnings for capital instead of relying on the money market. Carter believed that not only was this law a bad idea but that it also hindered recovery. He told Garner that, at a minimum, this tax law should be "amended to allow exemption of profits used to fortify the business—for the discharge of debts" accumulated for the purpose of expanding production. Such an amendment would encourage economic growth, whereas the law as it stood "has actually retarded recovery." In support of this, he cited a personal case in which the *Star-Telegram* decided against the construction of an annex to the current building and purchases of new equipment because the tax penalty made it too costly for the company to hold on to the profit necessary to fund this expansion.[50]

In this same letter, Carter asserted that the Roosevelt administration, with its reformist tendencies, was meddling with the economy, making business and industry uncertain about the future. He feared that the current recession would then spiral into another depression, the blame for which would have to be shouldered by Roosevelt. Carter advised that the federal government should revert back to April 1933, when the focus was on recovery, not on reform as Roosevelt's second administration was doing. This idea was not his own, of course, but stemmed from his initial beliefs as to what the government should do to alleviate the pain of the Depression. As early as April 1933, Carter told Garner what legislation the Roosevelt administration should focus on passing: "the currency measure, the banking bill, the security bill, the relief bill, the public works bill, and the farm credit bill." If legislation like this passed, the American people would then be "provided with the tools with which to work their way out." Essentially, Carter wanted the government to give "business and industry a chance to devote its industries to recovery and let reform take care of itself for a while." Yet despite any problems he had with the New Deal at this point, he remained a loyal Democrat and continued pouring his money into the coffers of the Democratic National Committee.[51]

As conservative Democrats like Carter became more disenchanted with Roosevelt, they began looking for a possible nominee for the 1940 campaign who would help steer the party rightward. After the 1938 midterm elections, in which Republicans gained more than eighty seats from the Democrats in the House of Representatives, Garner emerged once again as a possible candidate. By March 1939, he placed ahead of all other Democrats in a Gallup poll asking voters who they wanted to lead the Democratic ticket in 1940, assuming Roosevelt remained outside the fray by choosing not to run for an unprecedented third term. Roosevelt remained characteristically coy about the prospect of a third term, despite previously assuring James Farley that he would not run.[52]

In March 1940, the *Star-Telegram* published an editorial criticizing a movement in Texas to support a third term for Roosevelt at Garner's expense as well as a recent visit to the state by Ickes. A third Roosevelt administration, the editorial claimed, would ensure the continuation of a reform agenda, whereas Garner was assuredly a more conservative, safer option. At a time when several conferences supporting Roosevelt were being held in the state, Ickes appeared in East Texas to visit new oil fields after an invitation had been extended to him in his capacity as interior secretary. Ickes's trip to Texas was viewed with suspicion by many anti–third term Texans because of his reputation as an ardent supporter of a Roosevelt third term. The editorial accused Ickes of wanting to "take production control out of the hands of the State into those of his own department" while simultaneously calling him a "hatchet man," presumably for the pro-Roosevelt forces. The bulk of the editorial castigated Roosevelt supporters, mainly those who were traveling to Texas from other states. These people were "carpetbaggers" just the same as those Texans who refused to support Garner.[53]

Though Ickes was only mentioned once in the long editorial, he took umbrage at the "carpetbagger" term and responded with a scathing public letter. He accused Carter of sending his own "carpetbaggers" to Wisconsin and Illinois to skew the Democratic primaries in Garner's favor. Illinois politics, Ickes argued, were generally clean and open when compared to Texas's, plus they had no "disfranchising poll tax." Carter's opposition to federal regulation of the oil industry reminded Ickes of "a boy in short pants, playing with tin soldiers, and pretending that he is Napoleon." Despite these shortcomings on Carter's part, Ickes admitted that Carter was "a pretty good fellow" when he allowed himself to "function as a normal human being" and did not print editorials "which reflect the Ku Klux spirit."[54]

Thus began the Carter-Ickes tiff, an argument between two stubborn, vocal personalities. The two men had had some disagreements in the past about PWA funding, but it seems that at the heart of this clash lay disparate political views as well as disputed political territory. Carter promptly fired back at Ickes by publishing another editorial entitled "Mr. Ickes Irritates Easily and Quickly" while also printing another long letter that he had written the secretary. Carter defended his actions and denied that he was even officially involved in the "Garner for President" campaign. Referring to Ickes's comment that his previous editorial was illogical, he quipped, "That is pretty phraseology, but, fortunately, you are not the sole arbiter of whether they make sense or not."[55]

Word of this petty argument soon spread. "Efforts in Capital to Avert Roosevelt-Garner Showdown Tangle by Ickes . . . He Twits Amon Carter" read one *New York Times* headline. The *New York Herald Tribune* opined that Ickes showed some naïveté in engaging the "hell-for-leather old frontiersman" publisher from Fort Worth. The paper observed that Carter did not possess a reputation for backing down, and that Ickes was foolish to become involved in any manner in Texas politics because "Texans may make fools of themselves . . . but they insist upon doing it their own way." Dwight Marvin, editor of the *Troy Record* in Troy, New York, congratulated Carter for debating Ickes, and Joseph P. Cowan, a resident of Lubbock, defended Carter as the nominal leader of West Texas and claimed that Ickes had "figuratively evacuated" in his "mess kit." The Carter-Ickes controversy screeched to a halt after Carter published all the correspondence between himself and Ickes, and the publisher seemingly emerged from the wordy brawl unscathed yet no stronger politically. If anything, all Carter had demonstrated to the American public and to his readers was that he could play the sauntering Texan defending his state from marauding know-it-all Yankees.[56]

The uncertainty created by World War II only strengthened Roosevelt's political standing in spring 1940, and the Garner-for-president campaign quickly fell apart amid early primary losses across the nation. Two possible roadblocks to a third term for Roosevelt remained, however; Cordell Hull, Roosevelt's secretary of state, and James Farley were each mentioned as potential candidates, though neither one had a strong national following. As the Democratic Convention in Chicago neared, a worried Farley confided in Carter. The two had been discussing the election since 1939 when Farley, thinking ahead to his possible candidacy, inquired if Carter was going to throw his support behind Jesse Jones, Sam Rayburn, or Garner. Carter planned on attending the convention, and Farley, recognizing that Carter, if not completely supportive, was at least an anti–third term ally, proposed making him assistant sergeant-at-arms or assistant to the chairman. Being named to one of these positions was more than an honorific, as it would enable Carter to travel freely around the convention hall as a surrogate for the anti-Roosevelt forces. Ever the astute politician, Farley was under no illusion that Carter would work the floor solely on his behalf; after all, he joked, he probably had "more than one candidate running. You always did have an ace in the hole!"[57]

An illness forced Carter to cancel his usual attendance at the Democratic Convention, but it is possible other factors influenced his decision. With no nationally recognized figure like Garner in the running, he must have understood that throwing his support behind another individual would probably be fruitless as well as damaging to his relationship with Roosevelt. Whatever political differences he had with the president during the New Deal's later years, he did not want to endanger his access to the White House. Never one to stray too far from the seat of power and ever the gregarious companion, he maintained his bond with the president and continued to promote Fort Worth in the nation's capital. And as war with Germany and Japan loomed, Carter found himself criticizing the president less and calling for rearmament more. After all, Roosevelt's call for the nation to become the "arsenal of democracy" might mean further benefits for Fort Worth.

Though Carter had already earned a reputation as a vocal civic booster in the years prior to the New Deal, Roosevelt's transformative war on the Great Depression elevated the publisher's status as Fort Worth's unofficial representative to the nation due to the promotional opportunities the New Deal offered. In addition, his solidly Democratic credentials, combined with his ownership of the widely circulated *Star-Telegram*, ensured Carter access to the White House in ways previously not available to him. Even so, clearly there were limits to his influence within the Democratic Party and to his support for the New Deal. Yet no other Fort Worthian, or West Texan for that matter, could claim the extensive political and business contacts that Carter had, thus ensuring that as "Dr. New Deal" became "Dr. Win the War," he would continue to lobby President Roosevelt as the city's primary booster.

CHAPTER 6

WATERWAYS, AIRWAYS, OIL PRODUCTION, AND THE HOME FRONT

FOR AMON CARTER, the 1930s were about more than learning to adjust to a new style of government in Washington, D.C. The decade marked the beginning of his pursuit of a dream that never came to fruition: the canalization of the Trinity River from the Gulf of Mexico to Fort Worth. His efforts involved the marshaling of local, state, and federal political support, as well as the backing of the Dallas and Fort Worth business communities. The cause of aviation, never far from his mind since the arrival of the first airplane in Fort Worth, also received greater attention from Carter than ever before as he continued to work with American Airways/American Airlines in hopes of promoting Fort Worth as a major aviation center. Carter's dreams of achieving wealth through oil finally came to fruition in 1937 when he struck oil in West Texas. This subsequently allowed him to begin devoting more time and energy to philanthropic activities and, of course, added to the western persona he had been developing since the 1920s. On the domestic front, he continued to devote himself to his two children from Nenetta, Amon Jr. and Ruth. Yet not all remained peaceful for the publisher, because on the eve of the United States' entry into war, his marriage to Nenetta collapsed, threatening to upset the familial stability he had enjoyed for nearly two decades.

WATERWAYS

For twenty-five years, visions of freighters docking in Fort Worth and transforming the city into an industrial powerhouse consumed Carter and drove him to push for the construction of a canal up the Trinity River from the Gulf of Mexico to Fort Worth and Dallas. This was no one-man scheme, however; prestigious citizens of both cities joined the organization that worked tirelessly to create a canal that would create economic benefits for North Texas. Though the name of this organization changed a few times throughout Carter's life, the goal remained the same. Whether it was called the Trinity River Navigation Association (TRNA), the Trinity River Canal Association (TRCA), or the Trinity Improvement Association (TIA), this group of businesspeople lobbied the state and federal government to support the plan to make the Trinity navigable. Spearheading this effort was Carter, the eternal optimist, promoting the idea to politicians, businesspeople, and his community. From his early years as a salesman, Carter learned to be ever mindful of his audience and accordingly shifted his emphasis. Depending on with whom he was speaking, he alternately stressed the industrial or commercial benefits of building the canal. Once Roosevelt embarked upon his New Deal, Carter learned to couch the proposal in terms palatable to the administration. Little did he know that his extensive efforts would fall short, leaving Fort Worth no closer to the Gulf than before he began this endeavor.

Carter and his colleagues were not the first to foresee that a navigable Trinity River would benefit Texas. In a letter to Carter, Fort Worth oil operator George Hill wrote that he had stumbled upon Mexican correspondence in some Austin archives regarding making the Trinity navigable. A certain Francisco Madero, citizen of the Mexican province of Tejas y Coahuila, petitioned that the Trinity River be "navigable to steamboats, horse drawn vessels, sail boats, and boats propelled by oars from its mouth to Bull Hill." In a memo entitled "The Legislative History of the Trinity River," TRCA executive vice president Roy Miller outlined the historical discussion regarding the navigation of the Trinity. In the River and Harbor Act of June 18, 1878, Congress called for the deepening of the channel at the mouth of the Trinity for easier navigation and then appropriated $10,000 for the project. Congress earmarked additional funds for the improvement of the Trinity throughout the rest of the nineteenth century. The 1899 River and Harbors Act provided money for a survey of the Trinity from its mouth to Dallas while simultaneously approximating the cost of adding locks and dams along the way. Congress continued to appropriate hundreds of thousands of dollars

until the project was abandoned in the River and Harbor Act of 1922. The only accomplishment of these various acts was the widening and deepening of the mouth of the Trinity, which had little impact on Fort Worth's economy. Fort Worth and Dallas both possessed political and business communities that did not want to see canalization abandoned, and were therefore hopeful when, in 1930, Congress began debating the passage of a new rivers and harbors bill that might include funding for deepening the Trinity. In February 1930, representatives from the two cities met with army engineers in Dallas to present their case for canalization. Optimistic as the representatives were, they understood that the cities must address the reasons given for prior abandonment of canalization.[1]

According to TRCA vice president Miller, earlier projects were abandoned for two reasons: one, engineers doubted that the water supply would be sufficient to allow for consistent navigation; and, two, "the purely local character of the project . . . limited its possible services to the area immediately contiguous to the river." Miller, however, did not believe that these reasons should halt any future Trinity projects. Reservoirs had been completed since the initial project came under scrutiny, and the completion of the Mississippi River System along with the Intracoastal Waterway in Louisiana and Texas changed the project from a local one to one of national importance. Since the hearing was for army engineers, the arguments presented focused mainly on the alleged feasibility of the project, though some speakers did discuss the economic benefits that would be made possible by canalization. Through the efforts of Senators Morris Sheppard and Tom Connally of Texas, as well as Fort Worth Representative Fritz Lanham and Dallas Representative Hatton Sumners, Congress passed a rivers and harbors bill in July 1930 that included funding for a resurvey of the Trinity River.[2]

Carter's involvement with the canal began in the summer of 1930 with the formation of the TRNA. At first, he served the organization on the board of directors, but in this position he held little power in the association. He was simply one of many Fort Worth businessmen, such as department store owner William Monnig or oilman Ed Landreth, who were granted positions. His first assignment was to find a suitable young lady in Fort Worth to break a bottle of Gulf of Mexico water at the dedication of a hydraulic dredge in Dallas. This dredge was to begin digging in preparation for a turning basin in the Trinity River. Carter found a young woman for this ceremony and then prepared to give a speech at the ceremony entitled "Trinity River Navigation and Its Relation to the Development of the Southwest." In this speech, one of many given on this momentous day, Carter discussed how the building of a canal would benefit not only Fort Worth and Dallas but also the infinite stretches of West Texas with its vast agricultural and oil resources. Dallas and Fort Worth would be transformed into great inland industrial centers like Pittsburgh or Cleveland.[3]

It did not take long for Carter to begin exerting his power and influence over the association. The other members quickly recognized what an asset they had in Carter. His friendship with politicians in Texas and Washington, D.C., combined with having his own newspaper, was very attractive to the association. At an August 1930 meeting of the TRNA, Carter was named chair of a finance committee to raise $60,000 a year for five years for an educational program to increase local awareness about the project. By August of the same year, the TRNA changed its name to the TRCA, moved its offices from Dallas to Fort Worth (presumably at Carter's urging), and named Carter to the executive committee. He also hosted a meeting with TRCA members, Senator Sheppard, and Representatives Sam Rayburn, Lanham, and Sumners at his Shady Oak Farm in August that year to discuss the future of the project as well as to assure the continued support of Texas's congressional delegation.[4]

The new TRCA added Intracoastal Waterway board member Roy Miller of Corpus Christi as the executive vice president and selected Dallas businessmen John Carpenter as president and John Fouts as general manager. Miller was simultaneously involved in the planning of the Gulf Intracoastal Canal and was therefore valuable for his experience. Carpenter was a prominent Dallas businessman and the president of Texas Power and Light, and he often took the lead in civic affairs in much the same manner as Carter. In correspondence with Carter, Fouts detailed the move to Fort Worth and Carter's future role. With Carter's name on the official letterhead, Fouts hoped to capitalize on his presence, commenting that earning Carter's cooperation "moves mountains and canalizes rivers."[5]

Carter needed little persuasion to devote himself wholeheartedly to the project. Any operation that would boost Fort Worth and West Texas in the eyes of the nation was a worthy undertaking, even if it meant cooperating with Dallas. Later in 1930, at a meeting of the TRCA at the Fort Worth Club, Carter disclosed that he was already in talks with politicians regarding the Trinity. Having earned the cooperation of powerful politicians like Sheppard and Rayburn, Carter realized that the canal could become a real possibility. Later, Carter confessed that he had been reluctant to cooperate with Dallas because he doubted that it would commit to the project with the same fervor as Fort Worth. However, he was satisfied by the move of the offices to Fort Worth and the sincere cooperation of Carpenter and Fouts.⁶

As chair of the finance committee, Carter began sending letters to local businessmen to raise the money to fulfill Fort Worth's financial commitment. The TRCA planned to spend $300,000 over five years in raising awareness, hosting meetings, and lobbying politicians. Dallas was going to raise $30,000 annually, Fort Worth $20,000, and the rest was to be raised by other towns and cities along the Trinity. In a form letter sent to businesses such as Swift Meatpacking, Texas Electric, and Monnig's Department Store, Carter appealed to both their sense of pride in the community and their desire for a growing economy in the region. He claimed that Fort Worth's position at the head of the canal not only would bring business and industry but would also mean increased savings in freight rates. Carter assured the business community that the project would be national, not local, and pointed out that the president of the Mississippi Valley Association had noted at recent meetings that the Trinity Canal was to be an integral part of the internal waterway system of the United States. He could not resist infusing these letters with the booster spirit for which he was so well known, saying that "every sign points to success of the Trinity River project." To seal the deal, Carter pointed out a recent unnamed survey showing that the Trinity River shipping area had handled 450 million tons of freight; the survey had also calculated that the present ratio of river traffic to total traffic around the country revealed that the Trinity proper might handle over 5 million tons of traffic. The Southwest would profit by over $15 million annually; therefore, the approximate cost of construction to the federal government of $50 million would be easily justified.⁷

Carter believed that the easiest way to get fellow Fort Worthians on board with the idea was to focus on the impact of the canal on freight rates. In an article he wrote for a locally published book on canalization, Carter pointed to the absence of the steel industry in North Texas as proof of the harmful effects of high freight rates. Up to that point, he said, steel mills were unable to locate in the North Texas region because freight rates were too high to ship steel cost-effectively. Water rates were much cheaper, and with the canal, steel mills would be willing to build in North Texas. Carter believed that "canalization" (a word frequently used by proponents) was "the most far reaching proposition, in its ultimate benefits, that has been presented to the people of Fort Worth and North Texas since the advent of the railroads." Increased manufacturing would also mean larger population, more business, and more prosperity for the community as a whole, he claimed.[8]

Though freight rates were at the center of Carter's argument, he did not want his stand to be mistaken for an attack on the railroads. Carter recognized that the railroads were Fort Worth's lifeline. Building the canal would help, not hurt, the railroads because the canal would mean increased railroad traffic when many new industries shipped their goods to the canal for further transportation. In Carter's own words, "The canal will merely be a complementary form of transportation not a competitor of the railroads." Regardless of Carter's remarks, the railroads felt threatened by a new form of transportation in the region. Silliman Evans, executive secretary of the TRCA, informed Carter that the railroads were mounting opposition to any legislation that supported the canalization of the Trinity River. According to Evans, railroad attorneys were pressuring lawmakers to defeat any canal bill while simultaneously urging them to hold up favored legislation of those who supported the canal. Determined leadership was needed to rally canal forces, and he believed that Carter was the man for that job. With opposition to his dream mounting, Carter took action by using the pages of the *Star-Telegram* and by phoning many legislators in Austin urging passage of the Trinity River Canal District Bill, which provided for the formation of a tax district for the canal. The bill passed in May with a 21–6 vote, and Carter received much of the credit for its success.[9]

The TRCA faced more problems than railroad opposition. It was still debatable whether or not the Trinity's water levels could be maintained to allow navigation. In 1932, Colonel W. T. Hannum, a War Department engineer, reported that his preliminary survey of the Trinity disclosed that in fact there was not enough water for year-round navigation. However, this survey did not take into account two lakes currently under construction by Fort Worth. According to Fouts, the amount of water impounded by these two lakes would be sufficient for both Fort Worth's needs and the needs of shipping on the Trinity. In response to Hannum's report, the TRCA hired engineers and an attorney to prepare a feasible solution to present to the Board of Engineers in Washington in the summer of 1932.[10]

The TRCA was successful in convincing both the federal government and the state of Texas that a navigable Trinity was worth the research and investigation. The Texas Legislature created the Trinity River Canal and Conservancy District to comply with any demands the federal government would make to prepare the area for improvement. In 1933, the Department of Commerce completed an economic survey to determine if a navigable Trinity was necessary for the continued development of Texas. Commerce was also interested in knowing if the canal would be worth spending tax dollars to construct. In the fall of 1933, the Department of Commerce determined that the project would cost $120 million. Carter maintained, however, that it could be built for only $54 million and continued rallying local businessmen to the cause of a Trinity Canal. The canal would boost Fort Worth's population to a half million in time, and despite all the continued enmity from the railroads, it could be completed. Carter believed that Fort Worth's future as a big city hinged on the construction and completion of the canal.[11]

The flurry of activity that accompanied the creation of the TRNA and TRCA slowed down as the effects of the Great Depression reached Fort Worth and Dallas. The years 1932 and 1933 were especially slow, if the lack of correspondence between members signified anything. However, the arrival of Franklin D. Roosevelt, with his promise of increased federal spending, breathed new life into the canalization of the Trinity. Carter and his fellow board members apparently recognized that an increase in public works spending by the federal government could mean more money for the construction of a canal. Workers would be needed to build a canal and the economic benefits created by the canal would be a credible weapon to combat the Great Depression.

Others involved in the canal project recognized early in the Roosevelt administration that Carter would be a great emissary to the New Dealers in Washington. Hoping to exploit Carter's connections with Harry Hopkins and Harold Ickes, Carl Mosig of the *Dallas Morning News*'s Fort Worth branch notified Carter in December 1933 that $250,000 in public works money had been given to the National Planning Board for regional planning projects. Both Dallas and Tarrant Counties filed applications for this money with the hopes of hiring a prominent engineer to do preliminary planning for the canal project, but Mosig doubted that the money would be given to Dallas and Fort Worth unless Carter could persuade Hopkins or Ickes otherwise. Unfortunately for Carter and canal supporters, the two men believed that the money would be better spent elsewhere. Despite this initial failure to garner support from the federal government, canal boosters continued their efforts.[12]

John Carpenter, longtime Dallas booster and president of the TRCA, recognized Carter's lobbying skills and appointed him the chair of a TRCA delegation traveling to Washington for the 1934 meeting of the National Rivers and Harbors Congress. While at the session, Carter revealed the broadening plans of TRCA that would allow for a greater water supply. Flood control in the Upper Trinity

River Basin would be added to the designs so as to reclaim more than 1,000,000 acres of land. Surveys conducted by TRCA disputed claims made by railroad engineers, and Carter naturally took the side of the association. For example, TRCA surveys showed that yearly maintenance of the canal would cost approximately $500,000, whereas the Texas Railway Association stated it would cost in excess of $26 million. This estimate, Carter argued, was larger than the yearly maintenance of all the canals and rivers in the United States.[13]

The Roosevelt administration had more pressing matters, however, than building a canal in Texas, and it was well over a year before the federal government took specific steps toward addressing the Trinity Canal. On August 7, 1935, the War Department's Board of Engineers for Rivers and Harbors held a hearing in Fort Worth regarding the feasibility of the proposed Trinity waterway, and Carter presented the opening statement on behalf of the TRCA. Though not successful in the sense of persuading the U.S. Army Corps of Engineers of the immediate necessity of the plan, he did enjoy some limited gains. The Corps of Engineers agreed with Carter that canal construction was feasible from an engineering standpoint, but disagreed that it could be economically viable. Also, the federal government had rarely agreed to construct a waterway within the first few years of the initial proposal. In the face of this somewhat daunting news, the TRCA agreed to continue the struggle to make the Trinity navigable because the idea was "meritorious and sound," and, they argued, Fort Worth and Dallas could not continue their growth without the canal.[14]

As the TRCA's efforts stalled over the next few years, Carter decided that the best course of action would be an appeal to the top; if he could gain the ear of the most powerful man in America, President Roosevelt, he might have a chance of pushing his vision forward. Desperate for success, Carter personally appealed to President Roosevelt while he was visiting his son Elliott on his ranch just west of Fort Worth in July 1938. Carter arranged to meet with him to discuss the Trinity River project, and apparently piqued the president's interest. Roosevelt asked for maps and even made general engineering suggestions. Opportunistic as ever, Carter sent President Roosevelt not only the requested maps but also a letter containing a full outline of his ideas on the Trinity.[15]

Ever the salesman, Carter capitalized on his ability to take his audience into account. President Roosevelt's actions during the New Deal, especially his support for the Tennessee Valley Authority, had demonstrated that he was more favorable to projects that demonstrated both economic and social benefits, and Carter hoped Roosevelt would be swayed by the transformation of the Trinity canal project into a package that would holistically affect Texas. No longer was this merely a canal venture but a program for soil and water conservation; flood control; navigation; reclamation of flood lands; the alleviation of stream pollution; conservation of wildlife; and storage of water for municipal, industrial, and agricultural uses. Somewhat coincidentally, this meshed with the president's vision he shared in an address from Elliot's home in which he outlined the necessity of a federal land management program. The centerpiece of Carter's letter to Roosevelt was the canalization of the Trinity with a focus on the engineering feasibility, economic justification, and public necessity of the canal.[16]

Knowing that such a program needed input from the secretary of agriculture and the Army Corps of Engineers (and possibly wanting to defer making a decision that could offend an important ally like Carter), a somewhat supportive Roosevelt forwarded the letter to the relevant secretaries for further review. Harry Brown, acting secretary of agriculture, responded that he was pleased with the progress that had been made by the TRCA to further cooperation between federal and state organizations, especially with regard to soil conservation efforts. However, he cautioned, the state of Texas needed to pass a strong soil conservation law that would allow for increased agriculture in the Trinity watershed. Though this was not a statement specifically endorsing the idea of a canal, Carter had to have been pleased to hear that some aspects of the canal idea were well received in the higher levels of the government.[17]

Although Carter had the tacit support of President Roosevelt, this did not mean he was going to get his canal. Carter wrote Congressman Sam Rayburn that the imminent passage of the Wheeler-Lea Transportation Bill would mean that "Congress would cease to improve rivers for practical navigation." The Wheeler-Lea Transportation Act, introduced in 1939 by Montana senator Burton Wheeler, would place inland water carriers under federal jurisdiction for the first time and create a temporary transportation board that would monitor their condition. Carter feared government regulation, but he did not cite this reason for his opposition to the bill. There was little indication in the bill that the government was opposed to inland water transportation, but in Carter's case, he believed government regulation of the industry meant an attempt to halt the rise of a competitor to the railroads.[18]

Carter hoped that Rayburn would use his position to ensure that the Wheeler-Lea bill would not hurt the Trinity program. When it became apparent that the bill would pass, Carter pressured Rayburn to seek a thirty-day period in which the public could peruse the bill. The bill was so intricate, Carter claimed, that only an expert could understand the complexities. In those thirty days, Carter hoped that the legislators and the public would find some part of it distasteful and dispense with the bill. To Carter's chagrin, however, the Wheeler-Lea Transportation Bill passed in 1940, allowing for greater government regulation of inland waterway transportation. In reality, this legislation proved to be less damaging than the hydrological impossibility of canalizing the Trinity. Carter spent much of the rest of his life attempting to prove that the impossible could become reality with human perseverance and ingenuity.[19]

These canal-related activities during the 1930s are very revealing of Carter's goals, methods, and philosophy about government at the local, state, and federal levels. While not the originator of the Trinity River vision, he clearly believed that this program, if followed, could benefit not only his city but the whole region. Granted, that assumed the feasibility of canalizing a low-flow, narrow, shallow river, but considering the dream did not die until the 1970s, the possibility was tantalizing for many in the Dallas–Fort Worth region. Carter's support for the project even before the New Deal reveals a willingness to ask for and welcome federal support for internal improvements, as well as the width and breadth of his boosting. Urging New Deal work relief agencies to fund construction in Fort Worth was limited in scope compared to a project that would immediately affect the Trinity River from the Gulf of Mexico to Fort Worth. Like a typical New South booster with a business progressive philosophy, he found nothing to dissuade his support for canalization: government at all levels should encourage entrepreneurial development in as many ways possible, including supporting projects too large for private enterprise alone.

AIRWAYS

Carter continued his promotion of aviation in quite tangible ways during the 1930s that extended well beyond his hobby of collecting inscribed helmets from famous aviators such as Jimmy Doolittle and Benny Foulois. Through a position on the board of directors of American Airlines and through public advocation of air travel, he demonstrated a commitment to expanding the popularity of air travel even in the midst of the Depression. As with most causes he supported, he hoped that Fort Worth could reap some advantages from his promotion, especially in the construction of a modern airport, but he would pursue that cause in the future when the worst of the Depression had passed. In the meantime, he viewed it as his duty as a leading citizen to show the public that air travel was a safe and feasible means of transportation and that the aviation industry was a worthy investment.[20]

Carter's relationship with American Airways (later American Airlines) during the 1930s, while not tumultuous, certainly ebbed and flowed, as did the fortunes of America's aviation industry. In 1930, President Hoover's postmaster general, Walter Brown, seeking to encourage the development of passenger service, moved to consolidate what he regarded as an unwieldy patchwork of airlines delivering mail. From Brown's perspective, most airlines "were not really interested in developing passenger traffic, and never would be as long as they depended so heavily on mail pay, many of them for sheer survival. And Brown believed sincerely that the industry's future rested on passengers, not postal stamps." That same year, he persuaded Congress to pass the McNary-Watres Act, which ultimately "gave the postmaster general economic control over the airlines." This act (also known as the Airmail Act of 1930) paid airlines not by the pound-per-mile method, but by space available for mail. His hope was that carriers, motivated by this subsidy shift, would transition to using larger aircraft, thus providing space and a motive to fill up the excess room with passengers. Many smaller airlines did not have the resources to continue competing under these new rules, and a new wave of consolidation began. While carrying the mail retained its importance for many carriers, the larger ones realized the possibilities of carrying passengers and began developing more routes to market to travelers.[21]

American Airways, still operating under the umbrella of its parent company, AVCO, was one carrier that stood to benefit from this new legislation. After a flurry of mergers and acquisitions that followed the passage of McNary-Watres, three airlines dominated 90 percent of the industry: Trans World, United, and American. Carter, serving on American's board of directors, saw an opportunity for continued growth of the airlines as well as the possibility of greater gains for Fort Worth. For two years, Carter harangued and negotiated with AVCO chairman Averell Harriman and short-tenured president Frederic Coburn to move its southern operations from Dallas to Fort Worth. It certainly helped his case that former *Star-Telegram* reporter Silliman Evans served as vice president of AVCO's board. The Fort Worth city council, most likely at Carter's behest, offered a bonus to American if it agreed to the move: free use of the municipal airport, no gasoline fees, and no taxes for thirty-three years. This offer was made on the condition that American build a $150,000 building at the airport, a building that, unless the company exercised a twenty-year option, would belong to the city of Fort Worth after thirty-three years. In May 1932, two months after the board of directors deposed Coburn as president for what they believed were poor manufacturing decisions as well as a micromanaging style, American Airways and Fort Worth reached an agreement, much to the chagrin of Dallas city leaders and businesspeople. While there was clearly an element of Fort Worth boosterism to Carter's position, a part of it (as well as many of his other positions) was the desire to strike at Dallas. For example, when the Oil Well Supply Corporation announced in 1931 that it was moving its offices from Pittsburgh to Dallas instead of Fort Worth, Carter allegedly vowed "revenge will be mine if it takes forever." The truthfulness of the outburst aside, it cannot be denied that while Carter knew how to cooperate with Dallas on cases such as the Trinity River, when it came to aviation, he desired to outperform Fort Worth's eastern neighbor in every way possible and to benefit his own city.[22]

Carter's first tenure on American Airways' board of directors ended in 1933 amid the turmoil at AVCO over control of the company. Coburn's replacement, LaMotte Cohu, was soon ousted by AVCO shareholder Errett Cord in March 1933. Cord "felt [AVCO] was worrying too much about its bulging portfolio of stocks, too little about its basic business of flying airplanes." Though many Wall Street–associated directors like Robert Lehman of Lehman Brothers and Harriman resigned after Cord's takeover, Carter stubbornly remained on the board nearly two weeks after the reshuffling. He finally announced his resignation at the end of the month, claiming that this was "purely an act of principle, feeling a newspaper publisher should be identified with as few outside businesses as possible and that it is better to be left entirely free from any semblance of influence in connection with matters which the paper must discuss editorially, from time to time." To complete his severance, he also sold off his five hundred shares of stock in AVCO. Within five years, however, he would have a change of heart and once again join the board of directors after reinvesting in the company.[23]

In the interim, Carter did not abandon his aviation dreams and maintained solid relations with American, as demonstrated by his participation in a flight with Elliott Roosevelt on the company's first transcontinental flight from Los Angeles to New York. Yet his dabbling with flying and related activities was now no longer limited. Always the avid collector, he began to build up his collection of inscribed helmets gifted to him from famous aviators like Foulois and Doolittle. He forged a friendship with noted aviator Frank Hawks, which, on one occasion, nearly cost them their lives. On a flight from Fort Worth to New York, between Birmingham and Atlanta, Hawks, with Carter as his passenger, flew through what he called "the worst [storm] he had ever encountered in the air." Newspaper coverage of the flight reported that Hawks claimed that "at one time, he and Mr. Carter prepared to take to parachutes." Carter denied this in a letter to Hawks, declaring that he "did not know just what was happening when the motor quit on us" and had assumed that Hawks was finding a place to land. Even such a brush with disaster failed to quench Carter's love of flight; he told Hawks that he hoped to make the trip again, however under "more favorable circumstances." He continued to fly when he traveled, especially if doing so promoted aviation, such as his trip to South America in 1935 on Pan Am's "Brazilian Clipper," a flying boat piloted by Hawks.[24]

Carter rejoined American in 1938, a company that looked somewhat different from when he had left. In 1934, American Airways had undergone a name change in response to new government policies regarding airmail contracts, so it was now American Airlines. The president of this new corporation was Fort Worth's C. R. Smith, who had been active in the southern division of the company for some time. Even with this local connection, Carter was absent from American until 1938, when he was once again elected to the board of directors. He remained with American until his death, upon which it was noted that he was the longest-serving member of the company's board as well as the largest shareholder.[25]

Though not always involved in the day-to-day activities of the airline, he was generally considered to be "the most influential director of them all," partially because he "always expressed his opinions freely at board meetings and everywhere else." When Smith decided to remove the footrests from the airline's DC-3s, Carter "bawled [Smith] out." Sometimes his outspokenness could lead to positive gains for the airline, as it did in 1940 when he opposed a proposal to partner with an outside company to operate restaurants at airports American served. When the contract was presented to the board, every member except Carter approved. "If we're gonna operate restaurants, we should run 'em ourselves," he exclaimed. The result was Sky Chefs, a subsidiary of American Airlines that operated concessions at airports and cooked food for in-flight meals. One would expect that Carter would spend a considerable amount of time trying to persuade Smith to move the company's headquarters from Chicago to Fort Worth (where the company already had based its southern operations), but obviously his boosterism was limited by both his understanding that this might not benefit the airline and the fact that such an idea would most likely have been defeated by the other board members.[26]

Flying, of course, was still a relatively dangerous activity during the 1930s; after all, barely three decades had passed since Wilbur and Orville Wright had celebrated their initial flight on the desolate, sandy stretches of Kitty Hawk, North Carolina. Memories of Carter's own dangerous experience while flying with Hawks just a few years before must have surfaced as he sat inside the chapel at Forest Lawn Memorial Park in Glendale, California, on August 22, 1935, for Will Rogers's funeral. Rogers, still widely read and well respected, died in Alaska while flying with famed aviator Wiley Post. Nenetta wired him from her vacation spot in Colorado Springs (a favorite Carter destination for decades), saying, "I wish I could be there to alleviate your heartaches and sorrow." The Light Crust Doughboys, long a mainstay on Carter's WBAP radio, performed a tribute song over the air. The grieving Carter, in Washington, D.C., at the time of the crash, flew to Seattle to greet the body, an act for which Betty, Will's wife, expressed deep gratitude. "My dear, dear Amon," she wrote, "you're going to Seattle was the sweetest and most comforting of all the loving things that was done for him." "He loved you, we all do," she continued, "you are one of the finest." The grief-stricken widow closed mournfully, "Please come sometime to see us. It's lonely here but it seems I just can't tear myself away. Not yet. Maybe later sometime." And while there was little Carter could do that would assuage Betty Rogers's grief, he did, of course, ensure that his friend's memory would live on.

OIL BARON

While ownership of the *Star-Telegram* gained Carter a certain amount of political influence, he failed to achieve a considerable amount of wealth until the mid-1930s, when he finally struck oil after numerous previous attempts had ended in failure. Ever since the West Texas oil boom of the 1920s, Carter had been obsessed with drilling for oil, purchasing large tracts of land in the vast expanses of that region and drilling one dry hole after another. Once again, his tenacious personality paid off. Ever independent-minded, Carter seemed to personify the typical "wildcatter," a man who struck out on his own in pursuit of wealth without the backing of large oil corporations. In reality, he worked with oil companies to purchase leases from them that they had been unsuccessful with or did not desire to develop for whatever reason. His successful quest for oil added to his credibility as a typical Texan, making it easier for him to play the role he had begun to adopt in the 1920s. Now a member of what has been called the "big rich" (Texans like his friend and confidante Sid Richardson and H. L. Hunt), Carter became an oil legend in his own time and a celebrity of some stature. It is no accident that after his entrance into the status of the independently wealthy, his name appeared more often in gossip columns and rumor mills, especially after his second marriage to Nenetta fell apart. The sudden wealth he gained also enabled him to begin building a vast art collection, mainly centered on pieces related to the American West by artists such as Frederic Remington and Charles Russell. Most importantly, at least from his perspective, his wealth now enabled him to pursue his philanthropic dreams more than ever before.

In the midst of the Depression, drillers discovered more oil in the Permian Basin in far West Texas and across the border into New Mexico, and Carter believed that here lay his opportunity for success. Much of this work was done, not by the major oil companies, but by independents, or "wildcatters," like Carter. Many of the major players acquired leases in the region during the 1920s, but these were only valid for ten years unless production had begun. As oil prices dropped during the Depression, the major companies turned to the independents and offered them farmouts, defined as "a contribution of lease acreage in exchange for the drilling of a well." Like many independents, Carter found this to be a ready method of accessing what turned out to be productive oil fields in West Texas. By 1935, oil companies and wildcatters alike were rushing to West Texas in search of instant wealth, to the extent that the Humble Oil Company reported that year that over 40,000,000 acres of the state were under lease. Carter purchased a tract in Lea County, New Mexico, and in May 1935, found oil. Soon after, through his independent oil company, Crafton Oil, and a partnership with Fort Worth oilman William A. Moncrief, he received a farmout from the Pure Oil Company in the Keystone Field in Winkler County and struck oil once again. This considerable boost to his fortune allowed him to plow even more money into more wildcatting. Two years later, Carter negotiated with Continental Oil to obtain expiring leases in Gaines County and on June 19, 1937, brought in Wasson No. 1, the first of many productive leases for Carter in the region. Later that year, he "extended the Harper Field in Ector County with a 608-barrel well in another farmout," and in 1940, discovered two more wells on his lease in the Wasson Field. As the oil flowed in, so did the money, and Carter was now able to develop his wealth independently of his media empire. It would not be until 1945 that Carter would take a large portion of his oil income to form the Amon Carter Foundation, but the most important piece of the foundation was laid for a promising future in philanthropy.[27]

Of course, becoming an oil baron in his own right allowed Carter to add a new aspect to the Texas mystique he had carefully developed. As someone who bought into a concept of Texas exceptionalism, the Fort Worth publisher understood that being an independent oilman gave him an aura that just did not exist for those associated with larger oil companies such as Sinclair or Humble. The wildcatter image, one in which "oilmen could be heroic because they risked everything—a variation on the American pioneer or entrepreneurial spirit," fit flawlessly into Carter's vision of the West. Of course, this western mythos that so seamlessly incorporated a technologically advanced future based in part on oil consumption was also one in which the past, or at least one version of it, was never forgotten. And Carter, as much as possible, attempted to meld the western past, present, and future in his singular persona.[28]

Wanting to surround himself as much as possible with reminders of the heroic West of his imagination, Carter took advantage of his newfound wealth to begin pursuing a new hobby: collecting the art of famous western artists Charles Russell (1864–1926) and Frederic Remington (1861–1909). Russell and Remington each influenced Americans' image of the West through bronze and canvas, just as Buffalo Bill's arena spectacles and Will Rogers's and Tom Mix's silver screen adventures did. Carter was somewhat late in learning to appreciate these two artists, which was not really surprising, as he showed little interest in art before discovering their works, and even after, his taste remained limited to western art, especially art that conjured his concepts of the West as a region of heroic, rugged individualists battling nature and Indians. That said, according to his daughter Ruth (who later went on to oversee the Amon Carter Museum and sit on the board of the National Gallery of Art), he did have a keen sense of what made a quality piece of art. "Dad didn't have formal art training," she observed in a 1990 interview, but he "had a natural eye, an instinctive reaction, to something he liked. The quality of the Remington art he bought is an example. Most of it was from when Remington shifted from being a good technical illustrator to when he became a good artist." Though Carter's initial purchases were modest, the Wasson Field strike allowed him to begin a buying spree that continued for much of the rest of his life. By the time he died in 1955, he owned at least one hundred bronzes and over two hundred paintings from the two artists. As the art consultant Harold McCracken said in a visit to Fort Worth in 1953, "The finest collection[s] of Remingtons and Russells are owned right here by Amon Carter."[29]

Even though Carter had consciously developed a western orientation during the 1910s, and had spent much of the turn of the century traveling the region, it appears he had no knowledge of Remington and Russell until Will Rogers introduced him to their work sometime around 1929 or 1930. Rogers was something of an art collector himself, and was partial to Russell's work, since it reminded him of his own past on the dusty Oklahoma plains. Limited funds meant slow entry into art collecting, but by 1935, he had accumulated eleven Russell watercolors and his first Remington, the 1903 piece *His First Lesson*. Carter's purchase of *His*

First Lesson, a somewhat light-hearted 27 ′ 40-inch oil on canvas showing two cowboys trying to break a young horse, was a remarkable entry into the collecting world for the publisher, as it illustrates his careful attention to quality work. It is unknown how Carter first became aware of this work, though presumably he must have seen a reproduction of it in some magazine or newspaper. The next decade witnessed a flurry of purchases, usually from New York–based dealers such as David Findlay Galleries and Newhouse Galleries. As someone who traveled to New York frequently enough to keep a room at the Ritz-Carlton, Carter found it easy to cultivate a relationship with dealers who would then either show him the art on site or, in some cases, ship pieces to him in Fort Worth for a few weeks so he could determine if they worked for him.

Shady Oak Farm naturally played a leading role in Carter's western persona. Even during the depths of the Depression, he continued to use this farm overlooking Lake Worth as his special hosting center for celebrities, politicians, and leading business figures. When the journalist Alva Johnston wrote a six-page Carter profile for the *Saturday Evening Post*, he devoted one page to the farm's importance to Carter's boosting efforts. Calling it a "one-man Bohemian Grove," Johnston noted how figures as diverse as industrialist Otto Kahn, orchestral leader Paul Whiteman, and, of course, President Roosevelt, were all heartily entertained at the farmhouse that began to reflect its owner's rustic tastes. Charles Lindbergh and New York City celebrity mayor Jimmy Walker, a friend of Carter's since they met in Houston at the 1928 Democratic Convention, fished in the private ponds on its grounds. The homestead itself was, in the words of Fort Worth socialite Catherine Lehane Johnson, "a rambling, frame house encircled by towering oaks and a white picket fence." Near the farmhouse was a barn and a number of corrals, one of which was used to house the clichéd Texas longhorn steer. Some distance from the house and barn was another sign of Carter's cultivation of the western image: a log cabin lived in for some time by Cynthia Ann Parker after her time with the Comanche Indians. After the closing of the Frontier Centennial, he purchased the Silver Dollar Saloon and the front of the General Store building that stood on the fairgrounds and had them transported to the Shady Oak grounds. Carter's house itself, surrounded on three sides by a porch and a screened-in wing, was unpretentious, and its interior was designed less to impress and more to serve as a kind of men's club and a storage facility for his collecting habit. Here was a two-hundred-dollar mounted grizzly bear skin, and over there were six pair of longhorn steer horns for which Carter paid $850. On the flagstone fireplace mantel was a stack of hats left by visitors who exchanged them for their requisite "Shady Oak" hat, given to them by their gracious host. In the dining room were two reminders of Carter's youth: an old wooden dining table from Mrs. Jarrott's boardinghouse and the bell he rang there at dinnertime. None of this, of course, was designed to overwhelm or awe visitors but instead to relax and lull them into letting down their defenses. After all, would one be more likely to cave to Carter's entreaties while seated in an office or while fishing cheerily on a warm summer afternoon?[30]

Perhaps the culmination of Carter's public embracing of the western image's intersection with Hollywood came in September 1940 as the Hollywood and Worth Theatres in Fort Worth hosted the world premiere of the Gary Cooper vehicle *The Westerner*. This film depicted a fictionalized frontiersman's (Cooper's) interactions with the legendary Judge Roy Bean, played by Walter Brennan (who went on to win an Oscar for his performance). Odd as it may seem, premiering a film in a city like Fort Worth happened fairly often, starting in the 1930s. Before the Depression, movie premieres were generally lavish, glitzy affairs that happened at luxurious movie palaces like the newly opened Grauman's Chinese Theatre in Hollywood. However, the realities of the Depression created new opportunities for the film industry, for by "exchanging their early image of carnival splendor for a Depression-era spirit of civic festival, Hollywood movie premieres not only overcame hard times, but set the stage for a new interplay between movie fantasy and American culture." For a nation desperate for escape from the struggles of reality, these premieres offered an opportunity to peer behind the curtain and catch a glimpse of Hollywood in their own hometown. In 1940 alone, 100,000 people lined the streets of Salt Lake City for the premiere of *Brigham Young*, the same number as flocked to South Bend, Indiana, that year for the opening of *Knute Rockne, All American*.[31]

As might be expected, the germ of the idea to hold the premiere for *The Westerner* in Fort Worth sprouted from the mind of Amon Carter. When asked about how this came to be, Samuel Goldwyn replied, "I was at a publisher's luncheon in New York, and Amon Carter was there. I happened to mention I might hold the premiere in Dallas, and Mr. Carter said 'Why . . . ?'" Presumably, Carter worked him over until he relented, and thus, for the first time, Fort Worth got to experience a slice of Hollywood. As the day of the premiere dawned, three chartered planes touched down at Fort Worth's Meacham Field, and Gary Cooper, Walter Brennan, Lillian Bond, and Samuel Goldwyn, among others, disembarked. As was common with these kinds of events, the celebrities then paraded through Fort Worth's central business district in a variety of carriages and old cars or on horseback. Cooper, appropriately, bestrode Will Rogers's famous steed Soapsuds. The parade route took the stars to Will Rogers Memorial Coliseum, where Gary Cooper and Bob Hope then regaled the crowd of 7,500 orphans and old-age home residents with humorous anecdotes and signed autographs. Of course, no event like this was complete without a trip to Carter's Shady Oak Farm, where 150 guests experienced his famous "western hospitality" and ranch beans. Then, at 7:30, it was on to the theaters, where guests were greeted at the Worth by a façade of the Grand Opera House in old Fort Davis complete with a wooden boardwalk.[32]

Throughout the festivities, as one would expect, Carter and Fort Worth played gracious hosts, and Goldwyn complimented both on the welcome he and his stars received. Yet, a report surfaced that days before the event there had been a brief kerfuffle between Carter and Goldwyn. Apparently, Carter was flying back from a trip to Hawaii aboard the Pan Am Clipper and remarked to his seatmate that he was in a hurry to get back to Fort Worth for the premiere. The man responded that he understood, since he had seen *The Westerner* in Melbourne, Australia, three weeks before and thought it a worthy film. Upon landing in California, a fuming Carter "simply tore up Samuel Goldwyn's Hollywood place when he got there." Goldwyn replied that he knew nothing of the Australia release, and, as the *Dallas Morning News* film critic John Rosenfield put it, "he was probably telling the truth. One simply can't watch everything in this dizzy business of motion pictures." Anger aside, Carter was not about to let this detail ruin such an opportunity to host Hollywood royalty; after all, he had successfully snatched the premiere from Dallas.[33]

Somehow, amid collecting art, promoting New Deal spending, and trying to make the Trinity River navigable, Carter found time to indulge his love of sports. Just as he had adopted the Fort Worth Cats in the 1920s as his favorite local baseball team, in the 1930s he became the leading booster for the Texas Christian University Horned Frogs football team. His support for the team went beyond simple fandom when he embarked on a campaign to raise funds for a new stadium and later accompanied Heisman Trophy winner Davey O'Brien to New York City for the Heisman ceremony. His newfound wealth from the Wasson Field oil strike enabled Carter to give even more lavishly to the university in the future. Though instrumental in pushing for the creation of Texas Tech University, his support for that university did not extend to its athletic department, possibly due to the simple fact that Lubbock was much too far from Fort Worth to allow for ready attendance on his part; furthermore, Texas Christian played in the more prominent Southwest Conference, while Texas Tech was an independent in its earliest years. Plus, from Carter's perspective, he never had any desire to cheer against a team from Fort Worth, especially one that was enjoying as much success as the Horned Frogs.

Texas Christian was a small private university that, after some years in Waco, moved to Fort Worth in 1911 after a fire destroyed the main building. The Horned Frogs had been playing football as a member of the Southwest Conference since 1922 and were building a competitive program. Even though the university was still small, with an enrollment of fewer than two thousand students, the old stadium, Clark Field, found itself overcrowded at times, especially as they were beginning to be a powerhouse in the conference. In 1929, after a game in which over twenty-one thousand fans crammed themselves into the rickety wooden structure, "the *Star-Telegram* ran a big picture . . . saying that TCU needs a new stadium." By September 1929, the university formed a committee to "investigate the stadium proposition" and, fueled by the school's first Southwest Conference championship, decided by December that Carter was "the one and only man to head up his stadium drive or campaign or whatever you desire to call it." It was understood that few men in Fort Worth had Carter's reach when it came to fund-raising, and his expressed desire to see the university have a new stadium meshed well with this gift.[34]

While other committees focused on stadium planning and construction, Carter began drawing on his vast network of business contacts to raise the funds necessary to construct the stadium. A corporation, the Texas Christian University Stadium Association, was formed to sell $300,000 in bonds with Carter leading the sales drive. In January 1930, he hosted a dinner for faculty and trustees of the university at the Fort Worth Club and announced that the bonds would begin being sold as soon as they could be printed; he expected that the football team could begin playing its games there in the fall "if public spirited citizens take over the bonds without delay." His largest victory in the bond campaign came when he persuaded rancher and oilman W. T. Waggoner to purchase $25,000 in bonds. Though other prominent, active Fort Worthians peopled the sales committee, Carter led the way with over $110,000 in bond sales. By October, the stadium was completed and opened with great fanfare as the Horned Frogs slaughtered the Arkansas Razorbacks, 40–0. In recognition of his efforts to secure the funding for the stadium, the university named the structure Amon Carter Stadium. The stadium effort proved timely, for the Depression loomed on the horizon; it is hard to believe that Fort Worth citizens would have been as willing to purchase hundreds of thousands of dollars in bonds in 1931 or 1932. Fortunately for the city and the university, the Horned Frogs provided a good diversion during the Depression.[35]

Carter continued to form a close bond with Texas Christian University during the 1930s and helped in small ways wherever he could; for example, he purchased some new instruments for the marching band in 1937 before a showdown with Fordham University at the Polo Grounds in New York. Such support earned him a small reward; in 1937, band director Don Gillis composed "The Amon Carter March," a tune often played at halftime in Carter's honor. The decade witnessed the Horned Frogs thriving in the Southwest Conference, due in part to excellent coaching from Dutch Meyer and the presence of two excellent quarterbacks: Sammy Baugh and Davey O'Brien. Sammy Baugh, who hailed from Sweetwater in West Texas, led the Horned Frogs to the brink of a national championship in 1935 with a victory over Louisiana State University in the Sugar Bowl. "Slingin" Sammy Baugh, as he was known, left in 1937 to play for the Washington Redskins in the National Football League, but the Horned Frogs were in capable hands with Davey O'Brien at quarterback. A diminutive 150 pounds, O'Brien nevertheless was an exceptional athlete, leading Texas Christian to a national championship in 1938 and that same year became the first Southwest Conference player athlete to win the Heisman Trophy. Winning the Heisman Trophy, awarded annually to the best college football player, gave O'Brien an opportunity to travel to New York City for the ceremony. Carter, ever the avid booster, went as part of the O'Brien party, and found an opportunity to once again play the role of the blustering Texan. On the day O'Brien was due to receive the Heisman Trophy at the Downtown Athletic Club, Carter drove him down Wall Street on a stagecoach to the astonishment of the staid New York financial elite. The grateful O'Brien returned the favor and gave him his helmet, which then hung on Carter's office wall until his death.[36]

Somehow, amid the hectic schedule Carter maintained through what for him was a prosperous decade, he found time to engage in a bitter struggle with railroad conglomerate Burlington over the Fort Worth and Denver Railroad. The fight began when in the fall of 1939, the railroad giant announced that it was going to lease out its Fort Worth and Denver City Line to the Colorado and Southern Railroad. This proposed cost-cutting measure by Burlington would eliminate 189 jobs from Fort Worth and Childress, a possibility Carter found unacceptable. With his characteristic fire, he called this planned action "Burlington Blitzkrieg

Against Texas," a clear reference to the Nazi hordes currently sweeping across the Polish plains. When Burlington publicized its proposal, he immediately sprang into action using the two tools he had at his disposal: his newspaper and his correspondence. Carter wired Ralph Budd, then president of Burlington, to tell him the action was "shortsighted and uneconomical." Since the Burlington system had many rail lines under its umbrella, including the struggling Colorado and Southern, he argued that it would not make sense for the company not to put additional lines under its authority. In addition, Carter warned that what the railroad would "lose in good will and public support" would offset the supposed $300,000 in savings accrued by laying off 189 workers. Also overlooked, he suggested, was a federal law mandating that employers pay two-thirds of their wages to fifteen-year employees who had been laid off. This would cut the estimated savings to a mere $100,000, an amount Carter argued was so paltry that it might cause Burlington to waver in its commitment to the cuts and consolidation.[37]

Budd, of course, had a reply ready for Carter. In a letter to Carter, he claimed that the savings could actually end up being up to $350,000 annually and that whatever wages it might have to pay to laid-off workers would not be enough to cause him or the company any concern, as very few employees had been with the railroad for over fifteen years. Plus, some of the employees affected by the closure of the Fort Worth offices would end up being transferred elsewhere. Budd also argued that contrary to Carter's belief, this transfer would actually improve rail service in Fort Worth and the surrounding region by eliminating duplicate roles around the country. After all, most Burlington officials agreed that the wisest move would be to have the Fort Worth and Denver lines operated from Denver because most of the iron ore transported by the line came from Wyoming and the bulk of this important shipment went to Pueblo, Colorado, to an iron company.[38]

Not surprisingly, Carter refused to accept Budd's justifications and fired off a reply. He claimed that Budd's citation of over $300,000 in savings was false and that they had admitted as much in front of the Interstate Commerce Commission (ICC) at a recent hearing in Fort Worth. He was clearly irked by Burlington's new focus on its Colorado and Southern subsidiary, especially since the Fort Worth and Denver had been forced to give up some of its profits to keep it afloat. From Carter's perspective, not only was business better on the Texas half of the line, but Colorado's state income tax also made it more economical to remain in Texas. And, in case Budd felt too confident about the move, Carter warned that he and his supporters would not back down and that since "this concerns a matter of public interest," their exchange of letters would be published in the *Star-Telegram*.[39]

Whatever setback Carter's cause received, it was soon surpassed by the ICC examiner's initial approval of the proposition. The ever-optimistic Carter dismissed this as but a small obstacle to overcome because the agency had not yet given its formal approval to the consolidation. To him, that meant there was still time to work, and fortunately, he had a newspaper that could do his bidding. A February 1940 *Star-Telegram* editorial slammed the examiner's report as being full of omissions and oversights. The report focused on the benefits to Colorado while ignoring the loss of jobs and productivity in Texas. In addition, the editorial stated, it disregarded the fact that the Fort Worth and Denver consistently outperformed the Colorado and Southern. What about the tax difference between the states, the editorial inquired? Even though the Colorado and Southern had four hundred fewer miles, its tax bill was $400,000 more than the Fort Worth and Denver's. The *Star-Telegram* surmised that the ICC would see these numbers and rule that Burlington would only be hurting itself if it went through with the consolidation because, "the ICC is charged with the duty of protecting railroads against their own mistakes of management and policy as well as against unprofitable rates." The editorial concluded with the hope that Budd would recognize that taking the railroad from Texas would be a monumental mistake. If Budd went through with the consolidation, then "the inevitable diversion of traffic to other roads will be something that will have to be set down as offset to the savings of Burlington from firing Texans now employed by the road." Once again, Carter was illustrating his willingness to appeal to federal intervention if it meant benefits for Texas—and Fort Worth.[40]

In May, Carter traveled to Washington, D.C., where he joined Ed Byars of the Fort Worth Freight Bureau and Texas Assistant Attorney General Cecil C. Carmack in testifying in front of the ICC regarding the proposed consolidation. In a long speech peppered with Texas tales and country aphorisms, he spoke of the disaster that would befall Texas, Fort Worth, and Burlington if the deal was approved. He called Burlington's proposition "cold-blooded" and "unthinkable" for supposedly good people to do. He described what he saw as Burlington's betrayal of Fort Worth's trust by not even telling city leaders of the plan until they had filed the application with the ICC. Not only had they betrayed the city that had been so accommodating, but they were going to fire 189 people "without any ceremony" and transfer headquarters to Denver where "they were going to lose their shirt." Carter proceeded to tell of the public relations disaster that Burlington would experience if the ICC approved the proposal. By treating its "good friends" in this manner, the company was wasting whatever goodwill they had, and goodwill was hard to restore after it had been lost. He added, "It is a long ways from corn bread to caviar but it's just a short ways back"; Burlington was clearly about to find out what it was like to go from caviar back to cornbread.[41]

In his presentation in front of the ICC, Carter deliberately stayed away from statistics and figures because, "you can prove most anything by figures and disprove it by another set of figures." His strategy was to appeal to the humanity of the ICC by speaking of it as if it were a wayward lover or an erring friend. Texans, he argued, would see how badly they had been treated by the railroad and proceed to spurn it, for Texans were "deeply resentful of anybody that mistreats them no matter what it is." Carter then reached back into his childhood and told the commission how some of his first memories were of the Fort Worth and Denver Railroad that ran near his home. He had sold chicken and bread sandwiches to its passengers, fraternized with the brakemen and conductors, and ridden on nearly every spot on the line. If Burlington were allowed to go through with the consolidation, it would lose not only his affection but also that of Fort Worth and Childress, and Burlington would discover that it, too, had lost something in the transaction.[42]

The hearing over, Carter then used another source of leverage—his influence within the West Texas Chamber of Commerce (WTCC)—to apply pressure on Burlington. At a meeting in the West Texas town of Big Spring, Carter presented a resolution that opposed the removal of the railroad's headquarters from Fort Worth and the closing of the maintenance shop in Childress. Jay Taylor, one of the WTCC members and a member of the Texas and Southwestern Cattle Raisers Association, pointed to a case twelve years prior in which the Santa Fe Railroad had threatened to move office from Amarillo to Lawrence, Kansas. After the WTCC led a protest against the action, Santa Fe relented, moved the Lawrence headquarters to Amarillo, and built a twelve-story office building there. With confidence, Carter successfully urged the WTCC to draw up a six-point resolution detailing why the members protested Burlington's proposed actions. The resolutions made no new points but simply regurgitated positions already stated by Carter: that the move was unjustified due to the loss of jobs and the removal of what was considered a Texas railroad from the state. Once written, the resolution was then sent to Ralph Budd.[43]

Not surprisingly, the fight see-sawed back and forth between Carter and Burlington until Carter and his fellow Burlington opponents Byars and Carmack won another chance in front of the ICC after a number of appeals. At his final appearance before the commission, Carter switched tactics, preferring this time to base his arguments not on homespun aphorisms but instead on a keen analysis of the proposal's lack of economic feasibility for both the company and Texas. Regardless of how one looked at the situation, he argued, the evidence was stacked against the company. Simply put, taxes would be higher for Burlington, and the majority of its business was in Texas. Burlington consolidation would therefore not be in the interests of either the company, its clients, or Texas. Yet, he could not help but close his argument with a more personal note. "As an evidence of my sincerity," he declared, "I am bringing up a boy now 21 years old to carry on for me with the *Fort Worth Star-Telegram*. In my final papers to the young man I am leaving everything discretionary with one exception, namely, the Burlington Blitzkrieg against Texas. On this I have asked that he never relent in keeping the good folks of Texas continually informed through our newspapers and radio stations of just how mean the Burlington has treated us country folks."[44]

At a point when it best suited his cause, Fort Worth was no longer a great metropolis guarding the gateway to West Texas but had miraculously transformed into a simple country town. Though initially deciding that Burlington could close its Fort Worth and Childress locations and lease the Fort Worth and Denver to the Colorado and Southern, in June the ICC reversed its initial ruling in a move that must surely have shocked Ralph Budd and his cohorts at Burlington. The *Star-Telegram* featured an editorial celebrating the decision that certainly had Carter's fingerprints all over. Headlined "Burlington Blitzkrieg Collapses" (ironically positioned next to an editorial decrying Hitler's invasion of the Soviet Union launched two days before), the editorial claimed that Fort Worth "fought so hard because we felt we were defending our own."[45]

Carter's successful fight against Burlington did more than save nearly two hundred jobs. Arguably more than any other incident, his fight with Burlington reveals much about Carter's stubborn and sometimes irascible nature, and his doggedness when defending what he believed was his city to protect. Of course, these characteristics alone were insufficient to ensure success as a booster; this required a platform from which to speak. Budd and Burlington might well have numbers in their favor, but they could never win in the court of public opinion. Carter's language throughout this episode illuminates how he saw himself in relation to Fort Worth. By this point in his life, he clearly saw himself as Fort Worth's paternal protector, a guardian who could be counted on to intervene when an outside force threatened what he believed was its well-being.

THE HOME FRONT

In the decade leading up to the outbreak of the Second World War, Carter's personal life descended into turmoil once again as he found his marriage with Nenetta deteriorating to the point of divorce. Amid the chaos, he still found time to be a devoted father to Amon Jr. and Ruth, finding in the two of them not only heirs to his media empire but also a warmth that seemed to be missing from his relationship with his wife. As his children grew older, they became closer to their father; even while away at their respective boarding schools, there was a constant flow of correspondence between them. Amon and Nenetta, on the other hand, found the last years of their marriage to be a struggle as he became more deeply involved in his various causes and interests. Like his relationship with first wife, Zetta, Carter's marriage to Nenetta became more strained as his work kept him away from home on many occasions. With Zetta, the tension derived from his commitment to building the *Star-Telegram* into the dominant newspaper in Texas. By the 1930s, the newspaper was comfortably in the lead with regard to Texas circulation, but now there was more to catch Carter's eye. The whirlwind of politics, ever present since the 1928 Democratic Convention, took more of his attention because of the promise of the New Deal, as did his continued work in aviation, oil, and general Fort Worth boosting. From Nenetta's perspective, as much as she enjoyed the life of a socialite, an absent husband was no husband at all. Even when he was gone, he could still provide an insufferable presence; while on a trip to Washington at the start of the New Deal, he called numerous times to a friend's home where Nenetta was known to be attending a party. Evidently his constant telephoning was an annoyance and embarrassment to Nenetta, especially as she had left before the party was over and had heard the next day of how her husband was trying to track her down. Exasperated, she wired him at the Willard Hotel where he was staying. "I do not appreciate one bit all the telephone calls you put in for me last night," she began, explaining that the reason she had left the party was because it was a children's party. She added acerbically, "If you have any desire to embarrass me further by checking up on me I will be glad to furnish you with my whereabouts every hour in the day."[46]

By the late 1930s, Amon and Nenetta had drifted further apart, with young Amon and Ruth caught between them. A letter from Nenetta to Amon Jr. on his twenty-first birthday in 1940 contains thinly veiled references to his father's absences and preoccupation with his work:

> When the time comes for you to make your choice in the woman you want to share your life, your love and your name, make up your mind to put her next to your God. Let her play the most important role in your life and never allow your business, community, and civic, as well as other interests, to push her out of that special niche she deserves. Then you will have accomplished what so few men realize only after it is too late.

Increasingly frustrated, in October 1940, Nenetta moved out of the home she shared with Amon in Rivercrest Country Club and to New York City where she stayed at the Savoy Plaza. This temporary move put her at odds with her children, especially Ruth, who was particularly close to her father. Nevertheless, Nenetta believed that her relationship with Amon had moved beyond repair and filed for divorce, stating that Carter's "absence from home and failure to show proper affection toward her has created a form of cruelty" that "impaired [the] petitioner's health." Demonstrating the relative level of celebrity he had attained, the news spread rapidly across the nation. Most newspapers carried the Associated Press wire release with little to no editorializing, but *Time* magazine, with its history of Carter criticism, differed from most news outlets, reporting the divorce in its "Milestones" section and describing Carter as the "peripatetic . . . Dictator of Cowtown" who was both "fiercely hospitable" and "belligerently civic-minded." Nevertheless, the divorce had little impact on Carter's professional life, and by all accounts he considerably enjoyed his new bachelor status.[47]

Financially, Carter did not suffer a substantial blow to his newfound wealth or to his holdings in Carter Publications. The couple agreed in the divorce settlement that even though Nenetta was due 40 percent of the Carter estate, her portion would be controlled by him. Because of the complexities of the financial situation, it was contracted that Nenetta would receive $24,000 annually from Carter. Nenetta's major motivation in not pursuing more of Carter's empire was her desire for Amon Jr. to receive his holdings intact. As she had no desire for her son to lose a portion of his inheritance through a disastrous court fight, it seemed wiser to follow a more moderate course. A long-lasting effect of this property settlement was that it kept the couple financially intertwined throughout the rest of Amon's life. And while bitterness was understandably present in the years immediately following the divorce, in the long run, the once happy couple was able to overcome their previous animosity to collaborate for the cause of philanthropy.[48]

One would expect that a divorce based on grounds of "mental cruelty" would result in acrimony between the two, and for quite some time this seemed to be the case, especially regarding Nenetta's relationship with the children. Though discussions between the couple were limited at the time, the war between them could very easily be waged by proxies: Amon Jr. and Ruth. After the divorce, Nenetta traveled to sunny Miami Beach, where she stayed for some time at the Versailles Hotel. In between sunbathing on the hotel roof and enjoying the blooming flowers, she wrote Katrine Deakins, Amon's longtime secretary, of how she feared Ruth's loyalty lay more toward her father than her mother. "I am afraid I have just about lost my baby girl thru her dad's influences," she complained, "but as soon as he begins to treat her as he once did me, she will have her eyes opened." Nenetta felt that Ruth was enthralled by her father and did not care whether or not her mother was happy. "She is so much like him and falls for his generosity and attention that she has never seriously considered anyone's happiness but her own and has never once given me a thought as regards my happiness." As the months went by, some of these feelings bled over into her letters to both her children as she began to believe that they were both aligned against her. America's looming entry into the war and young Amon's enlistment would soon distract her from these issues, yet for a time she struggled to pick up the pieces of her life.[49]

The correspondence between Amon and his children at this time shows a close bond between a father and his children that extends beyond the niceties. Their letters to one another are full of conversation about family, friends, politics, sports, and school, and it is in these letters that one can dig deeper into the inner workings of the Carter family. The tone differs depending on the recipient; his letters to Ruth are intimate and caring, with more personal commentary and humor, while his correspondence with Amon Jr. is businesslike and professional, yet still fatherly. Like Amon's oldest daughter, Bertice, Ruth was sent to boarding school for her secondary education; she attended the prestigious all-female Madeira School in the Washington, D.C., suburb of McLean, Virginia. What letters exist between father and daughter while she was away at school show Ruth to be an intelligent, charming young lady who followed politics with the same devotion as her father. Politics did not dominate their correspondence, but her remarks and inquiries about people and issues like Jesse Jones, the Neutrality Act of 1939, and a humorous poem about the New Deal are liberally sprinkled among comments and questions about the family, school, and her social life. Despite being the daughter of a wealthy publisher, she refused to take advantage of her status by relying on her father's generosity. For example, her interests in chemistry led her to spend one summer interning for St. Joseph Hospital in Fort Worth, working in a lab with the hopes of securing a paying job in this field in the future. Obviously, there was never a chance that Carter would let his daughter completely fend for herself, and she was simultaneously raised to fulfill the demands placed on females of high society; yet he did want to ensure that she would have a job based on her own merit, not through the fortune of her last name.[50]

Carter groomed young Amon as the heir to Carter Publications but refused to treat him differently because of his status as the publisher's son. When Amon Jr. was only eleven, he started working for the *Star-Telegram* as a news boy, delivering and selling newspapers in Fort Worth neighborhoods during the summers, on vacation days, and on school days after school was out. Like the other newsboys for the *Star-Telegram*, he had scholastic requirements placed on him by the newspaper. A profile of Amon Jr. in the *Urbana Evening Courier* reported that "The paper and the school work together. If the boy is not punctual at school and it is found that selling or a route harms his school work, he is asked to temporarily drop his school work." When Amon Jr. stated that he was ready for employment, Carter "turned him over to the circulation manager [Harold Hough], stating to him that under no circumstances was he to show Amon Jr. favoritism in any way." Clearly, he believed that his own experiences as a young man had shaped his life in a positive way, and as much as possible, his son must learn how to make his own way in the world. *Star-Telegram* managers treated him as they would any other employee but generally commended him for his hard work and ability to sell newspapers. A responsible young man, Amon Jr. was trusted enough by Hough to represent the newspaper to news dealers in Colorado Springs responsible for delivering copies of the *Star-Telegram* while he was on vacation with his family in 1934 at the exquisite Broadmoor Hotel.[51]

The next year, Carter sent his son to the prestigious Culver Military Academy in Indiana in preparation to attend the University of Texas. Culver Military Academy attracted the sons of notable businessmen and politicians across the United States and combined a rigorous academic tradition with a regimented military lifestyle. Students, or cadets as they were called, were enlisted in the infantry, cavalry, or artillery for the duration of their time at the school, though military service was not required upon graduation. Carter stayed informed of his son's progress at school and did not hesitate to encourage his instructors to bear down harder. "I am ambitious to see Amon Jr. make good and the best way for him to make good is for you to keep after him and see that he toes the line in every respect." He encouraged his son to develop his business sense while at school and was delighted to hear that in his first year, Amon Jr. made extra money shining buttons for other cadets' Easter dress uniforms. Carter must have beamed with pride as he wrote his son, "This shows the right spirit and is an evidence that you are not afraid of work and that you are not stuck up or 'high-hat.' Nothing could please me more than for you to be Democratic, friendly, thoughtful, willing to work, and make your own way through individuality and conduct." If there was a philosophy Carter ascribed to throughout his life, this was it, and he wanted his son to imbibe deeply of the same values.[52]

When Amon Jr. turned eighteen in 1937, Carter wrote him a letter that, in a sense, welcomed him to manhood. He laid out his hopes for the future, telling his son, "I hope to see you step in and take Dad's place, provided you show sufficient aptitude, interest, and qualification to do the job." In case Amon Jr. had any thought of ignoring the insight and wisdom of some of Carter's longtime colleagues who helped build the *Star-Telegram,* Carter wrote, "I hope you will, when the time comes, give due consideration and thought to their views, the same as I have during all my years of association with them." Clearly Carter had dreams of ensuring the newspaper would be passed down into what he hoped would be the capable hands of his son. From his perspective, if his son sowed discord and ruin among Carter's longtime associates upon taking over the *Star-Telegram,* this would destroy everything he had worked so hard to build. In no way was the man who had once sold chicken and bread to train passengers going to see his hard work be all for naught. After graduating from Culver, Amon Jr. enrolled in the University of Texas with the idea that after completing his degree there, he would then begin to work full-time at the *Star-Telegram* as the heir to the Carter fortune. While this did ultimately happen, the road to his inheritance was longer than was expected, as war loomed on the horizon.[53]

CHAPTER 7

TRIUMPHS AND TRIALS IN PEACE AND WAR

ON THE EVE of the United States' entry into the Second World War, Carter could certainly lay claim to possessing a vast national network of business and political contacts that he could exploit whenever he deemed necessary. As the nation prepared for and then entered the war, he found ample opportunity to exercise his influence with the Roosevelt administration and corporate America. Carter's experience in forging relationships with politicians and bureaucrats for New Deal and canalization purposes continued to reap benefits for him, his city, and even his state as evidenced by his successful efforts in helping lead the campaign to create Big Bend National Park. A vocal supporter of rearmament as Germany and Japan waged war on their neighbors, he comprehended how his boosting activities intertwined with the needs of national defense. Thus was born his support for the building of a Consolidated Aircraft plant in west Fort Worth in 1941. But just as the war created new opportunities, older ideas such as the canalization of the Trinity River had to be temporarily shelved, and Carter-led efforts such as the construction of a major airport for Fort Worth were grounded for the time being. Meanwhile, on the home front, Carter dealt with the new realities of bachelorhood, and rumors of new loves abounded in newspapers and in family correspondence. Sadly, the war became very personal for the Carter family, as his son, Amon Jr., was captured by the Germans in North Africa in 1943 and held in a prisoner-of-war camp until near the end of the war. At the end of the war, Carter trekked to Europe per the request of General Dwight D. Eisenhower, documenting the horrors of Germany's concentration camps while also seeking reunification with his son.

NATIONAL PARK STATUS FOR BIG BEND

Though often critical of the reform-oriented aspects of the New Deal, Carter knew better than to completely eliminate all support for Roosevelt. His leadership in the creation of a national park at Big Bend in West Texas demonstrated his ability to simultaneously censure and cajole the Roosevelt administration. Even while arguing that Roosevelt's prolabor stance was detrimental to the health of the American economy and that Harold Ickes was intervening in Texas politics, Carter possessed the fortitude to press for national park status for Big Bend. Nearly a decade passed between the beginning of his campaign and Roosevelt's final approval that granted Big Bend national park status on June 6, 1944, demonstrating that Carter possessed a great amount of patience in pursuing his goal. Usually, the causes Carter supported and advocated provided some direct benefit for Fort Worth, but Big Bend was an exception to this rule. Still, he considered this a project that was connected to Fort Worth because, having boosted Fort Worth for years as the gateway to West Texas, he believed in the importance of nurturing the relationship between his city and the region by promoting the creation of Big Bend National Park.

Few of Carter's initiatives better reflect his ability to bring federal, state, and local personalities together than his push to create Big Bend National Park. This project required the partnership of public and private entities, something Carter had grown adept at fostering through projects such as the canalization of the Trinity River or his New Deal successes. Carter was able to bring a variety of groups together to raise the funds necessary for the federal government to accept Big Bend: Texas women's clubs, the Boy Scouts, civic boosters across the state—all while working to assure the state and federal governments that the money would be delivered. Though he was not solely responsible for the creation of Big Bend, his efforts were integral to the success of the project.

While Carter was instrumental in the creation of Big Bend National Park, the idea was not his own. The concept of a park of some kind for West Texas dated back as far as 1921 when "a group of civic officials petitioned the Texas state legislature to identify lands within the Davis Mountains for a state park." This venture and similar attempts failed throughout the 1920s from lack of organization and legislative support. One might assume the onset of the Great Depression would stifle plans for a West Texas state park, but the creation of the Civilian Conservation Corps in 1933 and the work of two state representatives from West Texas, Robert Wagstaff and Everett Townsend, provided the impetus for the creation of a state park in the region. West Texans and nature lovers rejoiced later that year when Governor Miriam Ferguson signed into law the legislation creating Big Bend State Park on 225,000 acres in and around the Chisos Mountains and the canyons of the Rio Grande.[1]

The region's boosters had little intention of keeping Big Bend relegated to state park status, especially Townsend. Throughout 1933, the former Texas Ranger and native of the region "sent a barrage of letters and photographs to the Park Service ... that captured the vastness and contrasting beauty of the area's desert, canyon, river, and mountain landscapes." Through Townsend's efforts, the National Park Service grew very favorable to the idea of Big Bend National Park, culminating with Interior Secretary Harold Ickes's final approval of the idea in February 1935. With local support for the project high, Texas's congressional delegation in Washington pushed through a bill giving federal approval for the creation of Big Bend National Park, a bill signed in June 1935 by President Roosevelt. Unfortunately for park supporters, there was still much work left to be done.[2]

The Big Bend Act of 1935 might have enabled the creation of Big Bend National Park, but it was contingent on one piece of action from Texas: the state "had to present to the federal government the title of all of the acres included in the park boundaries." Such a stipulation would not have been a major source of trouble if it was not for the fact that the Texas Public School Fund was guaranteed the mineral rights on these lands. In addition, since the state legislature had convened before Roosevelt had signed the bill, it would not be until 1937 that it could address its responsibilities. When the legislature reconvened in January 1937, the issue was immediately addressed but with serious barriers. Governor James Allred had endorsed the plan for Big Bend but was simultaneously trying to deal effectively with the state's budgetary problems. Citing the possible damage such spending might cause to the general fund, in June 1937, he vetoed a bill appropriating $750,000 to purchase land for the park. With the veto coming just before the legislature adjourned, it seemed that the dream of having a national park in Texas was further away than ever before.[3]

Allred's veto prompted swift action from private citizens of West Texas, including Carter. Once again using the *Star-Telegram* as an instrument of his will, he began encouraging individuals to do their part to ensure the creation of Texas's first national park. On June 11, 1937, the editorial page of the *Star-Telegram* called for Texans to emulate the people of Virginia, where nearly a million dollars had been raised to purchase Shenandoah National Park. If one million Texans gave one dollar each, the editorial surmised, then Texas would be able to purchase the land for the national park. Herbert Maier, a regional officer for the National Park Service, contacted James Record, the *Star-Telegram*'s managing editor, about sponsoring the fund drive, because the paper was "one of Texas' leading dailies," and Carter was "perhaps in the best position in the state to get this thing successfully going." The *Star-Telegram* agreed to sponsor the fund-raiser and cooperated with other Texas newspapers as well as various chambers of commerce across West Texas. Carter's paper led the way with numerous positive stories, donor lists, and even a picture of Governor Allred donating his one-dollar contribution. Though most Texans involved in the campaign did not lack for enthusiasm, and boosters traveled the state pleading their cause, money sprinkled rather than poured into the coffers; after four months, only $50,000 had been raised.[4]

Fortunately for Big Bend supporters, legislative support was forthcoming during the fall of 1937. Allred had always supported the idea of Big Bend National Park, given the right piece of legislation; he therefore took advantage of the special session of the state legislature that fall and signed a bill that "officially recognized the national park, approved the boundaries proposed by the secretary of the interior, and authorized the Texas State Park Board to receive donations of land and money." Even though state money was nowhere to be found in the legislation, "the legal and governmental machinery to establish Big Bend National Park was in place."[5]

Until this point, Carter's involvement with the Big Bend project had been minimal, content as he was to use positive coverage of the park to stir up public support for fund-raising. But, with the obvious failure of the first round of fund-raising, it was clear that park boosters needed a new approach. Governor Allred appointed an Executive Committee of fifteen (later expanded to twenty-six) prominent Texans to head this new drive: names included men like Jesse Jones of Houston, John Carpenter of Dallas, and Carter. Because of the *Star-Telegram*'s coverage of this West Texas project as well as Carter's "ability to achieve worthwhile objectives," his fellow committee members chose him to chair the committee. As a man who had become well known for his trademark yell of "Hooray for Fort Worth and West Texas!" this was an opportunity Carter had to exploit. Though civic-minded and philanthropic, he did believe that the creation of Big Bend National Park was not without its financial benefits. He called the project "one of the most constructive and beneficial things that could happen to Texas," since it would "bring millions of dollars of money into the State to be spent by the tourists each year," and he welcomed the "opportunity of attracting a great number of people through Fort Worth for the purpose of vacationing . . . in the Big Bend country of southwest Texas."[6]

At Governor Allred's request, the Executive Committee first met in Austin in May 1938 with the goals of "publiciz[ing] the national park and rais[ing] funds for land acquisition." With objectives like these, it was obvious why a man like Carter was chosen to be the head of the committee. The expanded committee included "heads of women's clubs, parent-teachers clubs, presidents of colleges and public school representatives, as well as leading business men and public spirited citizens." Understanding that one of the primary reasons for the failure of the first fund-raising attempt had been a lack of organization, the committee brought in Adrian Wychgel of Adrian Wychgel and Associates; this firm had raised $2 million for Shenandoah and Mammoth Cave National Parks in Virginia and Kentucky. The committee decided that to cover organizational expenses such as campaigning, supplies, and a headquarters, they would need $25,000. Carter offered $5,000 to cover Fort Worth's contribution, while the difference was to be made up by $5,000 each from Dallas, Houston, San Antonio, and West Texas. The state was then to be divided into districts, with local directors leading the campaigns in their respective districts. At the beginning, the committee estimated that $1.2 million needed to be raised, and all funds raised would be directed under the auspices of the Big Bend Park Association, the name of the organization the committee led. Once the requisite cash was raised, it would be "turned over to the State Park Board, which will negotiate the land deals."[7]

Carter spent much of the rest of the year pressing committee members to raise their money and deliver on their pledges while also encouraging them to wait for a statewide campaign policy to be set before attempting any major fund-raising so as to avoid returning to the same donors twice. As in the previous campaign, money slowly trickled in. According to Carter, the *Star-Telegram* had $35,000 "sent in voluntarily by readers in answer to [an] editorial appeal for subscriptions" from the unorganized effort begun in 1937, with small amounts still coming in. Obviously, this amount would have little impact on the campaign, but in a time of economic depression, it seemed there was precious little for people to give.[8]

By September, Dallas had only contributed $500 of its $5,000; Carter cajoled fellow committee member and Dallas banker Nathan Adams, "I realize you are tremendously busy and have many calls on your time and finances," but "I hope you will find the time to get a few friends together and raise the remainder of your pledge." Houston had only contributed $1,000 of its share, prompting him to attempt to wring the money from its business leaders by telling banker A. D. Simpson that Big Bend National Park would "be of more benefit to the South Texas cities than to those in North Texas." In November, with little headway being made, a clearly annoyed Carter told W. B. Tuttle of the San Antonio Public Service Company, "If it had not been for you and Del Rio, we would not have made much progress in October toward our $25,000 working fund goal." By the end of the year, only $15,500 had been raised, and grave doubts were arising that the goal could be reached, yet "Carter refused to proceed [with the fund-raising campaign] until the working fund had reached $25,000." Despite the clear lack of progress, he requested of incoming lieutenant governor Coke Stevenson that he quash any move to appropriate funds because "any effort to secure a legislative appropriation will interfere with our plans." Such a move seems odd in the face of clear signs of failure, leading some to suggest that Carter "had lined up a major donor" or "did not want to obligate himself to the new governor," Wilbert Lee "Pappy" O'Daniel. Speculation aside, it appears that he simply believed that the money could be raised by the end of the next legislative session in May 1939. To concede defeat at this point would be too much for the stubborn Carter.[9]

In a sign of Carter's influence on Texas politicians wary of crossing the powerful publisher, Lt. Governor Stevenson complied with Carter's request, and the legislature failed to pass any appropriations for the park. Executive and legislative leadership was forthcoming in other ways, however, thanks to the newly elected governor, "Pappy" O'Daniel. A Fort Worth flour merchant, O'Daniel emerged as a bona fide Texas celebrity in the late 1920s when he began emceeing a radio show featuring Bob Wills and the Light Crust Doughboys. Heard on stations like Carter's own WBAP, WOAI in San Antonio, and KPRC in Houston, O'Daniel's show "probably had more daily listeners than any other show in the history of Texas radio." He agreed to run for governor in 1938, "at the behest of radio fans," and running on a vague platform of the Ten Commandments, the Golden Rule, and an old-age pension, easily defeated his opponents, Texas Railroad Commissioner Ernest Thomson and Attorney General William McCraw. Though by most accounts one of the worst governors in Texas history, O'Daniel did make it a point to support the Big Bend campaign. The result was "the only real victory of his administration."[10]

O'Daniel first visited Big Bend in 1938 and then pledged his support for the project during the 1939 legislative session by urging the legislature to pass Bill 123, cosponsored by Lt. Governor Stevenson and state senator H. L. Winfield. Per Carter's request, the bill did not contain the requisite appropriations to purchase land, but it "granted the Texas State Parks Board the right of public domain and the power to acquire land through purchase, condemnation, and donation." Private land prices in the region were set at a maximum of two dollars per acre. As the Senate debated the bill, O'Daniel delivered a strong message to the legislature, declaring Big Bend to be a "'Gift of God' to Texas and our nation." Conjuring up his gifts as a former radio host, he spoke "lyrically of the beauty and grandeur" of the park and "claimed that 'from many large peaks the gorgeous scenery is as impressive as a vast fairy land.'" Worried that without protection the region's geological and natural wonders might be lost to future generations, O'Daniel warned that "an emergency existed at Big Bend," due to "acts of vandalism," and, "unauthorized collecting of botanical, archeological, and geological specimens." To seal his argument, he mentioned President Roosevelt's support for the bill and quoted from a letter from the president: "I am very much interested in the proposed Big Bend National Park in your State." Roosevelt stated that "'it would be very gratifying to me personally' if Big Bend 'could be dedicated during my Administration.'" For once, the legislature responded positively to O'Daniel, and the bill sailed through and onto his desk.[11]

Carter understood that a major task was at hand. Having ensured that no appropriations would be made, he (and, by extension, the Big Bend Park Association) had to deliver the privately raised funds. "It should be impressed on the public," he cautioned, "that this is only the first step toward getting the national park for Texas." Because "this bill was only enabling legislation," Carter stated, "we must raise $1,500,000 to pay for the land . . . Now it is up to Texans to complete the project." The response was a deafening silence, a fact encouraged by the lack of an immediate publicity blitz from the Carter camp. The only major Big Bend–related news during the summer of 1939 was an August announcement by Carter that the federal government had approved the exemption for income tax purposes of donations to the Big Bend Park Association. Though such a move was calculated to bring in donations, little was forthcoming. The onset of war in September 1939 actually seemed to briefly brighten the park's prospects, at least in the eyes of park boosters. The *Star-Telegram* published a story on September 12, claiming that since Europe was no longer a viable option for tourists, more Americans would have to travel at home. "Texas should not fail to seize the opportunity to become a greater tourist State and to profit from the increased travel that is to be diverted from Europe to this country," the article argued; therefore, it stood to reason that the Texas public should respond by donating funds to begin purchasing land.[12]

While the "wishful thinking" in Carter's paper was "accurate in the longterm," the immediate future did not hold much promise because of the war, the depressed economy, and Carter's perceived lack of attention to the project for much of the rest of the year. National Park official Maier contacted Carter in October, believing the campaign to raise the $1.5 million should begin very soon. Explaining that "due to the War, the oil and cotton industries are in very sound positions," so "the present . . . should be an opportune time for Mr. Carter to launch his appeal." Behind the scenes, many park supporters from the Park Service and in West Texas wondered if Carter had forgotten to launch the initiative. Even O'Daniel expressed skepticism about Carter's lack of attention to the Big Bend initiative and his inability to raise the promised funds. The governor believed that ultimately "it would be essential for the Texas legislature to appropriate all, or the major portion, of the funds necessary."[13]

Doubting the necessity of asking the legislature for the funds, Carter took action in November 1939 by asking Jesse Jones if he could assist the campaign in Houston by working to "prevail on someone in Houston who would be sufficiently influential to give some strength to the campaign." More than a year had elapsed since Carter had started his campaign to raise $25,000 for the initial campaign expenses, and he refused to start a statewide campaign without the funding. He noted to Jones that even Humble Oil had only contributed $1,000, a sign of the moribund economy and the unsettled world situation. The situation was no better in North Texas, where it took until December 1939 for Dallas businessmen to raise the $5,000 pledged from their area. Despite this apparent lack of momentum, Carter felt confident enough to announce in December 1939 that there were plans to start the fund-raising campaign in January 1940. Unfortunately, his (and the committee's) "desires to get all the money in hand" before starting the campaign undermined the committee's ability to begin fundraising in earnest. No imminent campaign was in sight when 1940 dawned. As national park historian Michael Welsh states, the year "had begun hopefully enough, when Governor W. Lee O'Daniel accepted the entreaties of President Franklin D. Roosevelt and championed the park with Lone Star lawmakers," but ended in disappointment for park boosters, because "the anxieties caused by war surrounded Big Bend."[14]

The year 1940 proved to be no better for park supporters, and the official fund-raising campaign appeared to be stalled. Boosters around the state, including Carter, made efforts to raise funds outside the auspices of the Big Bend Park Association. Clearly aware of the fund-raising capabilities of women's clubs, he occasionally turned to their leaders for support. In February 1940, Carter presided over a Fort Worth Garden Club rally held to raise money for and awareness of Big Bend. Color movies of the region were shown, a special dance, the "Big Bend," was inaugurated, and attendees dined on "Horsetail Cataract shrimp cocktail, Pack Saddle chicken, Paint Gap Hills green beans, Green Gulch Canyon salad," and other Big Bend–themed dishes. Though over two hundred women attended the meeting, only fifty dollars was raised for Big Bend. In November 1940, Carter suggested to Mrs. Louis Wardlaw, head of the Texas Federation of Women's Clubs, that she should "explain that the movement has been retarded by existing world conditions." In a sign of his continuing reliance on the Federation, he closed by saying, "We are confident we can rely upon the club women of Texas to cooperate with this movement when our campaign gets under way."[15]

Positive publicity and lip service from Texas's business community failed to overcome the financial hurdles erected by a weak economy. Though never said explicitly, it seems that the distance between Texas's major cities and the Big Bend region must also have played a role in the lack of proffered private funds. In this boosterish yet economically depressed era, few civic-minded citizens were willing to expend their wealth for a national park in the West Texas wilderness far removed from their urban centers. Fortunately, political efforts on behalf of Big Bend had taken a different turn, thanks in part to O'Daniel's reelection, and park supporters were forced to realize that private efforts to purchase land in Big Bend were going to fall short.[16]

O'Daniel marched easily to victory in 1940, soundly defeating his opponents, Ernest Thompson and a hopeful but weak Ma Ferguson. Carter was much more concerned with national politics and with promoting a possible Garner candidacy, so he did little to involve himself in the election. O'Daniel was a huge supporter of the park, so his win boosted the chances of making Big Bend National Park a reality. By 1941, many Texas politicians recognized that "the failure of the private popular subscription campaign left only one alternative: a state appropriation." After all, Carter's Big Bend Park Association had only raised just over $9,500 by the end of 1940. When the legislature was called in January, O'Daniel asked it to "honor its commitment to the federal government to acquire the Big Bend acres." In response, the legislature began moving through a bill to spend $1.5 million of the state's general fund to begin purchasing land. Despite O'Daniel's previous negativity toward Carter, the governor did little to impede the passage of the bill and continued to publicize the virtues of Big Bend. In February, he gave an interview on WBAP focusing on the economic benefits of Big Bend, claiming that "when properly developed with adequate facilities, [Big Bend] will do for Texas" what Shenandoah, Great Smoky Mountains, and Yellowstone National Parks were doing for their states. That same month, he claimed that "despite the effect of the international situation on economic conditions . . . the Big Bend national park may pass from the project stage to reality in less time" than other national parks.[17]

With little opposition, the legislature passed a bill appropriating $1.5 million to purchase land in Big Bend, and in July 1941, O'Daniel signed it into law. The bill "had given the state parks board only twelve months to complete all transactions," meaning that the land purchases had to go smoothly and quickly. Despite an attempt by some opponents to prevent the state comptroller from spending the appropriation, the purchases were well under way by 1942. Rather unexpectedly, the process moved fairly rapidly, but it was more expensive than projected. Running low on funds to pay for the administrative costs of the program, the state turned to Carter to see if he could release funds from what little had been raised through the park association's efforts. With little hesitation, Carter assented, and the state was able to keep the land acquisition functioning past the deadline. Thus, by November 1942, very little acreage remained unpurchased. Newton Drury, director of the National Park Service, agreed to recommend to Harold Ickes that "the federal government accept title to the acquired acres," and in June 1943, "Ickes concurred." The first national park in Texas was about to become a reality.[18]

By this time, O'Daniel had left the governorship for the U.S. Senate, having appointed himself to the deceased Morris Sheppard's seat in 1941. This brought Lieutenant Governor Coke Stevenson, a longtime supporter of the park, into the governor's seat. By the end of 1943, Stevenson had given the land deeds to the Park Service and presented Carter with the cession deed as well, with the instructions that he was to deliver it to Ickes. Carter, recognizing the value of formal ceremonies, insisted on waiting until Roosevelt was available to preside over the transfer. Because World War II captured most of Roosevelt's attention, it was some months before Carter was granted the White House ceremony he desired. Finally, on June 6, 1944, as Allied troops stormed the beaches of Normandy, a beaming Carter formally presented the title to 700,000 acres of land to Ickes and Roosevelt. In less than a decade, Carter had helped bring about the creation of Big Bend National Park.[19]

National park status for Big Bend did not occur through the massive outpouring of private monies as Carter had expected, but instead of continuing down what was clearly a failed path, he changed course. Though supporters of the National Park system could say that Carter should have pushed for public funds sooner, it appears from his perspective that there was little to be gained in such an endeavor. As president of the Big Bend Park Association and the publisher of the most widely read newspaper in Texas, the sight of one million Texans each subscribing one dollar to purchase land would have been seen as another major victory for Carter and cemented his legacy as philanthropist extraordinaire. Instead, the twin problems of the economy and the war sabotaged his efforts, forcing him to change his tone and accept a state appropriation. Carter did not seem to view this as a defeat, though it is not much of a stretch to believe that Stevenson's request for him to present the deed was mainly acknowledgment of his hard work to publicize Big Bend for much of the 1930s. What stands out in Carter's involvement in the Big Bend project is his ability to balance it with his other pursuits, as well as the recognition by others that he was an integral piece for the success of the project. One must keep in mind that during the late 1930s and early 1940s, he was simultaneously engaged in canalizing the Trinity, drilling for oil, landing Consolidated, waging a rhetorical war on both Ickes and Burlington Railroad, coping with the collapse of his marriage to Nenetta, and running the *Star-Telegram,* among other sundry ventures.

AVIATION AND NAVIGATION ON THE EVE OF WAR

As much as Big Bend, with its grand vistas and colorful panoramas, seemed to symbolize for Carter all that was great and good about the West, he could never forget the new frontier of his time: the skies. While Carter enjoyed a successful tenure at American Airlines and flew often (many times internationally), he was not content to let his aviation achievements stagnate. Instead, during the 1940s, he began helping Fort Worth in its efforts to secure a centralized location for a proposed airport that would serve both Dallas and Fort Worth. While Dallas and Fort Worth were served respectively by Love Field and Meacham Field, by the end of the 1930s it was clear that neither airport was able to fully serve their host cities. The issue for both Love and Meacham was the lack of longer runways to accommodate the new DC-4 airliners, and expansion would be an expensive undertaking. In addition, many airlines were unhappy about having to make two separate stops only thirty-five miles apart. The Civil Aeronautics Authority (CAA) intervened, suggesting that the two cities establish a single airport that could serve them both. The question was, where would this airport be? Dallas, with its much larger population and larger business community, believed it had a better claim to being the location for the proposed field, but of course Fort Worth leadership opposed the idea. With some strong encouragement from CAA assistant administrator Lucius Clay, the two cities agreed in an October 1941 meeting at the Fort Worth Club to have the airport built near Euless, a Tarrant County community about midway between Dallas and Fort Worth. Carter, of course, was present. The CAA agreed to construct the landing field if American and Braniff purchased the land, deeded it to the cities, and constructed the terminals. And while the country's entry into the war threatened to stall plans to move forward with construction, what ultimately created a logjam was what might appear to outsiders to be a minor disagreement.[20]

When the airport issue was broached in 1942, a controversy over the terminal location and orientation quickly erupted, creating instant acrimony between the two cities. Carter, who proved through the Centennial celebration and the Trinity canal issues that he could be simultaneously friends and rivals with Fort Worth's neighbor, led the charge on behalf of Fort Worth. The CAA decided that the terminal would be on the west side of the airport, facing west toward Fort Worth even though its original plans showed its entrance to the north with a highway connecting directly with downtown Fort Worth. Dallasites instantly raised a hue and cry, charging that Fort Worthians must have been engaged in secret negotiations with CAA regional administrator L. C. Elliott to ensure such a favorable decision; Dallas mayor Woodall Rodgers even raised the specter of Carter's involvement. After all, who would put it past him? Elliott, of course, vehemently denied such a charge, even going so far as to deny that there had ever been plans for the terminal to face north. Carter responded ferociously in an epic telegram to Rodgers, dutifully printed in the *Star-Telegram,* saying that the mayor had made "some pretty fantastic statements not in keeping with the facts. I am sorry you have worked yourself in a frenzy just because Fort Worth has the temerity to merely ask for a square deal or an even break regarding the location of the new airport." As he had in the Burlington case, he played up Fort Worth's rural identity with an added side of snark: "I realize it may be presumptuous of us country folks to raise our hand so to speak in any way against the ambitions of your fair city." Neither Rodgers nor the city of Dallas was amused, taking the position that if the CAA stood by its decision to leave the terminal on the west side of the airport, Dallas would not participate.[21]

Fort Worth's (and Carter's) insistence on the westward terminal location and Dallas's refusal to agree to such a demand frustrated CAA officials, and no decisions were made until March 1943. That month, Commerce Secretary Jesse Jones agreed to have a hearing to give Dallas officials a chance to voice their opposition. Dallas and Fort Worth officials and representatives dutifully trekked to the nation's capital, where originally they were to meet with Jones and CAA administrators separately. Carter, fresh from receiving news of his son's capture by the Germans in North Africa, and the Fort Worth delegation met with Jones first, whereupon Jones asked his old friend why Dallas and Fort Worth representatives could not meet in the same room. Carter agreed to such an arrangement, whereupon Jones flipped a coin to determine which side could speak first. Fort Worth won the toss, with Carter speaking on the city's behalf. "Fort Worth doesn't know what to speak on," he pled, adding, "We thought this was already settled, that the building was going to be built on the west side of the field." He then deferred to Mayor Rodgers, who again made the charge that the CAA had only made the terminal location decision after pressure from Fort Worth. "Mr. Elliott admitted there was no technical reason to change it from the north side to the west side," he claimed, "but he did say it was to appease Mr. Carter."[22]

Once again, Carter vehemently denied this charge, firing back that "Mayor Rodgers declares this a 'dirty steal.' Those are tough words—it's a fight on Amon Carter and Fort Worth. Those charges are made without proper thought or due consideration." Jones, presumably frustrated by the intransigence of both parties, ruled after hearing both presentations that the government would not make a decision until after the war was over. As Fort Worth mayor I. N. McCrary said to Jones, "Now is not the proper time for Fort Worth and Dallas to be fighting over who is going to get the white meat and who gets the dark meat, because we may both get it in the neck if we don't work together." This may have been a stay of execution, but it was certainly no reprieve. There would be no shared airport, at least for the time being. Unbeknownst to all present, that dream would not be realized for another three decades.[23]

Despite the passage of the Wheeler-Lea Transportation Act in 1940, the Trinity Improvement Association (formerly the TRCA) did receive good news. The completed reports from the Departments of War and Agriculture were favorable and created a detailed plan for the proper use of water and soil resources in the watershed. Also, the War Department committed itself to spending money for the deepening of the Trinity Channel from Galveston up to Liberty, and money was diverted for the clearing of sandbars and snags to Romayor, thus making over one hundred miles of the Trinity navigable. The Department of Agriculture also began cooperating with the Texas Soil Conservation Board to halt soil erosion along the Trinity. In addition to actions by the government, railroads began reducing freight rates in the Southwest because they feared that Congress would approve the canal.[24]

Though the Japanese attack on Pearl Harbor greatly diminished the debate over the canal, Carter still wanted to make sure that the issue remained in the hearts and minds of politicians. Ten days after Pearl Harbor, he asked Fort Worth City manager Sam Bothwell for continued assistance regarding the canal. As chair of the executive and finance committee of the TIA, Carter "found it to be a tireless, hard, up-hill job" that cost the *Star-Telegram* money and aroused great opposition by the railroads. If Fort Worth wanted to continue attracting manufacturers, a canal would have to be built, as railroad rates were still relatively high. Carter went so far as to claim that General Motors and the Continental Can Company would have located in Fort Worth instead of Houston had it not been for a lack of access to water. If the city of Fort Worth continued to give its full support to the project, Carter believed that it might be possible to persuade the government of the necessity of the canal. Carter then tied the canal to the war effort. Fort Worth was now a national defense center, and its central location was very attractive to the government. If men like Carter could personally spend thousands promoting the canal and flood control, then the city of Fort Worth should have had the motivation to call more loudly for its own improvement.[25]

As the United States prepared for and then entered the war, Carter and the TIA's efforts to persuade the government that the Trinity Canal would benefit the war effort continued. He specified to the other members that the TIA from then on would only couch its requests for federal funding within the context of national defense. This meant that the TIA had to present any further suggestions to the Departments of War and Agriculture as well as to various U.S. defense agencies. Any changes that these defense agencies recommended would have to be made by the TIA. In a further continuation of this theme of national defense, TIA General Manager John Fouts wrote to all the members of Congress, defending the passage of the 1942 Rivers and Harbors Omnibus Bill. Responding to the Association of American Railroads lobbying Congress for continued support, Fouts accused the railroads of "disloyal and pernicious activities" because their "subversive tactics in wartime are imperiling the freedom of our Nation and aiding our country's foes" by attempting to quash other forms of transportation such as inland waterways and highways. The bill passed, and the Axis powers were eventually defeated, but during the war, little progress was made on the canalization of the Trinity. Evidently, comparing the railroads to Japan, Germany, and Italy was of no avail, and the canal would have to wait for peace to be won.[26]

MOBILIZING FOR WAR

Although the United States' entry into the war postponed activity on the canal, Carter found ways to ensure that Fort Worth would benefit from wartime conditions. After all, the southern region as a whole discovered that the war was good business. During both world wars, the South not only contributed to but also benefited from the war effort as millions of southerners marched off to war and southern states became the homes to numerous military installations and armaments factories. Most scholars "point to World War II as the catalyst that catapulted Texas and the rest of the South and [W]est into a stage of unprecedented growth and urbanization." Even though "the South remained more campground than arsenal . . . war production increasingly found its way southward" as the federal government ended up spending $4 billion on defense contracts in the formerly impoverished region. The location of military installations and defense industry in the South was the result of a two-way relationship. From the perspective of the federal government, the South was seen as the nation's "number one economic problem," so choosing southern states as the location for much of the nation's wartime needs was part of a deliberate policy. And just as many southern supporters of the New Deal saw the advantage of supporting the program in its early stages, they also recognized that this new war offered many similar economic possibilities for the region.[27]

Historians generally agree that Texas, more than any other southern state, was transformed by the Second World War. As historian Kathryn Pinkney observes, "Possessed of abundant natural resources, deepwater ports, open spaces, a mild climate, and a central location, the state met many of the needs of wartime America." Having already been the location for numerous temporary army bases and airfields during World War I due to its abundant space and good climate, Texas emerged once again as a natural choice; changes to Texas's economic structure would arise, however, more as a result of sincere efforts by Texas politicians and boosters to industrialize Texas by partnering with the federal government. As the nation began rearming after 1940, Texas's strong congressional delegation worked to ensure that their constituents would receive a sizable portion of the government's largesse. Though one might expect that the most rapid economic growth would occur in Texas's traditional fields of oil and agriculture, Randolph Campbell notes that "the most dramatic economic changes wrought by war came in manufacturing." Therefore, "Texas entered World War II a largely impoverished, rural, agricultural state and emerged from the war decade thriving and far more urbanized and industrialized than ever before."[28]

These changes were not unwelcomed or unforeseen by many leading southerners. Historian Dewey Grantham writes, "Southerners, more than other Americans, generally adopted a bellicose attitude toward the national debate over foreign policy in 1940 and 1941." This was not necessarily a new development in southern history, as the region had "rallied around the flag" in the Spanish-American War and in World War I. George Brown Tindall attributes southern readiness to enter World War II to numerous factors: "sentimental identification with the British," the fact that "German conquests menaced the cotton and tobacco trade with Europe and Britain," and the demographics of the region: few Germans or Irish immigrants, groups that were notoriously anti-British, had settled in the South. In addition, he notes that "southern history had bred a psychology of danger and defense, and a military-patriotic tradition." Along with these factors, Anthony Gaughan points out that while many Americans during the 1930s were antagonistic toward the defense industry, believing its manufacturers to be "merchants of death," "southerners saw war as a source of regional economic growth." Therefore, "the prospect of intervention did not frighten southerners."[29]

The West, Fort Worth's other regional identity, was arguably transformed in greater ways than the South, especially when one looks more narrowly at the urban West. It is no exaggeration to say, along with Carl Abbott, that for the urban West, "mobilization for World War Two was the central event that introduced a new era of sustained-city building." Even more, "World War Two changed the growth curve for every Western subregion, reversing decline or stagnation in much of the West and accelerating growth in a few favored areas. The war and its aftermath mark the takeoff when Western cities as a group changed from followers to trendsetters." Fort Worth, with both feet astride the meeting of South and West and conveniently located as a gateway city to the Great Plains, stood to benefit from the war if civic leaders such as Carter aggressively courted the military and defense industries.

As the state's most prominent publisher, Carter understood the gains that could be made by supporting Roosevelt's call to make the United States the "arsenal of Democracy." In 1940, Roosevelt began a national defense program that would allow for greater coordination between business and government for the purpose of readying the United States' defense capabilities. Like many other southerners, Carter possessed a hawkish view of foreign affairs, as well as full awareness of the dangers of what he termed, in a Christmas 1940 letter to his employees, "a world gone mad." Therefore, he easily came to terms with the idea that the nation should prepare its defenses. When Roosevelt delivered his "arsenal" speech, Carter wired the president his praise. "America's duty and obligation must cover the requirement of Great Britain," he argued. Demonstrating his loathing of the opposition, he remarked, "The defeatists and isolationists are a hindrance to our welfare and happiness." Within the war readiness President Roosevelt was calling for lay the possibility for Carter to continue his campaign to modernize Fort Worth by relying on the political and business network he had created for himself and his city. Armed with this sensibility as well as a strong boosterish spirit, he turned his attention toward figuring out how the mobilization of the American economy might benefit Fort Worth. Carter and other prominent Fort Worth citizens believed the new opportunities provided by the Roosevelt administration would be one more way for Fort Worth to become an industrialized city and be pulled from the depths of the Depression. Carter took on the most important role in attracting the Consolidated Aircraft Corporation to Fort Worth by using his acquaintance with Reuben Fleet, president of Consolidated, to his and his city's advantage.[30]

The North Texas region seemed a logical place for the defense aviation industry: plentiful labor, no housing shortages, and distance from the more vulnerable coastal regions made that part of Texas very attractive to both government officials and industry leaders. Fort Worthians had long had aviation dreams, many of which, of course, had Carter somewhere in the middle. But with or without Carter, civic leadership aggressively courted airmail contracts during the 1930s with great success. The city's central location as both an east-west and north-south crossroads in the federal Fourth Airways District and the well-developed Municipal Airport (officially called Meacham Field) helped persuade federal officials to make Fort Worth a stopping point for airmail pilots. As a matter of fact, by 1935, Fort Worth ranked behind only New York and Chicago in terms of the volume of airmail handled. That said, considering the relatively small size of the aviation industry during the Depression, it was not until the threat of war loomed that the possibility of making Fort Worth a center of aviation manufacturing became even a remote possibility. In November 1938, President Roosevelt held a secret meeting with his military advisers, informing them that to arm Great Britain and France for what was certain to be a showdown with Hitler's Germany, the United States needed to begin producing at least twenty thousand warplanes over the next two years. Congressional intransigence due to isolationism and economic woes forced Roosevelt to revise his request downward to five thousand, but, at least in the eyes of aviation advocates, something was better than nothing.[31]

General Henry "Hap" Arnold, who had recently been named chief of the Army Air Corps by the president, met in January 1939 with Consolidated Aircraft, one of just a handful of major aviation manufacturers in the nation; he told Reuben Fleet, head of the company, that he needed a long-range heavy bomber capable of reaching a ceiling of 35,000 feet, a speed of over 300 miles per hour, and a range of 3,000 miles. By the end of the year, Consolidated's plant in San Diego had produced the prototype XB-24. As orders rolled in during the earliest years of the war, Fleet and federal officials looked to build new manufacturing locations around the nation in order to expand production. Consolidated briefly toyed with the prospect of moving to Grand Prairie, just east of Dallas near Hensley Airfield, but the plans never materialized. By September 1940, with the Roosevelt administration working to increase aviation production, the Defense Plant Corporation, a subagency of Jesse Jones's RFC, allowed North American Aviation, one of Consolidated's main rivals, to move to the site. Undaunted, Fleet turned his attention toward Fort Worth, a city that would be sure to offer favorable conditions to Consolidated.[32]

Amon Carter and Ruben Fleet began discussing some form of cooperation between Consolidated and Fort Worth in 1940. Fleet contacted Carter, stating his interest in expanding his company's operations outside San Diego, where they were currently headquartered. In phone conversations and in writing, Fleet outlined what material he was searching for in considering possible locations for a new plant: information about "wage scales, union activities, labor disturbances, labor supply . . . state, county, and local taxations" among other things. He was also wise enough to explicitly mention that Consolidated was interested in other sites around the southern United States. Not only did the Sunbelt states, as they would later be called, have better weather, but clearly their more conservative economic policies were much more attractive to companies like Consolidated.[33]

Consolidated soon had a new proposal for Amon Carter and Fort Worth. The city's officials and Carter were working on preparing for Consolidated's possible presence when the company's chief test pilot requested a favor from Carter and Fort Worth. The aviation manufacturer was in the process of building PBY seaplanes for Great Britain, and these planes needed a place to land on their way from San Diego to Great Britain. Since these flights were to begin in the winter, however, the planes needed to land in a warmer climate so as to avoid frozen water surfaces. Consolidated officials explicitly asked to land at Lake Worth, not far from the shores of Shady Oak, and they asked Carter to mediate between them and the city of Fort Worth.[34]

By December 1940, Consolidated's seaplanes were landing at Lake Worth on their way to Great Britain. Meanwhile, Carter urged local politicians to pressure the United States Army to allow Consolidated to locate in Fort Worth. Carter believed Fort Worth to be the ideal spot because it offered water for navy planes and plenty of land for the army. If Consolidated were to build in Tulsa or Oklahoma City, as had been suggested, the plant would be forced to only build army planes at the plant. Armed with this reasoning and confident of his sales abilities, Carter considered the deal with Consolidated to be done; all that was needed was the army's consent.[35]

Officials on both sides of the negotiations were confident that Consolidated would choose to locate in Fort Worth. Carter and the Fort Worth Chamber of Commerce were willing to give Consolidated anything it needed to build a functioning plant. William Holden, executive vice president of the Chamber of Commerce, listed what Fort Worth would grant Consolidated if they chose Fort Worth: 1,200 acres along Lake Worth, two runways with taxi strips, a water supply system with a sewer main and sewage disposal plant, necessary utility and railroad trunk lines (at no cost), highways, and housing. Holden also stated that the three bodies of the Fort Worth City Council, Tarrant County officials, and Chamber of Commerce representatives were united in their efforts to bring Consolidated to Fort Worth. Amon Carter would not be alone in this project.[36]

Once Carter had established a solid partnership with Fleet and Consolidated, he turned his attention to politicians and government officials. Carter again used his connection with Elliott Roosevelt to influence various people in the government, such as General Edwin M. Watson, secretary to President Roosevelt, and, of course, the president himself. He also contacted Texas Senator Morris Sheppard, Chairman of the Military Affairs Committee, urging him to lean on Assistant Secretary of War Patterson and President Roosevelt. To assist Sheppard in his duties, Carter sent him a brief detailing what Fort Worth had to offer. William S. Knudsen, of the National Defense Advisory Committee, was next on Carter's list; fortunately for Carter, he already had a working relationship with Knudsen. Knudsen had formerly worked for General Motors, and Carter had tried unsuccessfully to coax Knudsen into constructing an automobile plant in Fort Worth. The National Defense Advisory Committee recommended building four bomber plants, the third of which was to be built in Tulsa by Consolidated. However, Carter told Knudsen that Consolidated believed Fort Worth to be the better site; Tulsa could receive the fourth bomber plant to be run by some other aviation company.[37]

The federal government continued to press for a Consolidated plant in Tulsa, even though Consolidated officials had stated that Fort Worth would be a better location. Even so, the government insisted that factories should be given to states that had not already benefited from defense dollars. Texas already had a sizable military presence, and the Dallas–Fort Worth area had acquired a North American airplane plant in Grand Prairie. Fleet remained adamant that Fort Worth should be selected and continued to urge Carter and Fort Worth officials to mount a last offensive against the War Department. Carter capped this flurry of activity with a wire to President Roosevelt stating what both Fleet and he had been saying all along—that Fort Worth offered numerous advantages over Tulsa: better climate, more railroads, and a position along American Airlines' transcontinental route. Also, Consolidated was still using Lake Worth as a stop for flying boats. If the War Department deemed it necessary to build bombers and flying boats, Fort Worth would be the ideal site for a plant. Carter offered Roosevelt a solution. He suggested that Tulsa be granted a plant and that Consolidated be allowed to come to Fort Worth.[38]

On January 3, 1941, the government announced that both Fort Worth and Tulsa would be awarded the Consolidated plant. Fort Worth officials were ecstatic, and congratulations were showered on Carter for his effort throughout the whole ordeal. Two local businessmen lauded Carter for his "untiring efforts," noting, "All Fort Worth will rejoice in your achievement." Lt. Colonel A. B. McDaniel, an officer serving in the Office of the Chief of the Air Corps, was apparently well informed of Carter's history of getting his way in relation to the government, as he wrote, "You 'did your stuff' as usual." Carter fired off a telegram to President Roosevelt thanking him for his help and apparent influence over the situation.[39]

The existing correspondence indicates that those involved in the Consolidated efforts viewed Carter's role not only as important but also indispensable. Without his presence, it is likely that Fort Worth would never have received the Consolidated plant. Reuben Fleet was no friend of the New Deal, as evidenced by his numerous appearances before congressional committees to denounce high taxation, the plowing under of cotton, and the "super-intelligent, wonderful, brainy people, who have never themselves made a success of business." William Holden did not possess the presence or political connections of Carter and would not have received the same respect from Washington politicians. It was Carter who urged Senators Connally and Sheppard to speak on his behalf, and he also took it upon himself to write to Roosevelt about the controversy. His flurry of activity at the end of December 1940 was the decisive factor in the War Department's decision to build a Consolidated plant in Fort Worth.[40]

Bringing Consolidated to Fort Worth proved to be one of the most remarkable feats in Amon Carter's life solely because of the impact Consolidated had on the Fort Worth economy. In 1941 alone, Consolidated added six thousand jobs to the Fort Worth economy; to put that number in context, there were fewer than 10,000 manufacturing employees in Fort Worth in 1939. At the height of wartime production, 38,000 people were employed at the Consolidated plant building B-24 Liberators, one of the main workhorses of the strategic bombing campaign over Germany. Consolidated not only added jobs but also poured payroll dollars into Fort Worth, an amount that increased from $10 million in 1942 to $60 million in 1944. The end of the war did not halt production at Consolidated, because the United States remained militarily on alert throughout the Cold War. Consolidated underwent a few name changes and buyouts through the rest of the century, beginning with Convair, then General Dynamics, and finally Lockheed; regardless of the changes, Fort Worth continued to benefit from the presence of the plant.[41]

As the first bombers rolled off the production lines at Fort Worth's Consolidated plant, Carter continued his vocal support for the burgeoning war effort and criticized any gains by labor unions that might threaten defense capabilities. Like most other southern businessmen, he was wary of any strength labor unions might gain, especially in the middle of America's national defense preparations. Labor historian Irving Bernstein notes that strikes "became a critical issue during the defense period" as a consequence of "rising employment, growing inflation, residual resistance by management to unionization, the inexperience of new bargainers on both sides of the table, and the exploitation of unrest by communist leaders within the CIO unions they controlled." Even though Roosevelt created the National Defense Mediation Board in March 1941, it seemed little could stop the wave of strikes in the shipbuilding, steel, lumber, aluminum, coal, and other industries. In 1941 alone, more than five hundred strikes occurred in defense-related industries, leading to the loss of over 4.7 million man-days.[42]

One of the most crippling strikes of the period was a coal strike in the fall of 1941 ordered by John Lewis, former president of the CIO and, at the time, president of the United Mine Workers, in support of a union shop at steel-company-owned coal mines. When Senator Connally publically decried these strikes that harmed the war effort, Carter notified him of his full support. "A few selfish people are doing honest labor a great injustice," he fumed. Connally, ever mindful of the necessity of positive newspaper coverage, replied that he was "pleased to have your approval and commendation [, and I] hope you can give editorial and newspaper publicity to support." When the possibility of labor strife emerged once again in February 1942, Carter fired off a telegram to Senator Alben Barkley of Kentucky, Connally, and Congressman Sam Rayburn denouncing work stoppages in the midst of war. "If we cannot achieve unity of purpose to victory on the home front, how can we expect our soldiers to sacrifice their lives for victory on the battle front?" he queried. "Anything which delays, restricts in quantity, or in any way hampers the flow of machines and materials to our forces in battle, means that the war must last longer, that more American soldiers must be killed and wounded before we win." He went on to say, "When delays are deliberately engineered or concerted, it is treason, and nothing else." Lewis, constantly a thorn in Roosevelt's side, continued to threaten strikes throughout the war. Coal miners under his leadership walked out in 1943, forcing Roosevelt, through the War Labor Board, to order them back to work. Carter approved of his move, stating that the United Mine Workers actions "are lending aid and solace to our mortal enemies" and that "Mr. Lewis should promptly be brought to an accounting and definitely given to understand that neither the United States government nor the public will tolerate disloyal arrogance of this kind."[43]

THE CARTER FAMILY AT WAR

Amid war and rumors of war, Carter's personal life was marked by turmoil and tension as he attempted to deal with the aftermath of his divorce from Nenetta. Their children, particularly Ruth, found themselves torn between mother and father, a battle their indomitable father was sure to win. Reports in April 1941 of Carter being seen in the presence of other women did little to heal the scars of the recent divorce. Nenetta had taken refuge in New York, but even there, she could not avoid hearing rumors of her ex-husband's dalliances with women. Hurt as she was, she poured her swirling emotions out to Ruth in an effort to turn her against her father. She reported hearing of Amon's new female companion, a woman who "is my age, has blonde grayish hair, and is taller and larger than I am." Nenetta's friends witnessed Amon "coming out of a [New York] florist with [his new girlfriend] dripping orchids and then again dancing every dance with her at Monte Carlo Sat nite." The fact that this happened on a Saturday night was a blow to Nenetta: "You know full well," she complained, "he never took me to such places and was always too tired to get dressed for me."[44]

Nenetta claimed she still had feelings for Amon but disagreed with her daughter's belief that Amon wanted her back. She told Ruth, "You seemed to think your daddy was so hurt and still in love with me, and now you know differently," thanks to the new woman. Plus, she had "sent him a box of ties and lovely argyle socks . . . just to let him know how I felt, but he has never acknowledged them." Meanwhile, in an effort to assuage her hurt feelings, she took up with a gentleman named Eddie, much to her daughter's chagrin. An angry Amon forbade his daughter to be seen with Nenetta and Eddie, a fact that only stoked Nenetta's resentment toward the man. In a rage, she vented to Katrine Deakins, Amon's secretary, "I think he has a hell of a nerve to ask her not [to] be seen with me and a nice man." Matters took a turn for the worse the next week when he was witnessed in New York at the Stork Club, "with a cheap Mexican tramp he picked up in Paris." Even New York gossip columnist Walter Winchell wrote of the sighting in his "On Broadway" column, noting that Carter was seen in the club with "somebody newer, somebody truer, etc." That same week, Nenetta had lunch with a large group, one of whom, without knowing Nenetta was Amon's ex-wife, mourned that "it was a crime that Amon could not quit his tomcatting around as he had been doing for years and he guessed his wife must have found him out and left him." A wounded Nenetta got up and left the table. In her eyes, it only confirmed that he was "openly doing now what he has been doing on the sly all along."[45]

Understandably, Ruth was torn apart by the acrimony she witnessed through her mother's letters. In an attempt to get Ruth to "see my side," Nenetta wrote her a detailed letter about Amon's new girlfriend, a dancer and, in her eyes, "a cheap little tart." "With so many decent ones to go with," she sighed, "it breaks my heart" that he was with a lowly dancer. An exasperated Ruth wrote Katrine that "I am just getting sick and tired of them. I think I shall tell Dad and Mother both that I don't want to hear any more about anything." Regarding the allegations about her dad's past and present womanizing, she claimed, "I don't know what to believe. But I know Daddy would never do anything disrespectful." Either way, her mother's statements did little to loosen the bond between father and daughter, and Ruth was "mad as a wet hen at her accusations." The tension between Nenetta and Ruth continued until Amon Jr. was captured in North Africa in 1943.[46]

Sadly, Carter's war experiences were marred by the capture of Amon Jr. by the Germans in the North African campaign in 1943. After graduating from Culver Military Academy in 1938, Amon Jr. attended the University of Texas. His military interests acquired at Culver influenced him to maintain ties with the army, and upon turning twenty-one, he was granted a commission as a second lieutenant. As the nation prepared its defenses, Amon Jr. was called to active duty in July 1941 as a lieutenant in the First Armored Division at Fort Knox. When the United States entered the war after the Japanese attack on Pearl Harbor in December 1941, his unit was shipped to Northern Ireland, where it remained until the American invasion of North Africa. His military service caused his already patriotic father to take an even more intense interest in public support for the troops. When the Associated Press referred to American troops in North Africa as "green" after being dealt defeats by German forces at Kasserine Pass in 1943, the easily irritated Carter took offense. Partially motivated by his sense of patriotism, but mainly by Amon Jr. serving in the First Armored Division then fighting in Tunisia, he wrote a letter to Kent Cooper, general manager for the Associated Press, claiming that "the American boys are not lacking in guts or patriotism." Noting that his son was currently serving in North Africa, he closed, "I feel somewhat resentful in having these boys continually referred to as 'green troops' and I am rather confident they do not appreciate it themselves."[47]

Unbeknownst to Carter, Amon Jr. was nowhere near the fighting at Kasserine Pass that so bloodied American forces. The First Armored Division, then under the command of Major General Orlando Ward, was helping guard the Faid Pass, one of a select few passes through the Eastern Dorsal Mountains in Tunisia against which General Erwin Rommel was directing his Afrika Korps' offensive. However, the defenses were limited and were easily overwhelmed by the Axis assault on the morning of February 14, and on that day, Amon Jr., on observation duty for a battery, was reported missing. For the next nine days, he remained hidden behind German lines, desperately trying to make it back to his unit. Unfortunately, a group of Bedouins found him first; they knocked him unconscious, took his two cameras (including a movie camera), watch, money, and clothes and turned him over to the Germans. The Germans then transported him to a prison in Capua, Italy, on a Junkers 52 transport plane in a trip that nearly ended in his death when American fighter planes attacked his formation. Conditions on the ground in Italy were no better. "It was there," newspapers reported, "the Italians vented their spite on the American prisoners." Amon Jr. remembered, "They spat on us and threw rocks at us. It was the worst treatment we had from anybody." He was then taken to Germany and, finally, to Poland, where he spent eighteen months at an officer's prison camp at Oflag 64 near the town of Szubin.⁴⁸

For some time after his capture, his whereabouts were unknown and he was reported as missing. As word spread of Amon Jr.'s disappearance, his father found himself deluged with telegrams and letters from friends and associates nationwide praying and hoping for his son's survival. "A thousand girls and boys [send] a thousand wishes that you may soon hear that Amon Jr. is safe and well," students at Amon Carter Riverside High School in Fort Worth wired. J. C. Penney wrote, "I scarcely know how to write to you for it is difficult to know what to say to a man whose son has been reported as missing." The indomitable J. Edgar Hoover wrote that he "read with deep emotion the newspaper clipping concerning Amon." John Cowles of the Lend-Lease Administration attempted to soothe Carter's fears by reporting that a friend "told me he believed that nine out of the ten American soldiers who were reported as missing in action [in North Africa] had probably been captured, and that it would later be reported that they were all right." Full of hope for his friend, he closed: "When Rommel is destroyed[,] Amon will be released from a Tunis prison camp in good health." In an egregious error, Ickes wired Carter, "Report has reached me that your son has been lost in action." The rest of the telegram was replete with references to his death, with one line mentioning that "it was his privilege to die for his country." Carter's response is unknown, but receiving such a statement from someone as prominent as Ickes must have been a temporary blow to his already fragile state. Fortunately, correspondence from other people like Hap Arnold, Sam Rayburn, President Roosevelt, as well as a personal note from Eleanor, countered Ickes's comments about Jr.'s death and offered sincere hopes about his safety. Though newspapers reported young Amon's possible loss on March 11, Roosevelt, whose sons were serving in the war as well, waited until the 26th to write to Carter, claiming, "I have been wanting to write you but put it off hourly hoping that there might be some good news." He reassured Carter that he had "made repeated inquiries and that absence of any definite news does not lessen the possibility that he was taken prisoner—so do not lose hope." As Carter mourned the possible loss of his son and worried about his safety, he could at least rely on the support of his vast national network of friends and acquaintances.⁴⁹

The situation eased for Carter in April when he received word that his son was not dead but had been taken to Germany, where he was now in a prisoner of war camp. For the next two years, father and son kept up a flurry of communication. Letters from Carter to his son were full of information about life back home and updates on friends, family, and colleagues. Amon Jr., desperate for some semblance of comfort and ease in his barracks, constantly requested candy, cigars, and blankets, while also notifying his father of recent Texas arrivals to the camp so he could publish their names in the newspaper. All the while, Carter remained hopeful that the war would end soon, knowing that its end would mean reunion with his son. Never a devout man, he nevertheless received spiritual encouragement from chaplains and pastors, urging him to rely on his faith to see him through these dark days.

Always looking to exploit his Washington connections, Carter asked Connally in 1944 to add his support to legislation that called for the promotion of captured officers. He reasoned that the officers had suffered such great hardships at the hands of the Germans that they should get automatic promotions. Carter stressed that he was not doing this solely because of his son, but because he wanted the officers to be rewarded for their perseverance. In an attempt to make this an issue Connally would be willing to support, Carter added that as of May 1944, 10 percent of the American officers in German POW camp Oflag 64 were Texans. Connally contacted Secretary of War Henry Stimson regarding the issue, but Stimson refused to support the idea, observing that whatever the hardships the officers had endured, "none of those circumstances can be justified as the basis for promotion under sound military policy."[50]

The tension of Amon and Nenetta's recent divorce having worn off, the family found common ground with Amon's capture. In January 1945, a flustered Nenetta wrote Amon about a tip she had received from someone she wished to remain anonymous, warning her that she had recently been investigated by the FBI. She was warned to carefully monitor her "mail, telegrams, and phone conversations regarding news from, of and by Amon Jr." Though she had not gone to Amon for advice in "nearly four years," she begged Amon to handle [the situation] as you see fit." Upon receiving the letter, Amon wired J. Edgar Hoover a brief note from his New York hotel: "Will you please have one of your top men call on me here at the Ritz-Carlton at his convenience?" How the resulting conversation between Carter and the FBI unfolded is unknown; fortunately, the family did not have long to worry about Amon Jr.'s well-being because Germany was nearing collapse.[51]

On February 2, Carter received word from Connally that the camp near Stettin where his son was being held was moved farther into Germany as the Red Army advanced on its final offensive. Finally, Amon Jr.'s liberation appeared imminent. As Germany teetered on the brink of collapse, the opportunity soon arose to be reunified with his son. In early 1945, as American and British forces began encountering German camps such as Buchenwald and Dachau, General Dwight D. Eisenhower requested that a number of American newspaper publishers be sent to survey the camps to enforce upon the public the magnitude of German crimes as well as to dispense with any notions that reports of German atrocities were merely Allied propaganda. Carter was asked to accompany seventeen other publishers to Europe, where they encountered the horrific scenes of emaciated prisoners and piles of dead bodies. The photos taken of the press tour show the publishers repulsed and, in Carter's case, seemingly in sickened horror at the images. Amid the nauseating setting of the camps, he learned some inspiring news: his son had been liberated by the Soviets. One liberated American prisoner reported that "Carter was in charge of distributing Red Cross parcels and when I saw him last Tuesday he was in good shape and was staying in the Luckenwalde camp in compliance with the senior American officer's order that prisoners stay there until arrangements are made for them."[52]

While Carter encamped with the 83rd Division along the Elbe River in Germany, a special patrol was sent to acquire his son. On May 5, father and son saw one another for the first time in over two years as Amon Jr. "walked up behind his father and said quietly, 'Here I am[,] dad.'" The two embraced warmly, both attempting to hide their emotions from the gathering press and military men. Amon Jr. was adamant that his fellow prisoners be sent for as well. "We've got to go back and get those other fellows," he implored the officers present. Carter could not have been happier, as "Cowboy," as he called his son, was back home and ready to take the helm of his father's empire in the near future.

Joyous as he was, Carter could not shake his bitter feelings toward Germany. Already hawkish in his approach to the war, his experiences of having a son spend two years in German camps as well as witnessing the brutality of Dachau and Buchenwald brought him new beliefs about America's role in the world. Traveling through Germany's prisoner of war and "political atrocity" camps shaped his views both about how Germany should be treated after the war and how the United States should face the complexities of the postwar world. Like many of the publishers who traveled with him to Germany in 1945, he strongly believed that Germany should be harshly punished for its crimes and believed the United States should use its power to prevent similar events from ever happening again. Upon arriving back in Fort Worth, he wrote at length of his feelings toward Germany. Never one to keep his thoughts to himself, he exploded with anger. "We found the attitude of the Germans still arrogant, and they do not seem to feel that they have lost the war." Well aware that many Americans believed that

"Hitler and his gang of cutthroats were solely responsible for the war or atrocities," Carter fumed, "I am confident that the German people knew what was going on. They were a party to it. They were the beneficiaries of the loot drained from occupied countries; of thousands of slave laborers." He declared that "national sterilization would not be too severe," but recognizing the implausibility of this path, suggested that the best way to prevent such actions again would be for the United States to "have an Army, Navy, and Air Corps of such size and quality that no other nation would have the nerve even to think of starting another war."[53]

Such words, strong as they were, were not unexpected from a man of his personality. A proponent of preparedness before America entered the war, it made sense for him to support the concept that would later be termed "peace through strength." In his words, "If America keeps its powder dry, keeps itself ready for all emergencies, it will be the best preventive of war we can have." As the United States faced, not the specter of a resurgent Germany, but the increasingly menacing Soviet Union on the rise, Carter continued to advocate for a strong defense policy. Meanwhile, on the home front, the loss of Amon Jr. and subsequent reunion of the Carter family with him reaped great benefits for individuals and institutions in need. In 1943, Nenetta, "kneeling before the altar of the Blessed Mother at St. Patrick's Cathedral . . . made this promise: 'If God will give me back my son, I will spend the rest of my life trying to help others.'" The result would be the Amon G. Carter Foundation.[54]

CHAPTER 8

THE FINAL DECADE

CARTER'S TWILIGHT YEARS reveal a man comfortable with his status as a nationally recognized booster, yet still retaining the fiery drive that propelled him from his humble beginnings. Now an incredibly wealthy man, he established a philanthropic foundation with an initial endowment of over $8 million and was often involved in the minutiae of his charitable endeavors. He remained politically active at the national level as he sought to navigate the changes in the postwar political and economic landscape. Carter maintained the relationship he had cultivated with Lyndon Johnson since 1941, railed against Harry Truman for his stance on the Tideland oil controversy, vocally supported Dwight D. Eisenhower in his 1952 presidential run, but, toward the end of his life, suffered a humiliating political defeat at the hands of a young Jim Wright. His boosterish activities involving petitioning figures and organizations external to Fort Worth and Texas did not wane as he continued to lobby for support for Trinity canalization, helped bring about the opening of an international airport in Fort Worth, and succeeded in persuading General Motors to build a plant in Tarrant County. Finally, he seemingly achieved domestic peace with a third marriage, this time to Minnie Meacham Smith, all while continuing the friendly relationship he had constructed with Nenetta. Unfortunately, a series of heart attacks beginning in 1953 marred his usually frenetic activity, and he spent the last years of his life combating his failing health.

American newspaper publishers entered the postwar era generally with confidence. Nearly 49,000,000 daily newspapers circulated by the end of 1945, and that number continued to rise over the next few years. Increased circulation meant increased advertising revenues, and by 1949, "total newspaper employment grew faster than total US employment." But troubling signs bubbled just below the surface: higher production costs due to increased labor costs, technological advances, and, maybe most forebodingly, a possible challenge from a new medium—television. Not everyone saw television as a threat, and it was suggested by some that television would complement, not challenge, the dominant newspaper industry. The American Newspaper Publishers Association (ANPA), of which Carter had been an active member for some time, agreed with this assessment. It was therefore no surprise that a number of publishers nationwide began to purchase television stations; at one point in 1945, the FCC reported that "40 percent of the pending applications for new television stations came from newspaper interests." Ever watchful of developing trends in the industry, in 1948, Carter, leaning heavily on *Star-Telegram* vice president Harold Hough, decided to create the *Star-Telegram*'s television arm, WBAP-TV. The station, operating as an affiliate of both NBC and ABC, first aired on Channel 5 on September 27, 1948, broadcasting a short spot highlighting President Truman's brief stop in the city on his fiery reelection campaign. Regular programming began two days later when Carter kicked off the evening's lineup with a brief talk introducing viewers to the new medium. Texas and the Southwest had its first television station.[1]

Carter's oil discoveries in the mid-1930s shifted his philanthropic efforts toward a more organized approach as well as enabled an increase in art purchases. Access to millions of dollars enabled him to quit borrowing money or relying on his newspaper to support his charitable endeavors. Some of his first donations went to a summer camp for a local Boy Scout troop, the purchase of a light system for Amon Carter Riverside High School (a Fort Worth school named after him during the 1930s), and air-conditioning for polio patients at John Peter Smith Hospital. Even though Carter was able to give larger gifts more frequently, it was not until 1945 that he formally organized his philanthropy with the founding of the Amon G. Carter Foundation. Carter, along with his ex-wife Nenetta, formed the Amon G. Carter Foundation on April 7, 1945, with an original endowment of over $8.5 million. Upon his death in 1955, almost $7.5 million was added from his estate. The purpose of this foundation was to support "benevolent, charitable, educational, or missionary undertakings." The foundation was formed as a tax-exempt nonprofit organization originally housed in the *Star-Telegram* building. According to *Foundations of Texan Philanthropy* author Mary Kelley, Carter had numerous reasons for creating a foundation for "large-scale, organized philanthropy after more than thirty years of individual giving." Though maybe not a completely altruistic person, he sincerely loved Fort Worth and West Texas and wanted to promote their interests whenever possible. Post–World War Two tax increases influenced Carter to find a way to shelter his money and indulge his philanthropic acts. Concerns about his legacy and a genuine belief in Andrew Carnegie's ideal that the wealthy were obligated to give of their largesse appear to have been motivating factors as well.[2]

Given his devotion to Fort Worth, it is not surprising that the Carter Foundation's grants were restricted to Texas with a focus on the Fort Worth region. In an undated, untitled memo that gives some details as to how Carter wanted some of his foundation's funds to be directed, he specified not only some preferred recipients but also how much was to be given to them. He directed that money be given to Texas Christian University for a science building that could cost up to one million dollars, a new building for the Lena Pope Home (a Fort Worth home for homeless and abandoned children) that was expected to cost nearly $500,000, and a nurse's home at Fort Worth St. Joseph Hospital costing up to $250,000. Carter donated hundreds of thousands of dollars to these institutions before his death (and apparently after the memo was written).[3]

Now that Carter had money available to grant to grateful recipients, he seemed to throw himself into giving with greater enthusiasm. Proving that he was no absentee philanthropist, he and his trusted assistant Katrine Deakins consistently communicated with beneficiaries to ensure that their requests were properly handled. One of his favorite charitable recipients with which he maintained a steady correspondence was the Lena Pope Home. Lena Pope, a Fort Worth woman, opened a children's home in west Fort Worth in 1930 and often received monetary assistance from Carter. Before his wealthier days, he often gave gifts to the children at the home at Christmastime, but with the creation of the Carter Foundation, he was able to become more involved with the home and served on the advisory board.[4]

In 1945, Carter and the Lena Pope Home board of directors began working to obtain land in the Arlington Heights neighborhood for the expansion of the home. Buying the appropriate plots of land took several years of negotiations with the neighborhood and the Fort Worth City Zoning Ordinance, especially since eight blocks of land to be purchased belonged to hundreds of owners. By 1950, however, construction on the home's new nursery known as "Babyland" was under way. Carter consistently gave to the Lena Pope Home building fund beginning in 1944 (in 1944, the *Star Telegram* gave $10,000), and by 1949, had contributed over $50,000. In April of 1950, Carter wrote Lena Pope that he would like to contribute $25,000 more to the building fund, which would cover the costs of the 60 acres of land already purchased for the expansion. Until his 1955 death, Carter continued to help in small ways, even purchasing beds, mattresses, and sheets for the nursery when a small fire destroyed the existing bedding.[5]

Understandably, Lena Pope was very grateful for Carter's purchase of the land, especially since it apparently was somewhat unexpected. She wrote, "My first impulse was to tell the world about it through the newspapers. Mr. Leonard [local department store magnate] advised against this—said every agency in Ft. Worth, even broadened it into Texas, would be seeking a conference with you—and 'asking.' Hence I refrained." This strikes at the heart of much of Carter's philanthropy, especially to Lena Pope. The public often remained unaware that he was so involved, since his own newspaper rarely covered these examples of generosity. For one, he did not need the publicity, since he already had a reputation with the public for generosity; a reputation, it must be added, that ensured that he constantly received requests for assistance from individuals from all over the country. In addition to this unneeded publicity, it seems that these kinds of endeavors were genuine, heartfelt acts of philanthropy. While not an unwanted or orphaned child like those at the home, Carter was forever scarred by the loss of his mother at a young age, and helping children who were experiencing worse loss than he had must have provided some sense of comfort and joy.[6]

Another example of Carter's growing emphasis on charitable giving came in 1949, when, on May 17, the Trinity River flooded its banks and submerged a tenth of Fort Worth. Thousands of citizens were left homeless, ten people lost their lives, and damage estimates reached $25 million. The Red Cross rushed in to give aid and assist in the recovery from this devastating flood. In the middle of the crisis, Carter immediately took the lead in beginning a fund-raising campaign to counter the flood damage. He gave $10,000 to the fund and then used his newspaper to issue calls for help from the business community and Fort Worth residents.[7]

As money poured into the relief fund's coffers, so did appeals for assistance. Memos crossed Carter's desk notifying him of the hundreds of people who were in need. For a variety of reasons, the Red Cross was unable to assist some of the families; two intriguing cases involve the issue of race in the New South. Ella Patterson and Bea Steel, an African American mother and daughter, both appealed to Carter and the *Star-Telegram* for relief after being turned down by the Red Cross. Most of Ella Patterson's furniture and one recently built room were washed away by the flood. The Red Cross (reportedly represented by a woman from Wisconsin) told the seventy-year-old Patterson "that her two daughters could take care of her" and gave her fifteen dollars. Bea Steel, Ella's daughter, lived in a different location but suffered heavy damage to her house as well. She complained that the Red Cross was "helping many people . . . who never have and never will work a day in their lives and lost nothing in the flood." While Carter could never be mistaken for an advocate for racial equality and was someone who always functioned within the Jim Crow system, he had a history of making small contributions to the black community. The two women must have been aware of this and of his role as a kind of grandfather to the city and thus believed that he would give them fairer treatment than a Wisconsin woman representing the Red Cross. They, along with many other citizens both black and white, received help from the *Star Telegram* Relief Fund.[8]

The Flood Relief Fund succeeded in raising money for the hundreds of people who were in dire need of assistance. Texaco donated $5,000 after C. B. Williams, division manager of Texaco's West Texas Division of the Producing Department, conversed with Carter by telephone. Convair, by now one of the city's largest employers, donated $15,000 to the fund. Hundreds of citizens, from all classes of Fort Worth society, heeded Carter's calls for donations. Soon, Carter and the *Star Telegram* had raised over $335,000 and disbursed the funds to hundreds of families and businesses, repaired houses, and bought school books, clothes, bedding, and furniture for those who had applied for aid. By August 1949, the Red Cross had committed nearly $1.7 million in aid as well, and Fort Worth was soon on its way to recovery. Carter recognized the great help the organization provided and hosted a large party at his famed Shady Oak Farm for many of the workers; the chairman of the Fort Worth Chapter of the Red Cross commended him for "the invaluable aid rendered by the *Star Telegram* during the emergency period of the flood and throughout the many weeks of rehabilitation." Though the Red Cross with its national organization was able to give more assistance than the Relief Fund, Carter had proved that he was not going to rely on external help to bring the city through this natural disaster. His attitude is best expressed in a letter he sent to a Dallas banker: "Fort Worth made no appeal at any time for outside aid as the result of the flood. It felt that it was a responsibility of its own citizenship."[9]

Another of Carter's favorite beneficiaries was the medical field. He had a long fascination with osteopathic medicine and used the editorial page of the *Star-Telegram* to support legislation that allowed greater freedom for osteopaths. Recognizing that Fort Worth needed a better healthcare system if the city was going to continue to grow, he joined the Greater Fort Worth Hospital Fund as honorary president in June 1951. According to a pamphlet distributed by the fund, the purpose of this nonprofit organization was to "combine the needs of all our non-profit voluntary hospitals into a balanced plan and thus more economically finance at one time the construction of sufficient hospital facilities to meet more fully our total pressing needs." The organization would "conduct the federated appeal, collect the funds, and distribute them to the hospitals in accordance with their individual expansion programs within the master plan." The financial goal was to raise nearly $4,000,000 for five Fort Worth hospitals: All Saints, Cook Children's Hospital, Fort Worth Osteopathic Hospital, Harris Methodist Hospital, and St. Joseph Hospital.[10]

Due to his age and obviously hectic schedule, Carter was only serving as honorary president; his participation, while wholehearted, was not quite as vigorous as it had been in earlier campaigns. Much of Carter's support was financial, as denoted by his gift of $300,000 to the fund. Close friend and fellow Fort Worth philanthropist and oilman Sid Richardson donated the same amount. As the campaign neared its end in 1953, Carter did put a bit more effort into it to help the fund reach the expressed financial goal. One illustration of Carter's ability to exert pressure is shown in a letter to G. J. Coffey, president of the Chicago Pneumatic Tool Company. The company had recently opened a location in Fort Worth and committed to giving to the Hospital Fund, but Carter believed that the contribution of $1,000 over the course of five years was too little. Thus, he wrote Coffey a letter designed to shame him into giving more. Carter told him that other companies were contributing large amounts to the fund and, to press the point home, sent him a list titled "Out of Town Owned or Controlled Firms Who Have Subscribed to the Fund." Whether or not Carter was successful in getting Coffey to give more money is unknown, but the overall success of the campaign by 1954 seems to denote that these tactics must have been a boon to the campaign.[11]

Though Carter never expressed reservations about Jim Crow or disfranchisement, there were moments when his generosity crossed the color barrier. After

World War I, a number of black Fort Worthians moved west of the now-defunct Camp Bowie into a neighborhood along the shores of Lake Como, a small, human-made lake created by damming up a Trinity tributary. Como was once home to a resort and amusement center in the late nineteenth century, but those facilities were never rebuilt after being destroyed by a fire. Como then became a residential area sometime after World War I. Originally settled by those who served as servants and domestics for the wealthy white residents of nearby neighborhoods like Carter's own Rivercrest, Como was annexed by Fort Worth in 1922. By the 1940s, the community was something of a middle-class neighborhood that even had its own weekly newspaper, the *Lake Como Monitor* (later the *Lake Como Weekly*). Like many other black neighborhoods in the city, Como suffered from a dearth of parks. But in July 1951, the Fort Worth Board of Park Commissioners unanimously adopted a motion that the city send Carter a letter requesting that he give to the board 86.5 acres in the neighborhood that he owned "to be developed and used as a Negro park, subject to the approval of the City Council." The next year, Carter appeared before the city council and formally presented them with the parcel. Some 30 to 35 acres of this land was the actual lake, but the rest could be used for the park itself or sold as residential lots to help pay for the development of the park. In his short speech in front of the council, he remembered fondly that as a youth living in Bowie, he had once visited the old amusement park along the lake. He continued that he would be happy to do what he could to help the city develop the park, committing himself to "assist the city in fencing and landscaping the property to make it an attractive civic development." Such actions, impressive though they might seem, fit more into the tradition of local leaders in the New South acting more from a position of paternalism than from any effort to knock down the racial barriers erected by Jim Crow.[12]

Naturally, local concerns predominated in his philanthropic efforts, but at times distant causes took precedence, such as when France and Italy struggled to feed themselves in 1947; Carter donated six thousand 100-pound bags of flour (from Fort Worth of course). Even so, these efforts paled in comparison to those exerted on behalf of his community. The question remains: what do the Flood Relief Fund, the Good Fellows Fund or any of Carter's philanthropic activities tell us about his philosophy of philanthropy in his attempt to modernize Fort Worth? While Carter is not always explicit in his correspondence about his motivation for giving, one must look at his whole body of work. His preeminent goal was to promote not only his own interests but also those of the city of Fort

Worth. Running through his written and verbal philanthropic statements is a clear theme: he wanted Fort Worth to continue growing and become a major center of business and industry, and part of this effort meant enhancing the quality of life of its citizens. As has been demonstrated, this was balanced by a giving spirit that was not always publicly visible. It could be argued that few persons have ever held the level of devotion to a city that Carter held for Fort Worth; philanthropy meshed easily with this commitment, and as he wrote to a Dallas banker, "Fort Worth should take care of its own." As national as his outlook could be, Carter's goal was always Fort Worth progress.[13]

Though determined to keep his philanthropic efforts local, Carter could not help but be inundated with requests for donations from companies and individuals outside of Fort Worth. Mr. Octave Proer, a resident of Jumet, Belgium, wrote him in 1950 requesting that Carter purchase his property, which had been badly damaged in an air raid in the Second World War and was liable to be sold at public auction. Denied, but still desperate, Proer wrote again, this time offering to sell Carter a 1715 Stradivarius that had been handed down by his grandfather. Carter's answer remained the same. Proer's request was just one of countless appeals to Carter for assistance: from a Czech refugee in Canada hoping to start her own business creating artistic lampshades; from a twenty-five-year veteran of the Royal Navy who desperately needed a car but had spent most of his savings taking care of his aged mother; a plea from Tel Aviv for a new work truck. Sometimes the petition was minor, as in the case of L. Viney from Boscombe, England, who, after having read a profile of Carter in an English newspaper, requested only a copy of the *Star-Telegram*. Existing records do not reveal whether or not this specific request was fulfilled, but financial requests were always denied, though as gently as possible. Requesters could typically expect to receive a typed letter that assured them that their missives had been read, and though "nothing would give me greater pleasure than to be able to reply to these requests," it would be "financially impossible to do so" because of the sheer volume. Not surprisingly, these letters typically came flooding in after the sender had read something about Carter and his generosity. A *Time* profile might do wonders for his boosting efforts, but it also required effort (by either him or Ms. Deakins) to read and respond with the understandable answer: no. By 1952, these requests had become so common and numerous that Carter refused to appear on the *Garry Moore Show*, a CBS production. This came soon after *Time* had run an updated page-length profile of the philanthropist, triggering a flood of new requests. "Each time anything of this nature is done," Deakins wrote on his behalf, "he is besieged with every conceivable type of solicitation for funds, and help and crackpots, until he has definitely made up his mind never to appear on anything again."[14]

While Carter enjoyed providing assistance to local institutions and individuals, his passion for western art did not wane. By 1946, thanks to his oil wealth, he already possessed seven Remington paintings and bronzes, including the famous oil painting *A Dash for the Timber* and the large bronze sculpture *Coming through the Rye*. His Russell collection at that time was much larger, consisting of fifty-three bronzes and over forty watercolors and oils. Such a large collection could not be housed in his relatively modest home in Rivercrest, so many could be found hanging in his offices at the *Star-Telegram* or in his suite at the Fort Worth Club. Of course, with so many pieces, it was impossible for him to display all that he had in his possession. Carter's largest acquisition came in 1952 when he purchased the famous Mint Saloon collection of Russell pieces. This famous group of eighty watercolors, drawings, oils, and sculptures, found at the old Mint Saloon in Great Falls, Montana, showcased some of Russell's best, and in some cases, rarest, works. Already looking ahead to the opening of a museum, he knew he would probably never see, Carter purchased the entire collection through the Carter Foundation in 1952 for a whopping $165,000. It is not difficult to see why Carter lavished such attention on cultivating his already vast collection, especially the Russells. Russell believed he provided an accurate portrayal of the West; after all, he lived there for much of his adult life, and even spent eleven years as a cowboy as a young man. Western artist Maynard Dixon stated that for Russell, "Natural fact and historical accuracy were his aims; imagination, interpretation—a recreation of the subject matter—to him were nonsense." Such a perspective nicely intersected with Carter's own view that life was, in the main, not too complex. He lived what he believed to be a straightforward life of plain-speaking, existing strictly within social and cultural expectations; he preferred his art do the same.[15]

It was not as if Carter only owned the western art of Remington and Russell; apparently age not only mellowed his personality but also broadened his palate. To be fair, he was never going to be a connoisseur of modern or even impressionist art. That would be left to his daughter Ruth. But he did purchase some nineteenth-century European artists such as Emile Brisset, a Frenchman who specialized in oils, and a British watercolorist named George Henry Andrews. A particular favorite appears to have been Jean-Baptiste Lallemand, an eighteenth-century French landscape artist, since he owned no fewer than four of his pieces. It is of course possible that since these purchases came from his personal account, they could have been for his wife, Minnie. In a letter to the gallery owner, David Findlay, Katrine Deakins, Carter's faithful secretary, mentions these paintings along with some western pieces that were to be charged to the Carter Foundation. It stands to reason that the foundation purchased art for his hoped-for museum, while his personal account was to be used for purchases that would decorate the home. After all, Minnie was, by all accounts, not fond of western art and reportedly did not allow him to hang these pieces at home.[16]

Consumed as he was with philanthropic efforts and appeals, Carter still found time to continue efforts to lure national companies to set up operations in Fort Worth, including General Motors. Carter began working to lure General Motors to Fort Worth in 1935 in the middle of his campaign to canalize the Trinity River and secure PWA funding for Fort Worth. From time to time, Carter discussed with William Knudsen, executive vice president of General Motors, the possibility of reopening a defunct Chevrolet plant on Camp Bowie Boulevard in west Fort Worth. Coincidentally, Carter mentioned, Camp Bowie became Bankhead Highway, Fort Worth's link to West Texas, El Paso, and California. Dallas had its benefits with its perceived eastward-oriented culture, but Fort Worth, gateway to the Great Plains, had access to the markets of West Texas and beyond.[17]

The old Chevrolet plant was mostly vacant except for a portion that Frigidaire rented as a distribution center. Carter proposed two methods for General Motors to maximize their benefits from the building; the company could use it either as an assembly plant or as a distribution center. The city of Fort Worth recently had presented the latter option to General Motors, but the corporation declined, citing "unfavorable sentiment on the part of the citizenship of Dallas." Carter wrote, "This feature . . . was greatly exaggerated." A move from Dallas would actually be beneficial for General Motors, and Carter pointed to the Frigidaire Corporation as evidence. Frigidaire had been using the Fort Worth location for seventeen years, the most recent two as the distribution headquarters for northern Arkansas, North Texas, and eastern New Mexico.[18]

In case Knudsen and General Motors were concerned about freight rates, Carter sought to diminish whatever fears they might have had. He cited a recent study by the Traffic Department of the Fort Worth Chamber of Commerce showing an advantage by Fort Worth to twice as many points when compared to San Antonio, Dallas, and Houston. Because Fort Worth was the "railroad and transportation center of the Southwest," the city could afford to be in this advantageous system. In case Knudsen was unaware of the transportation statistics,

Carter provided them for him. Fort Worth had nine trunk-line railroads, nineteen rail outlets, and twenty-five motor freight lines. In addition to this, American Airlines had recently moved its southwestern headquarters to Fort Worth from Dallas. Also, Tarrant County, of which Fort Worth was the county seat, had a modern highway system that was well connected to nearby federal highways. From Carter's point of view, it was clearly beneficial for General Motors to reopen in Fort Worth, especially from a transportation perspective.[19]

As the owner of Carter Publications, Carter knew what appealed to large corporations when considering a move. Cutting costs was attractive, but many corporations were also interested in the quality of life in the new location. Carter loved enhancing Fort Worth's reputation, and he took advantage of a long letter to continue this practice. Fort Worth had a burgeoning population, was an oil center, had a large meatpacking presence, and a business-friendly, businessman-run city government. In addition to these physical positives, Fort Worth was a healthful city with one of the lowest death rates among Texas cities.[20]

Carter then moved to items directly related to General Motors by writing that a move to Fort Worth would not affect General Motors' sales. He maintained that people bought General Motors because of the name, not because they were located close by. Carter cited a recent traffic count conducted by Fort Worth near the proposed location, pointing out that nearly twenty thousand cars had passed in the space of one day with probably double that number of people in the automobiles. A General Motors presence would be great advertising for the company and would also be a central location for car dealers. Having presented Knudsen with an apparently invincible argument, Carter asked him if he was "going to continue carrying the meal in one end of the sack and the rock in the other merely because it has been a habit in the past? Or, will you go with the tide and move to Fort Worth, thereby taking advantage of the large investment you have here and, at the same time, be closer to the territory in Texas which is showing the greatest growth and development?"[21]

Having thrown down the gauntlet, Carter waited for a response. Unfortunately for Carter and Fort Worth, General Motors did not feel a pressing need to uproot its headquarters in Dallas and move to Fort Worth. This did not stop Carter from continuing to correspond with the company's employees. The next year, 1936, witnessed Carter scrambling for funds to pay for Fort Worth's Frontier Centennial, the Carter-driven response to the Texas Centennial in Dallas. In April of that year, Carter wrote Knudson again, and R. H. Grant, general sales manager for General Motors, about possibly advertising and setting up an exhibit at the Frontier

Centennial. In case General Motors was concerned that the Frontier Centennial was to compete with Dallas, Carter assured them that it was not. This centennial celebration was entertainment only, with no educational or scientific exhibits.[22]

Carter knew that General Motors had already committed to the Texas Centennial in Dallas, and he felt it would only be fair for General Motors to share some of their wealth with Fort Worth. Since the spirit and theme of the Frontier Centennial was the pioneer spirit that conquered the West, Carter believed that it would be highly appropriate for the pioneering company of General Motors to play some part in the proceedings. He proposed that General Motors construct their own building, provide their own exhibits, and put on whatever entertainment they saw fit. Whatever the cost of the exhibit was, General Motors would profit from being present at the Frontier Centennial.[23]

Carter proposed to furnish the land for the building if General Motors purchased $50,000 in 4 percent bonds that the city of Fort Worth was selling. Their main expense would be the construction and entertainment costs. The possibility of the bonds not being paid was slim because it was assumed that the Billy Rose spectacle would pay for the whole $750,000 in bonds. Carter was confident that attendance would be sufficient to cover everyone's costs; the Dallas show was estimated to attract over ten million people, and Fort Worth could expect to get at least half of those people. Finally, Carter told of one last advantage for General Motors. As there would be few if any exhibits to compete with, the General Motors exhibit would easily become the must-see building.[24]

General Motors declined to be as involved in the Frontier Centennial to the extent that Carter had hoped. Grant believed there would be too much overlap between the Fort Worth and Dallas celebrations and that the amount of money General Motors would have to spend would be too extravagant. However, General Motors did agree to be a major sponsor of the Frontier Centennial and also sponsored radio broadcasts of various events at the festival. Businessman that he was, Carter accepted this decision by General Motors and was happy to have them agree to sponsor a small part of the festivities. However, one wonders whether Carter believed his proposal was feasible. Clearly he must have known what General Motors' response would be, considering their present position in Dallas. It is possible that Carter never expected General Motors to mull over his proposition but only hoped to get some smaller amount from them. If that was the case, he was very successful.[25]

Amon Carter neglected to woo General Motors for the next nine years as he pursued other interests that he deemed more important. But, in 1944, Carter contacted Alfred P. Sloan, then CEO of General Motors, and John Thomas Smith, the company's vice president, and renewed his efforts to bring the company back to Fort Worth. His reasoning was that the economic status of Fort Worth had improved considerably in the last nine years. Again he was rebuffed, though General Motors did consider the offer a little more carefully this time. Instead, the company opted to build a plant for Buicks, Oldsmobiles, and Pontiacs in Kansas City. However, General Motors stated that future operations in Fort Worth might be a possibility, depending on the growth the Southwest underwent.[26]

Carter restrained himself from pursuing General Motors for an automobile plant for three years. In 1947, Carter wrote Paul Garrett of General Motors about a "railroad friend" who reported that General Motors was looking to build another assembly plant. Whether this was true or Carter was just seeking a way of bringing the topic up once more is up for debate, but the method worked. Carter told Garrett that Sloan had offered to build a plant in Fort Worth if freight rates would allow General Motors to ship as cheaply from Fort Worth as they could from St. Louis or Atlanta. Carter promised that if General Motors built a factory in Fort Worth, the city would arrange for friendlier freight rates.[27]

It would be another three years before General Motors made any more overtures to Fort Worth. Apparently Carter's attempt at bringing rumors to life had failed. However, by 1950, General Motors was serious about opening a plant in Fort Worth, and Carter began discussions with local railroads about freight rates, which had been the stumbling block to previous endeavors to bring General Motors to the city. D. V. Fraser, president of the Missouri-Kansas-Texas Railroad, wrote Carter concerning a conversation regarding General Motors they had had at a prior banquet. Fraser informed Carter that the railroad was offering rates at a price that would make Fort Worth an attractive site for General Motors. Not only that, but Fraser promised Carter that he would "help fulfill your ambition to locate the General Motors plant in Fort Worth." F. G. Gurley, president of the Atchison, Topeka and Santa Fe Railway, reported to Carter that he was discussing freight rates with the proper people in his company. He added that his was the last major railway on which General Motors had failed to place a plant. This would make the negotiations with General Motors much easier, as they would want to solidify their position by being located on all major American railways.[28]

Armed with these affirmations of railway assistance, Carter contacted Sloan one more time. Though he had invited General Motors twice before, Carter believed that this invitation would not slip by unheeded. His reasoning was that Fort Worth had grown considerably since his last push for a General Motors plant. Automobile registration in the Southwest region was booming, Fort Worth's labor force was increasing, and there were now over five times as many manufacturing employees as there were in 1940. More importantly, Carter claimed there were over two hundred thousand General Motors cars sold in the Fort Worth area in 1949. In addition to these facts, Carter presented Fort Worth as a large city with the heart of a small town, always ready to "run out the welcome mat for General Motors."[29]

During the fall of 1950, Carter instructed the Fort Worth Chamber of Commerce to draw up a report for General Motors detailing reasons why it would be a good decision for them to build a plant in Fort Worth. Included in the brief were two suggested locations that were along the Santa Fe Railway. Carter also asked Gurley, president of Santa Fe Railway, to contact Charles Wilson, president of General Motors, with positive information regarding Santa Fe and its freight rates. In December 1950, Amon Carter, along with William Holden, executive vice president of the chamber and former mayor of Fort Worth, traveled to Detroit to present the brief to General Motors. After the introduction of this latest report, General Motors began seriously considering the possibility of building a factory in Fort Worth.[30]

Carter continued exerting pressure on General Motors officials, hoping that this would persuade them that Fort Worth was a worthy site for an assembly plant. He was no longer concerned that they use the property located on Camp Bowie Boulevard because he was now touting a 2,000-acre tract south of Fort Worth that he happened to own. In a token of goodwill, Carter informed Garrett, vice president of General Motors, that he would be willing to sell the land at cost. However, Carter was open to the idea of the factory being located elsewhere, specifically along either the Rock Island Railroad (Chicago, Rock Island and Pacific Railroad) or the Santa Fe Railway. General Motors had something else in mind, however.[31]

After months of examination, and pressure from Arlington mayor Tom Vandergriff, General Motors purchased a 255-acre site in Arlington, Texas, halfway between Fort Worth and Dallas. The land was located along US Highway 80, a well-traveled road on which the plant would have high visibility. Not only was it not located on any land Carter owned, but it was also located along the Texas and Pacific Railway line, which went against Carter's previous suggestions. The site was purchased by the Buick-Oldsmobile-Pontiac Assembly Division, though "future plans for use of the property depend upon availability of materials for construction." Once it was clear that General Motors was moving to Arlington, Carter began decreasing his involvement with the project. In addition to this,

his deteriorating health and time spent in and out of hospitals prevented him from inserting himself further into the situation.[32]

Though Vandergriff succeeded in his efforts to bring General Motors to Arlington, Carter received much of the credit from other city leaders for bringing General Motors to Tarrant County. William Holden, the executive vice president of the Fort Worth Chamber of Commerce, invited E. C. Klotzburger, the future plant manager for General Motors, to Fort Worth for discussions on the relationship between the city and the corporation. In his letter, Holden praised Carter for his extensive efforts to bring General Motors to the area. Because of his patience and perseverance, he stated, six thousand North Texans would owe their employment to Carter. When General Motors broke ground on May 27, 1952, Carter was rewarded with turning the first shovel of dirt, an honor he had performed numerous times at other ceremonies.[33]

An analysis of correspondence between Carter and General Motors officials reveals that he rarely diverged from his straight-forward attempts at persuasion. Though no mention of his canal plans appears, it is possible that its proposed benefits entered his mind at some point. General Motors blamed their unwillingness to build in Fort Worth on high freight rates, something Carter believed could be reversed with the Trinity Canal. Though it took sixteen years to be partially successful, Carter was determined to bring General Motors to Fort Worth, a resolve that epitomized his highly optimistic worldview and sheer stubbornness. Both characteristics could readily be seen in other areas, of course, especially in his devotion to developing the Trinity River and his efforts to see a world-class airport constructed for Fort Worth.

Until 1945, the federal government did little work on the Trinity River. In February 1945, John Fouts saw fit to detail what the government had done regarding the Trinity River. Congress had authorized the Trinity soil and water conservation program, begun work on flood control by assisting in the building of lakes, and begun reclaiming formerly uncultivated land along the river for agricultural use. Though these were definitely steps in the right direction, Fouts still urged Carter to continue pressuring politicians to begin making the Trinity navigable from Liberty to Fort Worth. By 1948, the Corps of Engineers had begun work on four reservoirs on the Upper Trinity River. Carter's role in persuading the government of the necessity of the lakes earned him the right to preside over a couple of the groundbreaking ceremonies. Carter liked nothing more than to add to his silver spade collection from his numerous groundbreaking ceremonies, and to be able to assist in the opening of work that promised to make his dream a reality was to him a worthy reward. At the groundbreaking for Benbrook Lake just southwest of Fort Worth, Carter described for the crowd the ample benefits that the lake would bring. Imagine, he told them, the "cool cottages . . . the bathers . . . the boats . . . and the black-mouthed bass." Beyond these recreational advantages, he claimed the lake would prevent flooding in Fort Worth, provide water during drought, and, most dramatically, send industrial goods to the Gulf.[34]

At the fourth and final groundbreaking at Garza-Little Elm Reservoir, Carter rejoiced because this was the crowning reservoir for the Upper Trinity. Now, he said, soil conservation and flood control could begin in earnest, floods would no longer endanger cities and towns downstream, and farmers could begin cultivating previously unusable bottomland. Carter noted that in the near future, work was to begin on dredging the Lower Trinity from the Houston Ship Channel to Liberty. All that was needed was Congress's approval to begin the canalization of the rest of the Trinity.[35]

Satisfied that the federal government appeared to be committed to the idea of a navigable Trinity River, Carter spent considerable time asking local businessmen to continue giving to TIA. His gift for salesmanship that was developed in the chicken and bread business and the selling of picture frames continued to work as Fort Worth businesses responded positively to Carter's letters. Donating money, he touted, was a "most excellent business investment" that the region's "best citizens" would see as a wise move. Carter updated recipients on the status of the Trinity project, especially noting the millions of dollars the government was spending building reservoirs and working on soil conservation. Donors included national businesses like the local Coca-Cola Bottling Company, Southwestern Bell, and Gulf Oil. Local businesses like Cox Dry Goods Company, Chickasaw Lumber, and Washer Brothers also contributed to the TIA. Contributions ranged from $25 to $1,000, depending on the size of the company and the level of benefits it might receive from a navigable Trinity.[36]

Carter later noted that an improved Trinity would probably have saved Fort Worth from the devastating effects of the 1949 flood. Though construction on the reservoirs was under way in 1949, they were nowhere near complete, and the flood cost the city millions of dollars in damages and the loss of several lives. In addition to preventing future floods, the whole improvement program was an "efficient" and "democratic" development program, he argued. It was democratic because TIA had worked so long with Congress and finally earned that body's approval as well as that of several other federal agencies; it was efficient because work was under way conserving the soil and preventing future flooding. These aspects, combined with the government's imminent work on making the Trinity navigable from Liberty to Fort Worth, made contributing to the TIA a worthy investment from Carter's perspective. Sadly for Carter, his death came before he witnessed any future work on the Trinity Canal. Even if he had continued living well past the 1950s, it is doubtful that his efforts would have succeeded. The government began to view the project with alarm because millions of dollars were being spent with few results. Though the project did not die with Carter, the Trinity Improvement Association lost its most ardent advocate.[37]

Inevitably, the question will arise as to why this effort, failure that it was, is worth discussion. What relevance does it have to Carter's achievements if there never was a Trinity Canal? First, though the canal never became a reality, Carter's work resulted in some benefits for Fort Worth and North Texas. The Dallas–Fort Worth region now had lakes such as Benbrook Lake, Lewisville Lake, and Grapevine Lake to serve as recreational and flood control facilities. Also, a serious soil conservation program was begun in which farmers along the Trinity learned ways to prevent erosion while simultaneously being able to reclaim fertile bottomland. Finally, this project demonstrates the passionate devotion of Carter to his adopted city and to his state. Nowhere in the TIA correspondence did Carter appear to be chasing visions of grandeur for himself, though he was certainly guilty of perceiving his city as a kind of western Valhalla where cowboys and entrepreneurs were glorified as rugged individualists dominating their respective landscapes.

Cooperation with Dallas over the Trinity issue was starkly contrasted with the grudging realization that there would probably never be any agreement on a shared airport. Some development had occurred at the Midway site during the war when runways were paved for possible use by the military, but little more had been done. But in the years immediately following the war, Dallas continued to invest in expanding Love Field, while Fort Worth began to purchase land six miles south of downtown for a larger airport that could replace Meacham. All of that changed suddenly in October 1947 when the Fort Worth City Council revealed that it had been in talks with CAA officials and American, Braniff, and Delta Airlines to construct its own airport at the Midway site, to be named the Greater Fort Worth International Airport. City officials believed that even if it was solely owned and operated by Fort Worth, its location would make it the dominant airport in the region. The airlines and the CAA loved the location for economic and administrative reasons. Dallas, of course, was stunned, seeing this proposed airport as a direct threat to Love Field, but there was little it could do but hope to persuade the larger airlines not to abandon it. Groundbreaking for the terminal, facing west of course, did not take place until July 1950, but when it did, Fort Worth officials were determined to honor Carter for his commitment to bringing aviation to the city. In response to a petition signed by 172 "leading citizens," the city council moved to name the airfield and the administration building after Carter. In front of a crowd of nearly five hundred present for the groundbreaking ceremony, John Carpenter, president of the Dallas Chamber of Commerce, spoke warmly of Carter's contributions and called him "not only a citizen of Fort Worth and Texas, but one of the great Americans and the great men of the world." Carter, understanding that the success of Dallas and Fort Worth required cooperation, predicted somewhat presciently that in the future, "you won't know when you leave one [city] and enter the other." The rivalry, it seems, was neither perpetual nor permanently desirable. And as important as local issues were to the man now known by many as Mr. Fort Worth, it often seemed as if his passions increasingly took him far away from North Texas.[38]

On the national stage, Roosevelt's death in April 1945 forced Carter to forge relationships with new presidents. The postwar era witnessed Carter's older Washington-based friends leaving and new personalities being ushered in. Gone were the days when he could rely on men like Jesse Jones, Morris Sheppard, John Nance Garner, and, soon, Tom Connally. Though often at odds with Roosevelt over the more liberal aspects of the New Deal, he remained good friends with the president both for the benefits he could gain and his genuine desire for friendship. Without Roosevelt, one might expect Carter to indulge himself in the niceties of life and enjoy his twilight years, but he clearly was endowed with too strong of a boosterish personality to refrain from further political activity. Loyal Democrat that he was, he attempted to establish a firm friendship with Harry S. Truman, but was not able to curry the same favor with him as he was with Roosevelt. His acquaintance with Eisenhower blossomed into friendship during the late 1940s, and by the early 1950s, Carter became one of his most outspoken supporters. At the state level, Carter built upon the support he had given to Lyndon Johnson in 1941, and guaranteed that he would always have a voice in Washington by ensuring positive coverage from the *Star-Telegram* during and after Johnson's notorious senate run in 1948.

If Carter expected the Truman administration to cease the liberal trends begun under Roosevelt, he was sorely disappointed, and he let the president know of his displeasure with the administration's generally prolabor policies. Initially Carter attempted to ingratiate himself with Truman, going so far as to send the president a *Star-Telegram* editorial praising his support for streamlining and reorganizing duplicate government departments in the wake of World War II. When Truman appointed Averell Harriman, a former associate of Carter's in the early days of American Airlines, as his secretary of commerce, Carter commended the president for "selecting the right man for the right place at the right time." Carter's early belief that "America is extremely fortunate in having a competent, hard-hitting, square shooter at the helm" was soon replaced by disdain. In response to a United Auto Workers strike at General Motors plants in late 1945, Truman concurred with the union that "a company's earnings are relevant in wage disputes." In a letter to Truman, Carter wholeheartedly disagreed with him on the grounds that this would negatively impact a business's ability to save money or reinvest the money in the company, since workers could claim an increasingly greater share of the profits. "If all profits earned above a meager return to stockholders are paid out in wages and salaries," he argued, "it is a foregone conclusion that all business and industry will suffer, the progress of the nation will be retarded, and even the employees themselves will be injured in the long run." Foreseeing the impending backlash to the Wagner Act that culminated in the passage of the Taft-Hartley Act, he stated, "I do not believe the labor problem will be solved until the Wagner Act is amended so as to make labor and management equally responsible."[39]

Carter's opposition to Truman's prolabor position paled in comparison to his antagonism toward the administration's position on the tidelands oil issue. The controversy began when, in 1946, Truman vetoed a bill that would have given states ownership of offshore oil resources, and then accelerated when the Supreme Court ruled the next year against California's "claim to ownership of the oil-rich land off its shores from low tide to three leagues." The state of Texas claimed that it was exempt from the ruling due to its special status as having been an independent republic for nearly a decade. During the 1948 presidential election, Truman expressed what many interpreted as support for Texas's claim to the tidelands, stating during the campaign that "Texas is in a class by itself; it entered the Union by treaty." It became obvious after he won the election that Truman had no intention of recognizing Texas's claim, and soon thereafter the United States attorney general filed suit against the state. His actions against Texas's interests made it clear that this issue would influence Texas's position during the 1952 presidential campaign.[40]

As a conservative Democrat and Texas oilman, Carter firmly believed in Texas's claim to the tidelands and used the *Star-Telegram* to publicize his stance.

The administration's suit against Texas prompted Carter to order a chain of editorials defending Texas, an action repeated in 1952 when Truman vetoed a bill guaranteeing state ownership of the tidelands. Hoping to wield some direct influence on the White House, Carter wrote Truman before the passage of the bill and after his veto, arguing as other Texans had that one of his motivations in supporting the bill was his "deep interest in behalf of the school children of Texas, who would be the prime beneficiaries from the legislation." In an appeal to national defense, he argued that federal ownership of the mineral resources in the tidelands was delaying drilling because "the cost of finding and producing oil in the submerged area is so great that no one can be expected to undertake it while the present cloud of uncertainty remains." He wrote, "This result is one that could be of dire import if the nation should be plunged into a major war in the next few years." In his blunt manner, Truman responded succinctly to both pieces of correspondence, generally summing up his position as follows: "I am sorry to have to tell you the Texas viewpoint is not mine. I think those offshore oil reserves belong to the whole United States and that every State in the Union has an interest in them." Having taken such a stand, Truman ensured he would get no support from Carter or from many other Texans in the 1952 election.[41]

Carter's falling-out with Truman over the tidelands spurred his interest in supporting Eisenhower in his run for president in 1952. Carter was good friends with Eisenhower, a friendship that began in 1945 when the two met while Carter was in war-torn Europe. Though Eisenhower was a Republican and Carter, like most southerners at the time, was a lifelong Democrat, this did not stop Carter from loudly supporting him in his run for the presidency. This was not as odd a pairing as it might appear. For decades a one-party state, Texas was undergoing a political shift, and the state's support for Eisenhower during the 1950s was the first sign that the Democratic hold on the state was slipping. In his biography of Carter, Jerry Flemmons speculates that Carter and his friend Sid Richardson, oil magnate and Eisenhower confidant, talked Eisenhower into running for president while sailing on Carter's yacht, the *West Texan,* on Eagle Mountain Lake in late 1951 or early 1952. This seems unlikely, considering that in none of their correspondence did Eisenhower, Richardson, or Carter refer to this event, and Eisenhower did not even hint at this alleged interaction in his memoirs. Lady Bird Johnson claimed that Richardson paid a visit to Eisenhower apparently to pressure him into running, but could not remember "whether Amon Carter did or not." Her account meshes with the fact that many of Eisenhower's friends had been pressuring him to run for president since 1948, originally as a Democrat, so it is much more likely that Richardson and Carter were just two of many individuals pushing him to seeking the presidency—though not necessarily on the *West Texan* on Eagle Mountain Lake. Privately, Eisenhower was a Republican, and he supported Thomas Dewey in 1948, though he refused to publicly endorse the candidate. Biographer Stephen Ambrose notes that Eisenhower, "anticipating a Dewey victory, followed by Dewey's re-election in 1952 . . . believed that he had finally put politics completely behind him." But "that dream was shattered on election night, 1948," since "Truman's upset of Dewey thrust [Eisenhower's] name back into the forefront of politics."[42]

Though he was not actively pursuing the presidency of the United States in 1948, Eisenhower did accept an offer to become president of Columbia University that same year. The smattering of conversations between Carter and Eisenhower increased during this time, with phone calls and long letters moving back and forth between the two men. Well aware of Carter's philanthropic efforts, Eisenhower dangled in front of Carter the possibility of leaving behind some legacy at an institution like Columbia. "I personally think that the most magnificent kind of family memorial that any man of wealth could leave behind him would be an edifice or series of scholarships in a great university such as Columbia," he said enticingly. In another letter to Carter, he wrote, "I do hope that you will continue to give some thought to Columbia and the suggestions that I made to you concerning it." Some portions of his letters to Carter hint at developing a political platform, even as early as 1949. "The problem of our day and time," he mused, "is how to distinguish between all those things government must do now in order to perpetuate and maintain freedom for all—freedom from economic as well as political slavery—while, on the other hand, we combat remorselessly all those paternalistic and collectivistic ideas which, if adopted, will accomplish the gradual lessening of our individual rights and opportunities and finally the collapse of self-government." As a conservative Democrat who had grown tired of the increasingly liberal positions of the Truman administration, Carter could approve these words. Still, Eisenhower had a difficult time understanding Carter's obsession with the Trinity Canal. During a trip to Fort Worth, he attended a Chamber of Commerce meeting with Carter where he heard discussion of the project. From his recollection, "It was implied that the Federal Government should prosecute that Project energetically." How could Carter, someone who was "definitely opposed to unnecessary Federal intervention in state and local matters," support such a measure "merely because it promises temporary local advantage," he wondered. Regardless, such questions about his political philosophy did nothing to damage their friendship, and Carter positioned himself as one of Eisenhower's most steadfast Texas supporters.[43]

By 1952, the pressure on Eisenhower to run as the Republican nominee for president mounted, and he finally agreed to enter the party's primaries though he was now serving as the commander of the North Atlantic Treaty Organization (NATO). The *Fort Worth Star-Telegram* was the first paper in Texas to endorse him for president, publishing an editorial in February 1952 urging people to support Eisenhower as the candidate who could "appeal to the vote of those who make no fetish of party loyalty and who look to the man rather than the party." As a paper that had endorsed Democratic candidates without fail, such words were high praise and somewhat ironic. Carter, ever aware of the necessity of informing candidates of his unwavering support, sent Eisenhower a copy of the editorial and received in return a short note from a grateful Ike. "I shall always be proud that I have a friend of the warmth and courage of Amon Carter," he remarked, "for I realize that it takes courage in the South to go full out for any other than an avowed Democrat."[44]

As the 1952 campaign heated up, Carter and the *Star-Telegram* continued their support for Eisenhower. It must be stated that in the context of Texas politics this may seem odd, given the state's history as a Democratic stronghold, but Carter was not out of step with other members of the Texas political establishment. When the Democratic Party nominated liberal Adlai Stevenson from Illinois as their candidate, many other Texas Democrats shifted their support to Eisenhower, especially since he "promised to 'return' the tidelands to Texas and respect states' rights in general." This promised support for Texas's cause in the tidelands debate combined with his general popularity gave Eisenhower 53 percent of the Texas vote in the November election. Even when prominent Democrats Estes Kefauver, J. William Fulbright, and Paul Douglas, noticing the impending defeat of their candidate, fired off a last-minute telegram to Carter begging him to "write the largest possible check today," he refused to give any aid to the national Democratic Party. Eisenhower was his friend and candidate, and old party loyalties did little to sway his opinion. That being said, too much should not be made of Carter, or other Texas Democrats, supporting Ike the Republican. At the state level, Carter still endorsed Democratic candidates, and at no point were there any signs that he was prepared to begin pouring money into what was then a relatively defunct Texas Republican Party.[45]

As close as Carter was to Eisenhower, two things prevented him from exploiting having a close personal friend in the White House who shared most of his core beliefs. First, due to his death in June 1955, there was little time for Carter to establish a strong working relationship with the new president. His health began deteriorating in 1953 and the vigor with which he pursued his favorite causes was no longer present, thus diminishing his chances of making any great gains for his city. Second, while he did enjoy a warm friendship with Eisenhower, Carter did not have the same extensive network within the Republican Party as he did in his own Democratic Party or even a large measure of influence over the president personally. There was no serious state-level Republican Party in Texas for Carter to work with, and at the national level, most of Carter's longtime political friends and acquaintances were Democrats. As has been shown, his far-flung system within the Democratic Party ensured a fairly successful run for Carter during the Great Depression and World War II, but now that was gone, leaving him much less powerful within the corridors of power, though not without a friendly legislator as can be attested by his support of Lyndon Baines Johnson.

Carter's association with Lyndon Johnson began in 1941 when he first ran for the United States Senate in a hotly contested race against Governor Pappy O'Daniel. Senator Morris Sheppard died in April 1941, and O'Daniel, mulling a possible run for the seat himself, immediately named Sam Houston's eighty-six-year-old son, Andrew Jackson Houston, to the seat, knowing he would be much too weak to run in the special June election. Johnson, a strongly pro–New Deal, pro-Roosevelt congressman who had represented the 10th Congressional District in Central Texas since 1937, quickly entered the Democratic primary race, having gained O'Daniel's false promise that he would stay out. The governor changed his mind, prompting a hard-fought race on both sides, with Carter firmly supporting the young Hill Country representative. Sid Richardson, a Johnson confidant and financial backer, asked Fort Worth attorney Ray Buck, on retainer for American Airlines since its founding, to manage the Johnson campaign in a triangular region spanning from Tarrant County to Childress almost to El Paso (an area that, surely deliberately, was also the region where the *Star-Telegram* was widely read). Before long, Johnson asked Buck to arrange a meeting with Carter, since, in the words of Mr. Buck, "one of his vital objectives was to gain the friendship and support" of Carter. In a 1969 interview, Buck claimed that even though Carter generally expressed reluctance to get involved in campaigns "either personally or through his newspapers," he made an exception in this case in large part due to Johnson's persistence and persuasive skills. Though Buck was a close friend of Carter's who played dominoes with him every afternoon around five o' clock, he was clearly mistaken about this supposed reluctance, considering his long history of political action through the pages of the *Star-Telegram* and his own personal actions as a Democratic Party fund-raiser and delegate. Regardless, Buck evidently had reason to believe the publisher might hesitate to support Johnson and thus decided the best course of action would be to introduce him to Johnson without warning over drinks and a game of dominoes. One afternoon in 1941, Buck brought Johnson to the Fort Worth Club suite of Dr. Hodges McKnight, whose rooms adjoined Carter's, expecting full well that he would come in at the expected hour. Sure enough, Carter appeared in the suite on time, and Buck promptly introduced him to Johnson. Johnson immediately began talking to Carter, and according to Buck, "had made a friend and supporter of him" in half an hour. Asked if he remembered what the conversation was about, Buck replied that while he did not remember the specifics, he did "distinctly remember that Lyndon had his face within about twelve inches of Carter's face all that time."

Evidently Carter was unperturbed by Johnson's violation of traditional personal space and delivered on his promise to support Johnson's campaign. Two pro-Johnson *Star-Telegram* editorials stand out: one praising Johnson for his unwavering support for Roosevelt in national defense preparations, and a second excoriating O'Daniel for his demagoguery and insulting manner. As Election Day, June 28, came and went, it looked as if Johnson had pulled off a stunning victory over the popular, homespun persona of O'Daniel. Carter wired his congratulations to Johnson, comparing his apparent victory to that of David over Goliath, or even of TCU quarterback Davey O'Brien. The praise was premature, however, as over the next few days, votes trickled in from O'Daniel's East Texas base, enough to give him the victory by July 1. Fraud being evident on both sides, there was little Johnson could do to strike back at O'Daniel, and he emerged from the fight "convinced . . . as never before that politics was a dirty business in which a willingness to be more unprincipled than your opponents was a requirement for success." As for Carter's support for him, Johnson was grateful, writing him that "when a man of your affairs" supports a young candidate like himself, "there is not much a youngster can say except 'thank you very much.'"[46]

Johnson reemerged to run for the Senate in 1948, this time in a quest to replace the increasingly unpopular O'Daniel. His major opponent in the Democratic primary was former governor Coke Stevenson, a conservative who opposed New Dealism in general and the resurgent liberalism of the Truman administration in particular. Once again, Carter threw his support behind Johnson, who was running as something of a nationalist conservative, seeing in him a candidate who was more gifted than Stevenson at knowing how to ensure the continued flow of federal dollars into Texas. He was not alone among the Texas establishment in seeing something in Johnson. George and Herman Brown, of Brown and Root defense contractors, and Carter's friend and wealthy oil magnate Sid Richardson were among the many affluent Texans who, along with Carter, helped finance Johnson's campaign.

As Johnson maneuvered himself into position to run for the Senate, he voted for the Taft-Hartley Act and to override Truman's veto, two positions that ensured him the support of men like Carter. A string of editorials published in the *Star-Telegram* lauded Johnson for his "independent voting record" and his moderate votes on labor issues. Once again, Johnson was involved in a close race, this one much more hotly contested and clearly more fraudulent than the last. This time, however, Johnson was determined that he would win, and win he did, though most historians attest that determining the clear-cut winner in such a race is nigh impossible. As Johnson prepared to take his seat in the Senate, he wrote Carter a letter explaining how much he felt he owed him for his victory. "I just want to express to you my sincerest gratitude and appreciation for your unbroken and unwavering friendship and support," he gushed, "without which my success this year would have been impossible." "When a firm hand was needed to steady the ship," Carter "supplied it." When Johnson "steered too close to impetuous and intemperate action," Carter "pulled him back." Finally, Johnson was grateful for the favorable correspondents Carter assigned to his campaign and to editor Bob Hicks, whose "editorializing proved him a better strategist than most professional campaign managers." Granted, Johnson's victory hinged on much more than Carter's support, but he recognized that the man and the paper that had supported him for the Senate twice in seven years could provide him much more than he could ever produce for Carter. A wily politician, Johnson needed to ensure that he had a solid base on which he could rely to prevent the rise of any challengers. Having the largest newspaper in Texas at one's back was an insurance policy he could not take for granted. Carter, on the other hand, could now rest knowing that Texas once again had two solid senators who could act, to a certain extent, as his voice in Washington.[47]

For the first few years of Johnson's Senate career, Carter leaned on him for numerous favors, many of them relatively small. When Carter became aware of official statements being sent to American newspapers from the Rumanian legation lauding the "liberation" of the nation by the arrival of Soviet forces, he wrote Johnson hoping that he could influence the State Department to "call a halt to the crap of this kind." Johnson the Cold Warrior promptly forwarded the letter to the State Department but was told that in the interest of demonstrating freedom of the press, no action would be taken. Another example of his tendency to bog down the senator with small problems was Carter's request for a greater pipe allotment from the Petroleum Administration for Defense (PAD) for oil drilling. In this case, Johnson spoke with PAD administrator Bruce Brown and succeeded in getting Carter what he desired.

This period in Carter's life marked a shift from his actions of the previous decade and a half. With the Truman administration faced with a struggling economy and the heating of the Cold War, there was little desire to begin another round of New Deal spending. The reallocation of federal dollars for other projects meant there was little else for Carter to fight for beyond his usual tilting at the Trinity Canal windmill. In addition, Carter severed his connection with Johnson due to a dispute over the 1952 presidential election. As campaigning got under way, Johnson had no choice as a Democrat but to support Adlai Stevenson in his bid, thus losing his once warm friendship with Carter. Once again, Carter demonstrated that, at least for him, politics and friendship could sometimes make for a horrible combination. During the 1952 presidential campaign, Johnson not only campaigned with Stevenson, but accompanied him unannounced on a campaign visit to Fort Worth, or Carter's "fiefdom" as Lady Bird called it. In a much later interview, she remembered with a hint of sadness that Carter "was Lyndon's longtime friend and supporter, and I remember many good exchanges with him right up until about the time when Lyndon didn't go to see him and kind of ask his permission to keep on being a Democrat and support Adlai Stevenson." In a later interview, she expanded on this theme, remarking that losing Carter's friendship, which "had been a very good friendship, filled with admiration and respect on Lyndon's part and, I think, on Amon Carter's . . . was one of the saddest episodes of this sad fall."[48]

Despite his poor health, Carter found the time and energy for one last political fight in 1954. Jim Wright, the thirty-one-year-old "boy mayor" of Weatherford, Texas, and future speaker of the house, dared to challenge one of Carter's favorite congressmen, incumbent Wingate Lucas of the 12th Congressional District, in the Democratic primary in 1954. Lucas was not a formidable politician on his own, but he had Carter's support. Elected to Congress in 1946, Lucas became one of Carter's "rubber stamps" in Washington, ensuring that the publisher continued to have a vote on Capitol Hill. Once, when an obscure tax bill came up for a vote in the House, Lucas voted against the wishes of Carter. What the tax bill was or whether Lucas supported it is not known from the existing correspondence, but his vote angered Carter. Lucas wrote a letter to Carter apologizing for not having consulted with him first. After all, he wrote, "the only purely political action" he had ever taken "was done after consulting" Carter. A contrite Lucas sought to soothe Carter's displeasure by assuring him that he had never "consciously done anything as Congressman from our District that I thought you would disapprove" and that he would continue to seek Carter's approval.[49]

This being the case, clearly running against Lucas meant running against Carter, and Wright was determined to enter the fray. On July 22, 1954, the *Star-Telegram* published a front-page editorial entitled "The Voters Know Lucas' Record, but Where Does Wright Stand?" Up to this point, Carter and the *Star-Telegram* had ignored Wright's candidacy, but an apparent groundswell of support for the man attempting to overthrow the reigning figure in Fort Worth caused Carter to make a preemptive strike. The editorial accused Wright of refusing to voice his opinion on issues such as foreign aid and scoffed that "he is for avoiding atomic war . . . Who isn't?" According to the editorial, Lucas had greater political experience and had always "voted with sturdy independence for what he thought was best for the state and nation." Carter's lackey had evidently been transformed into a man of great conviction.[50]

Wright swiftly responded to this editorial with an "Open Letter to Mr. Amon G. Carter and the *Fort Worth Star-Telegram*" and spent $974.40 of his own money to take out a large ad in the *Star-Telegram*. When the newspaper's advertising manager asked Carter if the ad should be run, Carter simply asked if Wright's check was good; the check was good, and the ad was run. Wright told Carter, "You have at last met a man . . . who will not bow his knee to you and come running like a simpering pup at your beck and call." He added, "It is unhealthy for ANYONE to become TOO powerful . . . TOO influential . . . TOO dominating. It is not good for Democracy. The people are tired of 'One-Man Rule.'" Wright's main complaint against Carter was his refusal to cover Wright's campaign fairly and objectively. According to Wright, he had spoken out on many political issues with clarity and depth, something Carter's "private errand boy Congressman" had never done. Wright pointed to a recent rally for his campaign with nearly one thousand people in attendance that the *Star-Telegram* had covered. Carter had the story buried and reportedly "gave it less space than an obituary of some Chinese laundryman who once passed through Fort Worth."[51]

In his younger years, Carter might have taken these affronts much more seriously, but age seemed to have softened some of his earlier irascibility. The *Star-Telegram* published an editorial countering Wright's remark on the opposite page, and Carter also wrote an open letter to Wright. The *Star-Telegram* defended itself by saying that the paper had fairly treated Wright. His rally was not covered because it was a paid event; if it had been advertised as a campaign-opening rally, he would have received the proper coverage. The editorial claimed that Wright had been asked for specific ideas regarding Eisenhower's farm program, yet he had not been able to come up with any solutions to the problems he perceived. Regarding Wright's statements accusing Carter of having a stranglehold on what Fort Worthians could read, the editorial responded that the *Star-Telegram* would not be so successful if it had a history of covering up the truth.[52]

Amon Carter's personal letter was more conciliatory than the editorial. Writing after Wright's victory in the primary, Carter was full of congratulations and good wishes. However, he did respond to the allegations that he had his own personal congressman. According to Carter, he had only phoned Lucas three times and had never written him. A couple of the phone calls addressed funding for the Benbrook Dam, and one call came amid rumors of layoffs at the Consolidated Vultee plant. Research shows that Carter either suffered from memory loss or had a very selective memory. The aforementioned letter from Lucas to Carter implies that there were frequent conversations between Lucas and Carter, mainly consisting of Carter giving Lucas advice. The bill to which Lucas referred, though not specifically named, clearly did not refer to Benbrook Dam or Consolidated Vultee. Also, there is at least one existing wire from Carter to Lucas asking him to push H.R. 2319 pertaining to the unification of the armed forces. Evidence shows that Carter was much more involved in the legislative duties of Lucas than he remembered or cared to admit.[53]

Amid postwar philanthropic and political activities, and though permanent marital bliss had previously remained out of Carter's grasp, in 1947 he married his third wife, Minnie Meacham Smith. The daughter of former Fort Worth mayor and department store owner Henry Meacham and the widow of Glen Smith appeared to be a natural match for Carter, given her family's elite status. Her background being what it was, she circulated among the city's elite, and marrying Carter sealed her future as one of Fort Worth's leading ladies. Having attained political influence and great wealth, Carter had nothing to gain in marrying Smith. It appears that his marrying Smith, twenty-four years his junior, was based on a desire for companionship. As in his previous marriages, correspondence between the two is scarce, leaving it difficult to assess the relationship. What can be gleaned from existing documents is that the Carters thoroughly enjoyed their position in society, taking trips to Europe, continuing friendships with the nation's celebrities, and consistently circulating among Fort Worth's elite circles.

Oddly enough, the friendship that Carter developed with Nenetta upon their son's capture during World War II did not wane with his new marriage, though understandably their correspondence slackened. Their mutual interest in the success of the Carter Foundation as well as Nenetta's shares in Carter Publications ensured the former couple would continue to remain cordial. In addition, their shared memory of Amon Jr.'s imprisonment helped forge a bond between the couple, and the tension that was once present dissipated in the postwar years. When one of their son's fellow prisoners wrote a book in 1946 titled *Diary of a Kriegie* (a self-descriptive term used by ex-prisoners of war), she sent Amon a copy and remarked, "It tells much of what happened at Stalag III-A that Amon Jr. never did tell." Though there was much about Amon that Nenetta disliked, she did not seem to lose her admiration for the man. When, in 1953, Fort Worth named its new international airport after Carter, she wrote, "It is such a great tribute to you in every way, Amon, and again and again I am proud of the name of Carter." Having retained her married name and never remarried, her identity was still largely intertwined with her former husband's identity and accomplishments.[54]

Amon continued to remain close to his children, and seemed content to see both Amon Jr. and Ruth married and formally out from under his roof. Amon Jr. settled into his position as his second-in-command at Carter Publications and by all appearances adapted quickly to the demands placed on a media empire heir. Ruth married Fort Worth native J. Lee Johnson in 1946 and then lived for a time in South Bend, Indiana, where her husband studied law at Notre Dame before moving back to Fort Worth and settling into his law practice. But while domestic affairs with his two children and with Nenetta flourished, the same could not be said for his relationship with his oldest daughter, Bertice.[55]

Bertice had always had a strained relationship with her father extending back to her time at preparatory school and well into adulthood. Her marriage to her first husband, Harry Kay, collapsed, as he never seemed to be able to find a way to make a decent living. Having moved to Dallas in the late 1930s, Bertice entered the world of radio, where she worked for WFAA, the radio arm of the *Dallas Morning News,* during World War II, reporting on women's news under the name "Diana Dale." While working for WFAA, she met the station's foreign correspondent, Hugh Speck; they married in 1944. For unknown reasons, Carter did not particularly care for Speck, causing tension between father and daughter. Her querulous nature and general lack of maturity and self-confidence must have also bothered Amon. Her correspondence with her father by the late 1940s reveals a very insecure woman who made much of every slight, real or perceived, and yearned for constant affection from Amon. It appears their relationship was in constant flux, with periods full of a flurry of communication and visits interspersed with spells of drought usually brought on by Bertice's feeling isolated from the rest of the family. She believed, not without reason it seems, that she had become the "family pariah," a feeling exacerbated by Amon's inclusion of Ruth's husband, J. Lee Johnson, in the business affairs of Carter Publications. To make matters worse, she struggled with her weight and with alcohol abuse, both of which continued to take their toll on her health as she got older. Liver problems brought on by her alcoholism resulted in repeated hospital stints to try to revive her flagging health. During one stay in the hospital, she attempted to reassure her father: "Don't worry that I won't live up to the rules as laid down. They have me convinced that my life depends on the way I live, rest and no worrying." Sadly, liver disease took its toll on Bertice, and in September 1952, after ten days in the hospital, she passed away with Carter at her side. For the first time since his father died in 1915, he was confronted with the death of a close family member, but extant records do not reveal his reaction to losing his daughter.

Though he received a glowing health report from his doctor in 1951, Carter's health rapidly deteriorated over the next few years, much of it due to heart disease. He was first placed in St. Joseph Hospital for an extended period in spring 1953, where he spent over seven weeks recovering from what was rumored to be a stroke but turned out to have been two heart attacks. His son hastily denied it, saying that "Dad has just been run down and he is resting for a few weeks in the hospital." Word of this setback could not, of course, be prevented from spreading among a select few insiders. Oilman Clint Murchison wrote Lyndon Johnson, "Our mutual friend in Fort Worth who is a little miffed with you has had a heart attack. They are keeping it very, very confidential, so don't quote me and don't repeat it please." A concerned Johnson reached out to Carter, encouraging him to "relax a little and do just about what the men of medicine order you to do." When Fort Worth's Greater Southwest International Airport was finally dedicated that year in April, Carter had to be content with watching the proceedings on television from his hospital room. His ill health did more than impact his ability to attend ceremonies, however, as it also prevented him from mounting a vigorous campaign in support of a Tarrant County location for the proposed Air Force Academy. A younger, healthier Carter may not have been able to persuade Department of Defense officials to choose the shores of Grapevine Lake northeast of Fort Worth over Colorado Springs for the Academy, but he certainly would have waged a much stronger campaign.[56]

By June 1955, it was clear that Carter had failed to fully recover from his previous heart attacks, thus doctors ordered him to remain at home after his recent New York trip to attend the Associated Press and American Newspaper Publishers Association meetings. On June 23, two days after it was reported that Carter was at his home in Rivercrest suffering from a "critical illness," he passed away in his home at 8:20 P.M. The outpouring of grief at his passing and praise for his life was instantaneous and, by all accounts, a genuine expression of admiration and respect from all quarters. From President Eisenhower on down, government officials profusely extolled Carter's efforts to boost Fort Worth and Texas for much of his adult life. Lyndon Johnson, despite their recent falling out, took to the Senate floor to memorialize Carter the next day. Calling him "one of the great moving forces of our time," he noted that even though Carter was commonly known as "Mr. Fort Worth," "the impact of his personality was felt beyond the borders of Texas." In private, he wrote Amon Jr. that "despite differences we have had the last few years, I have always considered him among my closest friends and among those who have given me major inspiration." He then enclosed a copy of his recent remarks from the Senate floor on Carter's death, noting that they "came from the heart."[57]

Texas governor Allan Shivers wired the Carter family that his "drive and personality" enabled him "to do great things for his beloved Fort Worth and for his state." Prominent New Dealers like John Nance Garner and Jesse Jones added their statements to the sympathetic chorus. Dallasites, generally his competitors during his decades-long rivalry with Fort Worth's eastern neighbor, were unanimous in their acclaim for his accomplishments. Mayor R. L. Thornton called him a "gladiator" and a brilliant leader, while John Carpenter declared that he "Ranked with the top statesmen and business men." Celebrities and other public figures who had developed friendships with Carter mourned his death, including comedian Edgar Bergen, boxer Gene Tunney, and orchestra leader Paul Whiteman. Publisher that he was, it was fitting that others in the industry, like Arthur Sulzberger and Henry Luce, each contributed statements of consolation to the Carters' ever-growing pile of telegrams.[58]

As might well be expected for the man many called "Mr. Fort Worth," Carter's funeral on June 25 took on the air of a state funeral, with much of the city closing that day in his honor. Many downtown stores shut down at funeral time, and Texas Christian University, longtime Carter beneficiary, cancelled classes on that day. Two days later, with flags throughout the city flying at half-staff, what were reported to be "the largest crowds of mourning" ever seen in

Fort Worth visited his grave site at Greenwood Cemetery just west of the city's central business district. Cemetery officials observed that "hundreds of cars were waiting" at 6:30 the morning of his graveside tribute, and by the day's end, an estimated fifteen thousand people had paid their last respects to Carter, whose grave was "blanketed with a 60-foot cross" of flowers as well as orchids from the Eisenhowers and a Shady Oak hat made of flowers contributed by Broadway producer Billy Rose.[59]

Carter's philanthropic practices, only recently organized, garnered greater attention upon his death, for his will revealed much about his philosophy of philanthropy. Many telegrams that poured in to his family mentioned his generosity, and the public learned more about what Carter believed about giving. His will, filed for probate on July 1, contained a long statement from Carter, which is best described as his shortened version of Andrew Carnegie's *Gospel of Wealth*. "As a youth," he remembered, "I was denied the advantages which go with the possession of money and, therefore, I am endeavoring to give to those who have not such advantages but who aspire to the higher and finer attributes of life those opportunities that were denied me." Clearly, as much as he had fond memories of his childhood, the sting of having to begin work at such a young age still lingered. And even in death, his Texas identity still prevailed. "I am a part of the heritage of Texas," he proudly proclaimed, and, "its pioneer spirit that peopled the wide spaces and laid the foundations of a happy future comes down to me in the strain of the blood, and I wish to share it with others who would make Texas their home and their inspiration." The Carter Foundation's generosity, it should be no surprise, would be limited to within Texas's borders. "I have come to realize," he mused, "that they who acquire wealth are more or less stewards in the application of that wealth to others of the human family who are less fortunate than themselves." Carter admitted that "money alone, nor broad acres . . . nor estates of oil and gas" can "bear testimony to the fine quality of man or woman." Since "the grave is a democracy for all of human kind," he contended that the wealthy should not "refuse to heed the pleading voice of humanity," but understand that true happiness "comes from doing good to others." Carter's declaration was obviously meant for posterity and to ensure a positive legacy for his life, but at the same time, it is clear that he was putting into words what he had been doing over the latter portion of his life.[60]

And what to do with all that western art? Carter's will made official the idea of opening a museum, to be named the Amon G. Carter Museum of Western Art, to showcase his grand collection. Its importance to the deceased publisher is evident by the fact that he preferred that establishing the museum be one of the first projects undertaken by the foundation. Appropriately, he wished for it to be built next door to the Will Rogers Memorial Coliseum, a complex that served both as a shrine to his long-dead friend and as a monument to his own boosting capabilities. Not only would the museum be operated as a nonprofit initiative, but it was also to be perpetually free to all comers: a lasting reminder of his philanthropic desires as well as his genuine love for "his" city.[61]

Much can and should be made of Amon Carter's contributions to Texas's transition into urban modernity, a transition mirrored by the details of his own life. His contemporaries understood the contributions he had made throughout his life, and obituaries around the nation noted the many industries and institutions that came to Fort Worth as a result of his efforts. During his tenure, he helped lead his adopted hometown from a glorified market town to a major hub of business and commerce that truly served as a gateway city to West Texas. Carter was able to accomplish much of this by focusing his attention outward, understanding that in so doing, the state and national network he was building could and would ultimately help modernize Fort Worth. While verbally championing Texan concepts of individualism and self-help, he understood that his region's destiny would be shaped by its ability to fit into a much larger national network both politically and economically and, in many cases, by partnering with a more expansive federal government. This is not to say, however, that Carter was an altruistic man. His obituary in the *Star-Telegram* noted that "his passion for fostering and promoting this civic and regional interest was undoubtedly born of the realization that his own business could prosper only as Fort Worth and West Texas prospered." But where other civic boosters in the region might have narrowed their sights to building up themselves and their empires within the boundaries of their regions, Carter's expansive vision enabled him to become a nationally known figure, a fact that undoubtedly made him one of the most influential boosters of his time.[62]

NOTES

CHAPTER 1

1. *Fort Worth Star-Telegram,* June 24–25, 1956 (all quotations from June 25 issue); *Fort Worth Magazine,* July 1955.
2. Ben Proctor, "Amon Carter," in *The New Handbook of Texas,* ed. Ron Tyler (Austin: Texas State Historical Association, 1996), 1:998.
3. Ibid.
4. Randolph B. Campbell, "History and Collective Memory in Texas: The Entangled Stories of the Lone Star State," in *Lone Star Pasts: Memory and History in Texas,* ed. Gregg Cantrell and Elizabeth Hayes Turner (College Station: Texas A&M University Press, 2007), 271; Carl Abbott, *The Metropolitan Frontier: Cities in the Modern American West* (Tucson: University of Arizona Press, 1995), 179.
5. Blaine A. Brownell, *The Urban Ethos in the South, 1920–1930* (Baton Rouge: Louisiana State University Press, 1975), xix; "Personality," *Time* (February 25, 1952), 45; Patrick Cox, *The First Texas News Barons* (Austin: University of Texas Press, 2005), 3.
6. Edward F. Haas, review of *New Men, New Cities, New South: Atlanta, Nashville, Charleston, Mobile, 1860–1910,* by Don Doyle, *Journal of Southern History* 77, no. 4 (March 1991): 1370–71; George Green, *The Establishment in Texas Politics: The Primitive Years, 1938–1957* (Norman: University of Oklahoma Press, 1979), xi. The most recent biography of the father of the New South movement, Henry Grady, is Harold Davis's

Henry Grady's New South: Atlanta, a Brave and Beautiful City (Tuscaloosa: University of Alabama Press, 1990). On Richard Hathaway Edmonds, see Yoshimitsu Ide's dissertation, "The Significance of Richard Hathaway Edmonds and his *Manufacturers' Record* in the New South" (PhD diss., University of Florida, 1959).
7. Abbott, *Metropolitan Frontier*, xiii.
8. Ibid., 43–44.
9. Victoria Buenger and Walter L. Buenger, *Texas Merchant: Marvin Leonard and Fort Worth* (College Station: Texas A&M University Press, 1998), 143; Char Miller and Heywood T. Sanders, *Urban Texas: Politics and Development* (College Station: Texas A&M University Press, 1990), 18.
10. Samuel Kinch Jr., "Amon Carter: Publisher-Salesman" (Master's thesis, University of Texas at Austin, 1965); Jerry Flemmons, *Amon: The Life of Amon Carter, Sr., of Texas* (Austin, Tex.: Jenkins, 1978); Jerry Flemmons, *Amon: the Texan Who Played Cowboy for America* (Lubbock: Texas Tech University Press, 1998); Cox, *First Texas News Barons*; Mary L. Kelley, *The Foundations of Texan Philanthropy* (College Station: Texas A&M University Press, 2004).

CHAPTER 2

1. *Dallas Morning News*, May 16, 1955; David Minor, "Crafton, TX," *Handbook of Texas Online*, accessed December 4, 2016, http://www.tshaonline.org/handbook/online/articles/hncah; B. Jane England, "Wise County," *Handbook of Texas Online*, accessed December 4, 2016, http://www.tshaonline.org/handbook/online/articles/hcw14; Cliff Donahue Cates, *Pioneer History of Wise County: From Red Men to Railroads—Twenty Years of Intrepid History* (St. Louis, Mo.: Nixon-Jones,1907), 20.
2. *Time*, February 25, 1952, 45; "Texas, County Marriage Records, 1837–1977," database with images, *FamilySearch*, accessed March 7, 2016, https://familysearch.org/ark:/61903/1:1:QV14-CSV1; Amon Carter to Mrs. J. P. Hagler, Nov. 29, 1937, Box 36, Amon Carter Personal Activities File, 1937, Amon G. Carter Papers, Special Collections, Mary Couts Burnett Library, Texas Christian University, Fort Worth, Texas (hereafter cited as AGC Papers, Burnett Library); Victor J. Smith, *The State of Texas Book: One Hundred Years of Progress* (Austin: Bureau of Research and Publicity, 1937), 247; Flemmons, *Amon*, 39; Rondel V. Davidson, "La Reunion," in *The New Handbook of Texas*, http://www.tshaonline.org/handbook/online/articles/uel01. Further research on Josephine Ream Carter indicates that reports of her past at La Reunion are inaccurate. According to the *New Handbook of Texas*, the colony at La Reunion was dissolved in the late 1850s and was completely broken up by 1860. Josephine was born in 1859 in Arkansas and still lived there when the 1860 census was collected.
3. Josephine Carter to Mary Bondred, June 20, 1880, Box 45, Josephine Carter File, AGC Papers, Burnett Library.
4. Alva Johnston, "Colonel Carter of Cartersville," *Saturday Evening Post*, November 26, 1938, 31; Frank X. Tolbert, "On Amon Carter and the Bells," *Dallas Morning News*, May 16, 1955.
5. Johnston, "Colonel Carter of Cartersville," 31.

6. Johnston, "Colonel Carter of Cartersville," 31; Fort Worth Petroleum Club, *Oil Legends of Fort Worth* (Fort Worth: Taylor, 1993), 93.
7. Carter to Hagler, Nov. 29, 1937, Box 36, Amon Carter Personal Activities 1937, AGC Papers, Burnett Library; Ream Family Bible, AGC Papers, Burnett Library.
8. Carter to Hagler, Nov. 29, 1937, Box 36, AGC Personal Activities 1937 File, AGC Papers, Burnett Library; Kinch, "Amon Carter: Publisher-Salesman," 8; *"Personality," Time*, 45.
9. Melvin E. Fenoglio, ed. *Story of Montague County, Texas: Its Past and Present* (Montague County, Tex.: Curtis Media, 1989), 52; "Queen's Peak," *New Handbook of Texas*, 5:384; "Race Rider," unpublished manuscript, n.d., Box 36, AGC Personal Activities, 1938 File, AGC Papers, Burnett Library.
10. Johnston, "Colonel Carter of Cartersville," 31; Flemmons, *Amon*, 40.
11. Fenoglio, *Story of Montague County*, 52; Flemmons, *Amon*, 41; Johnston, "Colonel Carter of Cartersville," 31; "He Kept Faith With City, West Texas," *Fort Worth Star-Telegram*, June 24, 1955.
12. "Knife Board," unpublished manuscript, n.d., Box 37, Amon Carter Personal File 1938, AGC Papers, Burnett Library.
13. Ibid.; U.S. Bureau of the Census, 1900 Census; Johnston, "Colonel Carter of Cartersville," 31.
14. Oliver Knight, *Fort Worth: Outpost on the Trinity* (Norman: University of Oklahoma Press, 1953), 218; "Personality," *Time*, 45.
15. Amon Carter to W. W. Ince, June 28, 1899, Box 108, W. W. Ince File, AGC Papers, Burnett Library; Amon Carter to W. W. Ince, Sept. 29, 1901, AGC Papers, Burnett Library; "Personality," *Time*, 45; "Carter's Talk," July 3, 1903, Box 35, File 18, AGC Papers, Burnett Library.
16. "Carter's Talk," July 3, 1903.
17. Ibid.
18. Zetta Carter/Amon Carter Divorce Petition, Box 35, Amon Carter Personal Activities 1920–1923; Amon Carter to W. W. Ince, Sept. 29, 1901, Box 108, W. W. Ince File, AGC Papers, Burnett Library.
19. Flemmons, *Amon*, 44; W. J. Graham and A. L. Utz to Amon Carter, Sept. 1, 1903, Box 35, File 18, AGC Papers, Burnett Library; W. J. Graham and A. L. Utz to Carter, Dec. 27, 1904, Box 35, File 18, AGC Papers, Burnett Library; Carter to J. Eppinger, May 13, 1905, Box 35, File 18, AGC Papers, Burnett Library; Edgar Swasey to Carter, May 35, 1905, Box 35, File 18, AGC Papers, Burnett Library.
20. Ty Cashion, *The New Frontier: A Contemporary History of Fort Worth and Tarrant County* (San Antonio: Historical Publishing Network, 2006), 24.
21. David R. Goldfield, *Cotton Fields and Skyscrapers: Southern City and Region, 1607–1980* (Baton Rouge: Louisiana State University Press, 1982), 90.
22. Knight, *Fort Worth*, 25.
23. Ibid., 82–86.
24. Ibid., 123–127; J'Nell L. Pate, *Livestock Legacy: The Fort Worth Stockyards, 1887–1987* (College Station: Texas A&M University Press, 1988), 21, 42.

25. Richard F. Selcer, *A History of Fort Worth in Black and White: 165 Years of African-American Life* (Denton: University of North Texas Press, 2015), 98, quotations on pages 138–39.
26. Cashion, *The New Frontier*, 24–26, "Personality," *Time*, 45; Johnston, "Colonel Carter of Cartersville," 32.
27. Michael Hooks, "The Struggle for Dominance: Urban Rivalry in North Texas, 1870–1910" (PhD diss., Texas Tech University, 1979), 52.
28. Kinch, "Amon Carter: Publisher-Salesman," 20–21.
29. Johnston, "Colonel Carter of Cartersville," 32; Knight, *Fort Worth*, 186–87.
30. Flemmons, *Amon*, 46–48; "Personality," *Time*, 45; Johnston, "Colonel Carter of Cartersville," 32.

CHAPTER 3

1. C. Vann Woodward, *Origins of the New South, 1877–1913* (Baton Rouge: Louisiana State University Press, 1951), 371; Kinch, "Amon Carter: Publisher-Salesman," 33; Brownell, *Urban Ethos in the South*, 47–48; Cox, *First Texas News Barons*, 6.
2. Richard Selcer, *Fort Worth: A Texas Original* (Austin: Texas State Historical Association, 2004), 58–63; United States Census, 1920.
3. Selcer, *Fort Worth*, 57; Knight, *Fort Worth*, 165–70; Rich, "Beyond Outpost," 201.
4. Selcer, *Fort Worth*, 61; Knight, *Fort Worth*, 184.
5. Diana Davids Hinton and Roger M. Olien, *Oil in Texas: The Gusher Age, 1895–1945* (Austin: University of Texas Press, 2002), 75–79.
6. Ibid., 79–90; Bryan Burrough, *The Big Rich: The Rise and Fall of the Greatest Texas Oil Fortunes* (New York: Penguin Press, 2009), 17.
7. Selcer, *History of Fort Worth*, 287–90; "Effort to Get Negro Followed by Riot," *Dallas Morning News*, May 16, 1913.
8. Michael Phillips, *White Metropolis: Race, Ethnicity, and Religion in Dallas, 1841–2001*, (Austin: University of Texas Press, 2006), 77; Herbert Shapiro, *White Violence and Black Response: From Reconstruction to Montgomery* (Amherst: University of Massachusetts Press, 1988), 113; *Memphis Commercial Appeal*, n.d., 9.
9. Kinch, "Amon Carter: Publisher-Salesman," 29, 33–35; Cox, *First Texas News Barons*, 96.
10. Kinch, "Amon Carter: Publisher-Salesman," 25; Cox, *First Texas News Barons*, 95; "Editorial Comment," *Editor and Publisher*, January 3, 1914; "Southwestern Progress," *Fourth Estate*, April 26, 1913; cover, *Fourth Estate*, May 19, 1913.
11. Louis J. Wortham to Carter, Oct. 2, 1916, Box 35, Amon G. Carter Personal File 1916–1919, AGC Papers, Burnett Library; Carter to Wortham, Oct. 5, 1916, Box 35, Amon G. Carter Personal File 1916–1919, AGC Papers, Burnett Library. J. Frank Norris was possibly the most controversial American fundamentalist preacher in the first half of the twentieth century. In 1912, he was accused of setting his own church (First Baptist Church of Fort Worth) on fire, though this was never conclusively proved. In the 1920s, he stood trial for murder and was acquitted. For more information on Norris, see Barry Hankins's *God's Rascal: J. Frank Norris and the Beginnings of Southern Fundamentalism* (Lexington: University of Kentucky Press, 1996).

12. Amon Carter to William Randolph Hearst, Dec. 31, 1918, Hearst File, Box 100, AGC Papers, Burnett Library; Carter to E. M. Swasey, Mar. 5, 1917, Correspondence File, Box 303, AGC Papers, Burnett Library.
13. Carter to J. A. Moore, Jan. 27, 1918, Correspondence File, Box 303, AGC Papers, Burnett Library; Moore to Carter, Jan. 29, 1918, Correspondence File, Box 303, AGC Papers, Burnett Library; Moore to Carter, Jan. 30, 1918, Correspondence File, Box 303, AGC Papers, Burnett Library; Carter to Moore, Jan. 30, 1918, Correspondence File, Box 303, AGC Papers, Burnett Library; Carter to Swasey, Apr. 15, 1918, Correspondence File, Box 303, AGC Papers, Burnett Library.
14. Joseph A. Moore to Amon Carter, Feb. 8, 1919, Hearst File, Box 100, AGC Papers, Burnett Library; David Nasaw, *The Chief: The Life of William Randolph Hearst* (Boston: Houghton Mifflin, 2000), 257, 281.
15. Moore to Carter, Mar. 11, 1919, Box 100, William Randolph Hearst File, AGC Papers, Burnett Library.
16. Moore to Carter, Dec. 16, 1921, Box 100, William Randolph Hearst File, AGC Papers, Burnett Library; Carter to Moore, Dec. 22, 1921, Box 100, William Randolph Hearst File, AGC Papers, Burnett Library.
17. Cox, *First Texas News Barons*, 95; Kinch, "Amon Carter: Publisher-Salesman," 37–39; Nasaw, *The Chief*, 315–16.
18. Johnston, "Colonel Carter of Cartersville," 34.
19. Kinch, "Amon Carter: Publisher-Salesman," 43–44.
20. *Fort Worth Star-Telegram*, June 24, 1955, 3; Kinch, "Amon Carter: Publisher-Salesman," 43–44.
21. Kinch, "Amon Carter: Publisher-Salesman," 40, 148; "Finest Newspaper Plant in Southwest Ready," *Editor and Publisher*, May 28, 1921.
22. Ibid., *Fort Worth Star-Telegram*, May 31, 1921.
23. Knight, *Fort Worth*, 194–95; Anthony Rudel, *Hello, Everybody! The Dawn of American Radio* (Orlando, Fla.: Harcourt, 2008), 46–50; Johnston, "Colonel Carter of Cartersville," 32.
24. Selcer, *Fort Worth*, 82; Knight, *Fort Worth*, 195; Michael Stamm, "Newspapers, Radio, and the Business of Media in the United States," *Organization of American Historians Magazine of History* 24, no. 1 (January 2010): 25; Clay Reynolds, *A Hundred Years of Heroes: A History of the Southwestern Exposition and Livestock Show* (Fort Worth: Texas Christian University Press, 1995), 126.
25. Kinch, "Amon Carter: Publisher-Salesman," 31.
26. Ibid., 31; *Fort Worth Star Telegram, Jr.*, January 6, 1915; *Fort Worth Star Telegram*, December 4, 1994; Sanders, *How Fort Worth Became the Texasmost City*, 156.
27. Pacific Region Finance Newsletter, June 1922, Box 227, YMCA File, AGC Papers, Burnett Library; *Fort Worth Star Telegram*, April 15, 1924.
28. Amon Carter to R. N. Watts, Sept. 20, 1922, Box 227, YMCA File, AGC Papers, Burnett Library; Amon Carter to Mrs. Winfield Scott, Mar. 14, 1923, Box 227, YMCA File, AGC Papers, Burnett Library; *Fort Worth Star Telegram*, March 29, 1925.
29. A. C. Best to Amon Carter, Feb. 6, 1911, Correspondence File 1902–1923, Box 303, AGC Papers, Burnett Library; Elks Lodge Tablet memo, n.d., Correspondence File

1902–1923, Box 303, AGC Papers, Burnett Library; "Southwestern Progress," *Fourth Estate,* April 26, 1913.
30. "The Commercial Club," *Fort Worth Daily Gazette,* June 27, 1885, 5; Irvin Farman, *The Fort Worth Club: A Centennial Story,* (Fort Worth: The Fort Worth Club, 1985), 36–37.
31. Leonard Sanders, *How Fort Worth Became the Texasmost City* (Fort Worth: Texas Christian University Press, 1986), 153–63; Selcer, *Fort Worth,* 62; Darwin Payne and Kathy Fitzpatrick, *From Prairie to Planes: How Dallas and Fort Worth Overcame Politics and Personalities to Build One of the World's Biggest and Busiest Airports* (Dallas: Three Forks Press, 1999), 13–15. Cal Rodgers did successfully make it across the United States, but it took him eighty-four days to do so, thus he was unable to claim the prize. He died a few months later in a plane crash in California.
32. Selcer, *Fort Worth,* 60; Knight, *Fort Worth,* 220; Johnston, "Colonel Carter of Cartersville," 8, 34.
33. Divorce Request, n.d., Box 35, Amon Carter Personal File, AGC Papers, Burnett Library.
34. Nenetta Carter, to Bertice Carter, n.d., Box 35, Amon Carter Personal File, AGC Papers, Burnett Library; Ruth McAdams, "Mudholes, Fairy Godmothers, and Choir Bells," in *Grace and Gumption,* ed. Katie Sherrod (Fort Worth: Texas Christian University Press, 2007), 95.
35. Bertice Carter to Amon Carter, n.d., Box 35, Amon Carter Personal File, AGC Papers, Burnett Library.
36. Amon Carter to Bertice Carter, Nov. 5, 1920, Box 35, Amon Carter Personal File, AGC Papers, Burnett Library.
37. Bertice Carter to Amon Carter, Dec. 10, 1914, Scraps Folder, Box 303, AGC Papers, Burnett Library; Amon Carter to Nenetta Carter, June 24, 1920, Amon Carter Personal File 1920–1923, Box 35, AGC Papers, Burnett Library.
38. W. H. Carter to Amon Carter, Jan. 27, 1909, Box 35, Amon Carter Personal File, 1906–1910, AGC Papers, Burnett Library; W. H. Carter to Amon Carter, Oct. 2, 1909, Box 35, Amon Carter Personal File, 1906–1910, AGC Papers, Burnett Library; W. H. Carter to Amon Carter, Dec. 8, 1911, Box 35, Amon Carter Personal File, 1911–1915, AGC Papers, Burnett Library;
39. W. H. Carter, to Amon Carter, Dec. 2, 1911, Box 48, William H. Carter File, AGC Papers, Burnett Library; Amon Carter, to W. H. Carter, Dec. 6, 1911, Box 48, William H. Carter File, AGC Papers, Burnett Library.
40. Amon Carter to Hettie Scott, Mar. 30, 1916, Box 48, William H. Carter File, AGC Papers, Burnett Library; The Carter Family Files in the AGC Papers, Burnett Library, contain this correspondence and provide excellent insights into the relationship between Amon and his stepmother.
41. Amon Carter to Roy Carter, May 24, 1916, Box 48, Carter Family File, AGC Papers, Burnett Library; Amon Carter to Roy Carter, May 29, 1916, Box 48, Carter Family File, AGC Papers, Burnett Library; Amon Carter to Roy Carter, July 22, 1916, Box 48, Carter Family File, AGC Papers, Burnett Library; Roy Carter to Amon Carter, Feb. 26, 1917,

Box 48, Carter Family File, AGC Papers, Burnett Library; Amon Carter to Roy Carter, May 21, 1918, Box 48, Carter Family File, AGC Papers, Burnett Library; Roy Carter to Amon Carter, May 25, 1918, Box 48, Carter Family File, AGC Papers, Burnett Library.
42. Addie Brooks, to Amon Carter, Sept. 29, 1912, Box 35, Amon Carter Personal File, AGC Papers, Burnett Library; Addie Brooks to Amon Carter, May 16, 1916, Box 48, Carter Family File, AGC Papers, Burnett Library; Amon Carter to Addie Brooks, May 18, 1916, Box 48, Carter Family File, AGC Papers, Burnett Library; Amon Carter to Mrs. W. H. Carter, Nov. 3, 1919, Box 48, Carter Family File, AGC Papers, Burnett Library.
43. Amon Carter to Mrs. W. H. Carter, Nov. 6, 1918, Carter Family File, AGC Papers, Burnett Library.
44. Johnston, "Colonel Carter of Cartersville," 8–9, 31; undated clip from *Pittsburgh Post*, Correspondence file, Box 303, AGC Papers, Burnett Library; Claude S. Fischer, "Changes in Leisure Activity," *Journal of Social History* 27, no. 3 (Spring 1994): 455; James Gilmore to Amon Carter, Sept. 14, 1914, Correspondence file, Box 303, AGC Papers, Burnett Library; Carter to Gilmore, Oct. 20, 1914, Correspondence file, Box 303, AGC Papers, Burnett Library.
45. Charles Comiskey to Amon Carter, Apr. 15, 1915, Correspondence file, Box 303, AGC Papers, Burnett Library; George S. Robbins, "Texas Calls to Sox; Four Teams to Florida," *Chicago Daily News,* February 4, 1919; *San Antonio Evening News,* October 7, 1919; Johnston, "Colonel Carter of Cartersville," 31. *San Antonio Evening News,* October 7, 1919.
46. Louis D. Rubin Jr., Review of *The Texas League: A Century of Baseball, 1887–1987,* by Bill O'Neal, *Southwest Historical Quarterly* 92, no. 2 (October 1988): 383; Charter Train Bulletins, Box 194, Special Trains File, AGC Papers, Burnett Library; *San Antonio Express,* November 16, 1922; Amon Carter to Calvin Coolidge, Mar. 23, 1925, Calvin Coolidge File, Box 63, AGC Papers, Burnett Library.
47. "Purely Personal," *Fourth Estate,* December 9, 1922; Golf scorecard, Nov. 22, 1914, Box 303, Scraps File, AGC Papers, Burnett Library.
48. Amon Carter to Mrs. Amon Carter, June 24, 1920, Box 35, Amon Carter Personal File, 1920–1923, AGC Papers, Burnett Library; Tarrant County, Texas, Tax Rolls, 1920.

CHAPTER 4

1. Contribution Receipt, Nov. 14, 1912, Correspondence File, Box 303, AGC Papers, Burnett Library; George N. Green, *The Establishment in Texas Politics: The Primitive Years, 1938–1957* (Norman: University of Oklahoma Press, 1984), 165.
2. Francis B. Simkins, *A History of the South* (New York: Alfred P. Knopf, 1963), 474, quoted in George Brown Tindall, *The Emergence of the New South, 1913–1945* (Baton Rouge: Louisiana State University Press, 1967), 232; Randolph B. Campbell, *Gone to Texas: A History of the Lone Star State* (New York: Oxford University Press, 2003), 369.
3. Norman D. Brown, *Hood, Bonnet, and Little Brown Jug: Texas Politics, 1921–1928* (College Station: Texas A&M University Press, 1984), 16–17; Campbell, *Gone to Texas,* 344, 358–59.

4. Campbell, *Gone to Texas*, 371.
5. Robert Rutland, "The Beginnings of Texas Technological College," *Southwestern Historical Quarterly* 55, no. 2 (October 1951): 231–33.
6. Ibid., 232–34; Brown, *Hood, Bonnet, and Little Brown Jug*, 142; *Fort Worth Star-Telegram*, August 29, 1923; *Fort Worth Star-Telegram*, November 9, 1924.
7. Rutland, "Beginnings of Texas Technological College," 234–36; Brown, *Hood, Bonnet, and Little Brown Jug*, 142–44.
8. Rutland, "Beginnings of Texas Technological College," 234–36; Pat Neff to Amon Carter, Feb. 19, 1923, Box 125, Pat Neff File, AGC Papers, Burnett Library; Carter to Neff, Feb. 23, 1923, Box 125, Pat Neff File, AGC Papers, Burnett Library; *Fort Worth Star-Telegram*, March 3, 1923; *Fort Worth Star-Telegram*, August 29, 1923; *Fort Worth Star-Telegram*, June 28, 1924; *Fort Worth Star-Telegram*, May 27, 1930.
9. Campbell, *Gone to Texas*, 348–352.
10. Brown, *Hood, Bonnet, and Little Brown Jug*, 218–19, 250.
11. Ibid., 270–71, 284–85.
12. Ibid., 292; Cox, *First Texas News Barons*, 168.
13. *Wichita Falls Record News*, November 28, 1925.
14. Brown, *Hood, Bonnet, and Little Brown* Jug, 272–73; *Dearborn Independent*, February 27, 1926.
15. *Dallas Morning News*, December 1, 1925.
16. *Fort Worth Press*, December 1, 1925.
17. Sidney Hardin to Amon Carter, Dec. 2, 1925, Box 78, Ferguson File, AGC Papers, Burnett Library; H. M. Marks to Amon Carter, Dec. 1, 1925, Box 78, Ferguson File, AGC Papers, Burnett Library; Edward Jordan to Amon Carter, Dec. 25, 1925, Box 78, Ferguson File, AGC Papers, Burnett Library; *Miami Tribune,* December 12, 1925; Pat Neff to Amon Carter, Dec. 2, 1925, Box 78, Ferguson File, AGC Papers, Burnett Library; P.M. Horn to Amon Carter, Dec. 5, 1925, Box 78, Ferguson File, AGC Papers, Burnett Library.
18. *Fort Worth Star-Telegram,* January 26, 1926.
19. Campbell, *Gone to Texas*, 375.
20. Brown, *Hood, Bonnet, and Little Brown Jug,* 354–55, 358; Paul Lucko, "A Missed Opportunity: Texas Prison Reform during the Dan Moody Administration, 1927–1931," *Southwestern Historical* Quarterly 96, no. 1 (July 1992): 45.
21. John B. Rae, "Financial Problems of the American Aircraft Industry, 1906–1940," *Business History Review* 39, no. 1 (Spring 1965): 106–7.
22. *Dallas Morning News,* February 6, 1928; November 1, 1928; February 10, 1929.
23. Darwin Payne and Kathy Fitzpatrick, *From Prairie to Planes: How Dallas and Fort Worth Overcame Politics and Personalities to Build One of the World's Biggest and Busiest Airports* (Dallas: Three Forks Press, 1999), 40–41; Robert J. Serling, *Eagle: The Story of American Airlines* (New York: St. Martin's Press, 1985), 11–12, 15–16.
24. Amy Henderson, "Media and the Rise of Celebrity Culture," *Organization of American Historians Magazine of History* 6, no. 4 (1992): 49; "Shady Oak Fading After Shining Hours," *Nashville Tennessean,* March 11, 1965.

25. "Paris Day by Day," *Charleston Gazette,* September 17, 1924; "Once Overs," *San Antonio Light,* June 6, 1933; "New York Day by Day," *Waterloo Courier,* April 1, 1929; "New York Day by Day," *Waterloo Courier,* June 15, 1928.
26. Amon Carter to W. W. Richardson, Dec. 20, 1923, Box 119, O. O. McIntyre File, Amon Carter Papers, Burnett Library; O. O. McIntyre to Amon Carter, n.d., Box 119, O. O. McIntyre File, Amon Carter Papers, Burnett Library
27. Adam Fairclough, *Better Day Coming: Blacks and Equality, 1890–2000* (New York: Penguin Books, 2001), 149–50.
28. Undated newspaper clipping, Box 156, Will Rogers 1923–1925 File, Amon Carter Papers, Burnett Library; Ben Yagoda, *Will Rogers: A Biography* (New York: Knopf, 1993), 276.
29. Don Graham, *State Fare: An Irreverent Guide to Texas Movies* (Fort Worth: Texas Christian University Press, 2008), 14–16.
30. Gary Clayton Andersen, *Will Rogers and "His" America* (Boston: Prentice Hall, 2011), 116–17; H. L. Mencken, *Thirty-Five Years of Newspaper Work: A Memoir by H. L. Mencken* (Baltimore: Johns Hopkins University Press, 1994), 171–75.
31. Ibid., 174–75, 177–79.
32. Ibid., 176–77.
33. Graham, *State Fare,* 14–16.
34. Darwin Kingsley to Amon Carter, November 18, 1928, Box 222, West Texas 1921–1938 File, Amon Carter Papers, Burnett Library.
35. Amon Carter to Darwin Kingsley, November 26, 1928, Box 222, West Texas 1921–1938 File, Amon Carter Papers, Burnett Library.
36. Brian Hart, "George Lewis Rickard," in *New Handbook of Texas* ed. Ron Tyler, Douglas E. Barnett, and Roy R. Barkley (Austin: Texas State Historical Association, 1996), 5:576–77; *Dallas Morning News,* April 22, 1926; *Dallas Morning News,* January 9, 1929.
37. Transcript of Amon Carter broadcast on WBAP radio, Feb. 1, 1923, Correspondence File, Box 303, AGC Papers, Burnett Library; Harry Kay to Amon Carter, n.d., Box 45, Bertice Carter File, AGC Papers, Burnett Library.
38. Ruth McAdams, "Mudholes, Fairy Godmothers, and Choir Bells," in *Grace and Gumption: Stories of Fort Worth Women,* ed. Katie Sherrod (Fort Worth: Texas Christian University Press, 2007), 96.
39. Individual Income Tax Return For Calendar Year 1928 including Schedule C, Income Tax File, Box 108, AGC Papers, Burnett Library.

CHAPTER 5

1. Jesse Jones to Amon Carter, Nov. 1, 1935, Box 34, File 7, AGC Papers, Burnett Library (first quotation); Johnston, "Colonel Carter of Cartersville," 8.
2. Roger Biles, "The Urban South in the Great Depression," *Journal of Southern History* 56, no. 1 (February 1990): 72 (first and second quotations).
3. *Fort Worth Star-Telegram,* October 30, 1929; *Dallas Morning News,* October 30, 1929.
4. *Dallas Morning News,* April 27, 1930; *Fort Worth Star-Telegram,* July 15, 1930.

5. Amon Carter to Ross Sterling, Aug. 24, 1930, Box 195, Ross Sterling File, AGC Papers, Burnett Library; Campbell, *Gone to Texas*, 380.
6. Lionel V. Patenaude, *Texans, Politics, and the New Deal* (New York: Garland, 1983), 2–4.
7. Victoria Buenger and Walter L. Buenger, *Texas Merchant: Marvin Leonard and Fort Worth* (College Station: Texas A&M University Press, 1998), 74; Paul Mason, *The First: The Story of Fort Worth's Oldest National Bank* (New York: Newcomen Society in North America, 1977), 8.
8. Johnston, "Colonel Carter of Cartersville," 35; J. M. Davis to Amon Carter, Feb. 20, 1930, Box 78, First National Bank Run File, AGC Papers, Burnett Library.
9. *Fort Worth Record-Telegram*, February 19 1930; *Dallas Morning News*, February 19, 1930; Carter to Will Rogers, Feb. 19, 1930, Box 156, Will Rogers 1930 File, AGC Papers, Burnett Library.
10. Campbell, *Gone to Texas*, 378.
11. Betty Rogers, *Will Rogers* (Norman: University of Oklahoma Press, 1979), 244; Selcer, *History of Fort Worth*, 170.
12. Carter to Herbert Hoover, June 11, 1930, Box 104, Herbert Hoover File, AGC Papers, Burnett Library (first and second quotations); Charles M. Dollar, "The South and the Fordney-McCumber Tariff of 1922: A Study in Regional Politics," *Journal of Southern History* 39, no. 1 (February 1973): 45.
13. Carter to Hoover, Jan. 15, 1931, Box 104, Herbert Hoover File, AGC Papers, Burnett Library.
14. Ibid.
15. Campbell, *Gone to Texas*, 381; Knight, *Fort Worth*, 211; Selcer, *Fort Worth*, 77.
16. Will Rogers, *Will Rogers' Daily Telegrams*, Vol. 3: *The Hoover Years, 1931–1933*, ed. James M. Smallwood and Steven K. Gragert (Stillwater: Oklahoma State University Press, 1979), 192; Norman D. Brown, "Garnering Votes for 'Cactus Jack': John Nance Garner, Franklin D. Roosevelt, and the 1932 Democratic Nomination for President," *Southwestern Historical Quarterly* 104 (October 2000): 163.
17. Brown, "Garnering Votes for 'Cactus Jack,'" 165; Jordan A. Schwarz, "John Nance Garner and the Sales Tax Rebellion of 1932," *Journal of Southern History* 30, no. 2 (May 1964): 162, 176.
18. Carter to John Nance Garner, Feb. 29, 1932, Box 92, John Nance Garner File, AGC Papers, Burnett Library; Will Rogers, *Will Rogers' Weekly Articles*, Vol. 5: *The Hoover Years, 1931–1933*, ed. Steven K. Gragert (Stillwater: Oklahoma State University Press, 1982), 141–42 (quotation).
19. Rogers, *Will Rogers' Weekly Articles*, 143 (quotation); Russell M. Posner, "California's Role in the Nomination of Franklin D. Roosevelt," *California Historical Society Quarterly* 39, no. 2 (June 1960): 132.
20. Steve Neal, *Happy Days Are Here Again: The 1932 Democratic Convention, the Emergence of FDR—and How America Was Changed Forever* (New York: Harper Perennial, 2005), 4; Lionel V. Patenaude, "The Garner Vote Switch to Roosevelt: 1932

Democratic Convention," *Southwestern Historical Quarterly* 79, no. 2 (October 1975): 193–94 (second quotation), 198 (third and fourth quotation).
21. Neal, *Happy Days Are Here Again,* 280–82; "Texans Given Warm Thanks by Roosevelt," *Dallas Morning News,* July 3, 1932; Neal, *Happy Days Are Here Again,* 282.
22. Neal, *Happy Days Are Here Again,* 289; *Dallas Morning News,* July 5, 1932.
23. Mencken, *Thirty-Five Years of Newspaper Work,* 219.
24. Campbell, *Gone to Texas,* 381; Amon Carter to Ross Sterling, Feb. 25, 1932, Box 78, Ferguson Controversy File 1930–1932, AGC Papers, Burnett Library.
25. Amon Carter to Harry Wiess, Apr. 27, 1932, Box 78, Ferguson Controversy File 1930–1932, AGC Papers, Burnett Library; Amon Carter to D. D. Grubb, Aug. 1, 1932, Box 78, Ferguson Controversy File 1930–1932, AGC Papers, Burnett Library.
26. Campbell, *Gone to Texas,* 381; Rogers, *Will Rogers' Daily Telegrams,* 185.
27. *Dallas Morning News,* November 1, 1932; *New York Times,* December 9, 1932; Rogers, *Will Rogers' Weekly Articles,* 5:203–4; *Fort Worth Star Telegram,* January 29, 1933.
28. "Texas Party," *Time,* October 30, 1933, 15; "Letters," *Time,* November 20, 1933, 4.
29. Carter to Franklin D. Roosevelt, Dec. 24, 1933, Box 269, Franklin D. Roosevelt File, AGC Papers, Burnett Library.
30. Anthony J. Badger, *The New Deal: The Depression Years, 1933–1940* (New York: The Noonday Press, 1989), 66, 74.
31. "To supporters and critics alike, General Johnson's NRA, a vast scheme for delegating governmental authority to private cartels, seemed akin to the 'corporativism' of Italian Fascism," wrote James Q. Whitman in "Of Corporatism, Fascism, and the First New Deal," *American Journal of Comparative Law* 39, no. 4 (October 1991), 747–48.
32. "Text of Codes Offered by Daily Newspaper Publishers," *New York Times,* August 9, 1933; Paul Y. Anderson, "Johnson and the Freedom of the Press," *The Nation,* August 30, 1933, 234.
33. J. F. Young to Carter, Nov. 30, 1933, Box 26, File 14, AGC Papers, Burnett Library; John Kennedy Ohl, *Hugh S. Johnson and the New Deal* (DeKalb: Northern Illinois University Press, 1985), 116.
34. Elisha Hanson to Howard Davis, Nov. 22, 1933, Box 26, File 14, AGC Papers, Burnett Library; "Newspaper Code Altered for NRA," *New York Times,* August 16, 1933.
35. "Newspaper Code Is Expected Today," *New York Times,* December 23, 1933 (quotations); Ohl, *Hugh S. Johnson and the New Deal,* 150; Ronald Edsforth, *The New Deal: America's Response to the Great Depression* (Malden, Mass.: Blackwell, 2000), 186.
36. Brown, *Hood, Bonnet, and Little Brown Jug,* 7.
37. Johnston, "Colonel Carter of Cartersville," 8; Amon Carter to Harold L. Ickes, May 9, 1935, Box 34, File 7, AGC Papers, Burnett Library.
38. Application of Fort Worth for Federal Appropriations for a Livestock Centennial, n.d., Box 34, File 7, AGC Papers, Burnett Library.
39. Harold L. Ickes, *The Secret Diary of Harold L. Ickes* (New York: Simon and Schuster, 1953), 1:444; Ickes to Carter, Sept. 27, 1935, Box 34, File 7, AGC Papers, Burnett Library; Jones to Carter, Nov. 1, 1935, Box 34, File 7, AGC Papers, Burnett Library.

40. Jan Jones, *Billy Rose Presents ... Casa Mañana* (Fort Worth: Texas Christian University Press, 1999), 27.
41. Ibid., 8, 34–35, 46; Kenneth Ragsdale, *The Year America Discovered Texas: Centennial '36* (College Station: Texas A&M University Press, 1987), 211–12.
42. Jones, *Billy Rose Presents,*, 53; Steven Fenberg, *Unprecedented Power: Jesse Jones, Capitalism, and the Common Good* (College Station: Texas A&M University Press, 2011), 133–34; David M. Kennedy, *Freedom from Fear: The American People in Depression and War, 1929–1945* (New York: Oxford University Press, 1999), 84; Carter to Jones, July 8, 1936, Box 17, File 10a, AGC Papers, Burnett Library; Jones to Carter, July 10, 1936, Box 17, File 10a, AGC Papers, Burnett Library; Jones, *Billy Rose Presents*, 55.
43. Jones to Elliott Roosevelt, July 12, 1936, Box 17, File 10a, AGC Papers, Burnett Library; Jones to Carter, July 16, 1936, Box 23, File 5, AGC Papers, Burnett Library (quotation).
44. Carter to Marvin McIntyre, Nov. 4, 1936, Box 119, Marvin McIntyre File, AGC Papers, Burnett Library (quotation).
45. Irving Bernstein, *Turbulent Years: A History of the American Worker, 1933–1941* (Boston: Houghton Mifflin, 1971), 553–54; Amon Carter to Garner, Apr. 7, 1937, Box 92, John Nance Garner File, AGC Papers, Burnett Library (quotation).
46. *Fort Worth Star-Telegram*, April 7, 1937.
47. Carter to Roosevelt, Jan. 31, 1937, Box 32, File 2a, AGC Papers, Burnett Library; "Proposed Amendments Not Ratified by the States," U.S. Government Printing Office, accessed January 21, 2014, http://www.gpoaccess.gov/constitution/pdf/con002.pdf; "Informal Remarks of the President from the Rear Platform of His Special Train," *The National Archives Catalog*, accessed July 8, 2015, https://catalog.archives.gov/id/197802 (quotation).
48. Carter to Roosevelt, Jan. 31, 1937, Box 32, File 2a, AGC Papers, Burnett Library (quotation). See also Jeremy P. Felt, "The Child Labor Provisions of the Fair Labor Standards Act," *Labor History* 11, no. 4 (Fall 1970): 467–81.
49. *Fort Worth Star-Telegram*, April 16, 1937; Kennedy, *Freedom from Fear*, 351.
50. Carter to Garner, Nov. 29, 1937, Box 92, John Nance Garner File, AGC Papers, Burnett Library (quotation); Arthur M. Schlesinger, *The Politics of Upheaval* (Boston: Houghton Mifflin, 1960), 505–6.
51. Carter to Garner, Nov. 30, 1937, Box 92, John Nance Garner File, AGC Papers, Burnett Library.
52. Patrick Cox, "John Nance Garner," in *Profiles in Power: Twentieth-Century Texans in Washington*, ed. Kenneth Hendrickson Jr., Michael L. Collins, and Patrick Cox (Austin: University of Texas Press, 2004), 58–59.
53. *Fort Worth Star-Telegram*, March 27, 1940.
54. Ickes to Carter, Apr. 18, 1940, Box 107, File 13b, AGC Papers, Burnett Library.
55. *Fort Worth Star-Telegram*, April 29, 1940.
56. *New York Herald Tribune*, April 29, 1940; Dwight Marvin to Carter, May 4, 1940, Box 107, File 13b, AGC Papers, Burnett Library; Joseph P. Cowan to Ickes, Apr. 29, 1940, Box 107, File 13b, AGC Papers, Burnett Library.

57. Cox, "John Nance Garner," 60; Frank Freidel, *Franklin D. Roosevelt: A Rendezvous with Destiny* (Boston: Little, Brown, 1990), 343; James Farley to Carter, Apr. 17, 1939, Box 74, 1934–39 File, AGC Papers, Burnett Library.

CHAPTER 6

1. Roy Miller, "The Legislative History of the Trinity River," Box 41, File 7, AGC Papers, Burnett Library.
2. Ibid.; *Dallas Morning News,* February 4, 1930.
3. *Dallas Journal,* July 14, 1930.
4. *Dallas Dispatch,* July 14, 1930. The documents in the AGC Papers, Burnett Library, make no mention of the Trinity Canal until Carter was officially named to the board. However, the depth of Carter's correspondence makes it appear that Carter had thought through the possible benefits of the canal before his involvement.
5. John Fouts to Carter, Aug. 22, 1930, Box 41, File 7, AGC Papers, Burnett Library; *Handbook of Texas Online,* s.v. "Carpenter, John William," accessed February 2, 2005, https://tshaonline.org/handbook/online/articles/fca60; Lynn M. Alperin, *History of the Gulf Intracoastal Waterway* (Washington, D.C.: Institute for Water Resources, 1983), 27. Carter's notorious hatred of Dallas was put aside whenever the whole state could benefit.
6. Minutes from TRCA meeting, approximately November 1930 (no specific day given), Box 41, File 7a, AGC Papers, Burnett Library.
7. Ibid.; Carter to L. P. Swift Jr., Dec. 15, 1930, Box 41, File 7a, AGC Papers, Burnett Library. To clarify, Carter defined the Trinity River area very loosely and included ports like Galveston and Houston, while the tonnage given for the Trinity itself is referring to what the river was capable of handling up to Dallas and Fort Worth.
8. Carter, manuscript, Jan. 12, 1931, Box 41, File 8, AGC Papers, Burnett Library.
9. Ibid.; Evans to Carter, Feb. 23, 1931, Box 41, File 8, AGC Papers, Burnett Library; Evans to Carter, May 8, 1931, Box 41, File 8, AGC Papers, Burnett Library; Fouts to Carter, May 13, 1931, Box 41, File 8, AGC Papers, Burnett Library.
10. Fouts to Carter, June 14, 1932, Box 41, File 8, AGC Papers, Burnett Library.
11. Fouts to Carter, Jan. 18, 1933, Box 41, File 8a, AGC Papers, Burnett Library; Carter to Morris Berney, Oct. 26, 1933, Box 41, File 8a, AGC Papers, Burnett Library.
12. Carl Mosig to Carter, Dec. 14, 1933, Box 41, File 8a, AGC Papers, Burnett Library. The National Planning Board was created to implement the PWA's public works spending. See Paul Conkin's *The New Deal* (New York: Thomas Crowell, 1967), 48.
13. John Fouts to Carter, Apr. 14, 1934, Box 41, File 9, AGC Papers, Burnett Library; "Trinity Canal Plan Includes Flood Control," *Dallas Morning News,* May 2, 1934.
14. Fouts to the Board of Directors, Jan. 30, 1936, Box 41, File 9, AGC Papers, Burnett Library; *Dallas Morning News,* January 30, 1936 (quotation).
15. Carter to Fouts, July 18, 1938, Box 41, File 10, AGC Papers, Burnett Library.
16. Carter to Franklin D. Roosevelt, July 9, 1938, Box 32, File 2b, AGC Papers, Burnett Library; Franklin D. Roosevelt, "Remarks at Fort Worth, Texas," July 10, 1938, online by Gerhard Peters and John T. Woolley, *The American Presidency Project,* http://www.presidency.ucsb.edu/ws/?pid=15676.

17. Harry Brown to Carter, Sept. 29, 1938, Box 41, File 10, AGC Papers, Burnett Library.
18. Carter to Sam Rayburn, Sept. 18, 1939, Box 41, File 10b, AGC Papers, Burnett Library (quotation); David Porter, "Representative Lindsay Warren, the Water Bloc, and the Transportation Act of 1940," *North Carolina Historical Review* 50, no. 3 (July 1973): 277.
19. Carter to Rayburn, Sept. 18, 1939, Oct. 24, 1939, Box 41, File 10b, AGC Papers, Burnett Library.
20. "Aviation Helmets Inscribed," n.d., Box 35, Amon Carter Personal File 1930–1933, AGC Papers, Burnett Library.
21. Tim Brady, "U.S. Airlines from 1930 to World War II," in *The American Aviation Experience: A History*, ed. Tim Brady (Carbondale: Southern Illinois University Press, 2000), 174; Serling, *Eagle*, 32.
22. ,Serling, *Eagle*, 34–35; *Fort Worth Star-Telegram*, May 4, 1932; *Dallas Times Herald*, May 5, 1932; "Cohu for Coburn," *Time*, March 28, 1932.
23. "Cord in Control," *Time*, March 27, 1933; Carter to L. B. Manning, Mar. 31, 1933, Box 12, American Airlines File 1, AGC Papers, Burnett Library; "Aeronautics: Farley's Deal," *Time*, April 23, 1934.
24. "Against Time," *Time*, January 28, 1935; *Providence Journal*, March 31, 1932; Amon Carter to Frank Hawks, May 30, 1932, Box 35, Amon Carter Personal Papers File 1930–1933, AGC Papers, Burnett Library; Boyce House, "Amon Carter: Range Boss of West Texas," unpublished manuscript, Box 36, Amon Carter Personal File 1938, AGC Papers, Burnett Library.
25. Serling, *Eagle*, 72–73; "Personality," *Time*, February 25, 1952.
26. *Dallas Morning News*, January 14, 1935; "Against Time," *Time*, January 28, 1935; Serling, *Eagle*, 72–73, 148.
27. Roger M. Olien and Diana Davids Hinton, *Wildcatters: Texas Independent Oilmen* (College Station: Texas A&M University Press, 2007), 71, 73–74; *Dallas Morning News*, June 1, 1935; *Dallas Morning News*, April 7, 1935.
28. Robert Lifset and Brian C. Black, "Imaging the 'Devil's Excrement': Big Oil in Petroleum Cinema, 1940–2007," *Journal of American History* 99, no. 1 (June 2012): 137.
29. *Fort Worth Star-Telegram*, April 15, 1990; *The Korea Herald*, January 26, 2011; *Fort Worth Star-Telegram*, January 3, 1953.
30. Johnston, "Colonel Carter of Cartersville," 9; Catherine Lehane Johnson, Shady Oak Farm manuscript, n.d., Shady Oak File, Box 105, AGC Papers, Burnett Library.
31. David Karnes, "The Glamorous Crowd: Hollywood and Movie Premieres between the Wars," *American Quarterly* 38, no. 4 (Autumn 1986), 563–64.
32. *Fort Worth Star-Telegram*, September 19, 1940; *Fort Worth Star-Telegram*, September 20, 1940; *Hattiesburg American*, October 10, 1940.
33. *Dallas Morning News*, January 28, 1941.
34. *Fort Worth Star-Telegram*, December 4, 2010; Jerome Moore, *Texas Christian University: A Hundred Years of History* (Fort Worth: Texas Christian University Press, 1974), 98; Athletic Committee/Board of Trustees of Texas Christian University to Amon Carter, Dec. 13, 1929, Box 198, 1929 File, AGC Papers, Burnett Library.

35. *Fort Worth Star-Telegram,* January 8, 1930; Carter often targeted the wealthy Waggoner for his charities and fund-raisers, prompting the old rancher on one occasion to hold up a quarter and comment to a photographer, "Here, take a picture of this quarter; it's the one thing Carter hasn't taken from me yet" (Cashion, *New Frontier,* 56).
36. Moore, *Texas Christian University,* 215–16; Amon Carter to Amon Carter Jr., Oct. 11, 1937, Box 38, Amon Carter Jr. 1937 File, AGC Papers, Burnett Library.
37. "Burlington Blitzkrieg Against Texas," pamphlet, n.d., Box 25 File 22a, AGC Papers, Burnett Library. This pamphlet is a collection of telegrams and editorials regarding the Burlington case that Carter compiled.
38. *Fort Worth Star-Telegram,* November 5, 1939.
39. Ibid.
40. *Fort Worth Star-Telegram,* February 28, 1940.
41. "Argument of Mr. Carter," Transcript of ICC Hearing, May 8, 1940, Box 25, File 22, AGC Papers, Burnett Library.
42. Ibid.
43. *Fort Worth Star-Telegram,* May 18, 1940.
44. "Oral Arguments of Amon Carter," Feb. 5, 1941, Box 26, File 23, AGC Papers, Burnett Library.
45. *Fort Worth Star-Telegram,* June 24, 1941.
46. Nenetta Carter to Amon Carter, July 5, 1933, Box 35, Amon Carter Personal Files 1933, AGC Papers, Burnett Library.
47. Nenetta Carter to Amon Carter Jr., Dec. 23, 1940, Box 30, Amon Carter Jr. File 1940, AGC Papers, Burnett Library; Amon and Nenetta Carter Divorce Papers, Sept. 30, 1941, Box 36, Amon Carter Personal File 1940, AGC Papers, Burnett Library; "Milestones," *Time,* January 20, 1941.
48. Divorce Settlement, Jan. 3, 1941, Box 36, Amon Carter Personal Papers File 1941, AGC Papers, Burnett Library.
49. Nenetta Burton to Katrine Deakins, Mar. 7, 1941, Box 41, Ruth Carter File 1941, AGC Papers, Burnett Library.
50. Amon Carter to Ruth Carter, Nov. 9, 1939, Box 46, Ruth Carter File, AGC Papers; Ruth Carter to Amon Carter, Oct. 6, 1940, Box 46, Ruth Carter File, AGC Papers; New Deal poem, n.d., Box 46, Ruth Carter File, AGC Papers; *Fort Worth Press* clipping, "Ruth Carter Wants Job So Much She'll Work for One," Box 46, Ruth Carter File, AGC Papers, Burnett Library.
51. *Urbana Evening Courier,* July 28, 1934; Amon Carter to Lt. Col. G. L. Miller, Mar. 30, 1936, Box 38, Amon Carter Jr. 1936 File; Harold Hough to Amon Carter Jr., Aug. 11, 1934, Box 38, Amon Carter Jr. 1919–1935 File, AGC Papers, Burnett Library.
52. Amon Carter to Lt. Col. G. L. Miller, Oct. 23, 1935, Box 38, Amon Carter Jr. 1919–1935 File, AGC Papers, Burnett Library; Application for Admission to Culver Military Academy, Box 38, Amon Carter Jr. 1919–1935 File, AGC Papers, Burnett Library; Amon Carter to Amon Carter Jr., April 11, 1936, Box 38, Amon Carter Jr. 1936 File, AGC Papers, Burnett Library.

53. Amon Carter to Amon Carter Jr., Dec. 23, 1937, Box 30, Amon Carter, Jr. 1937 File, AGC Papers, Burnett Library.

CHAPTER 7

1. Michael Welsh, *Landscape of Ghosts, River of Dreams: An Administrative History of Big Bend National Park* (National Park Service, U.S. Dept. of the Interior, 2002, www.nps.gov/bibe/learn/historyculture/upload/BIBE-ADHI-2008.pdf), 19; John R. Jameson, *The Story of Big Bend National Park* (Austin: University of Texas Press: 1996), 22–25.
2. Ibid., 29–30.
3. Ibid., 30–35.
4. Ibid., 36–37; Herbert Maier to James Record, July 13, 1937, Box 21, 1937 File, AGC Papers, Burnett Library.
5. Jameson, *Story of Big Bend*, 38.
6. H. W. Morelock to Amon Carter, Mar. 10, 1938, Box 21, 1938 File, AGC Papers, Burnett Library; Amon Carter to Houston Harte, June 1938, Box 21, 1938 File, AGC Papers, Burnett Library; Charles Cotton to Amon Carter, May 27, 1938, Box 21, 1938 File, AGC Papers, Burnett Library.
7. Jameson, *Story of Big Bend*, 38–39; "Minutes of Meeting of the Executive Board, Texas Big Bend Park Association," May 23, 1938, Box 21, 1938 File, AGC Papers, Burnett Library; Amon Carter to Nelson Rockefeller, June 18, 1938, Box 21, 1938 File, AGC Papers, Burnett Library.
8. Amon Carter to Nelson Rockefeller, June 18, 1938, Box 21, 1938 File, AGC Papers, Burnett Library.
9. Amon Carter to Nathan Adams, Sept. 19, 1938, Box 21, 1938 File, AGC Papers, Burnett Library; Amon Carter to A. D. Simpson, Sept. 24, 1938, Box 21, 1938 File, AGC Papers, Burnett Library; Amon Carter to W. B. Tuttle, Nov. 8, 1938, Box 21, 1938 File, AGC Papers, Burnett Library; Jameson, *Story of Big Bend*, 40.
10. Green, *Establishment in Texas Politics*, 22–23; Jameson, *Story of Big Bend*, 42.
11. Welsh, *Landscape of Ghosts*, 156; Jameson, *Story of Big Bend*, 40–41.
12. *Dallas Morning News*, May 13, 1939; Welsh, *Landscape of Ghosts*,160.
13. Welsh, *Landscape of Ghosts*, 165.
14. Amon Carter to Jesse Jones, Nov. 10, 1939, Box 21, 1939 File, AGC Papers, Burnett Library; *Dallas Morning News*, December 8, 1939; *Alpine Avalanche*, December 1, 1939; Welsh, *Landscape of Ghosts*, 167.
15. Welsh, *Landscape of* Ghosts, 170; *Dallas Morning News*, February 8, 1940; Amon Carter to Mrs. Louis Wardlaw, Nov. 11, 1940, Box 21, 1940 File, AGC Papers, Burnett Library.
16. *Dallas Morning News*, December 9, 1938; Amon Carter to Mrs. Louis Wardlaw, Nov. 11, 1940, Box 21, 1938 File, AGC Papers, Burnett Library; Jameson, *Story of Big Bend*, 39, 42.
17. Green, *Establishment in Texas*, 42; Jameson, *Story of Big Bend*, 42; Script-Texas Big Bend Park Association's Program, WBAP, Feb. 16, 1941, Box 21, 1941 File, AGC Papers, Burnett Library; *Temple Telegram*, February 14, 1941.

18. Jameson, *Story of Big Bend*, 43; Welsh, *Landscape of Ghosts*, 312.
19. Jameson, *Story of Big Bend*, 43-44; "FDR Accepts Final Title to Big Bend National Park," *West Texas Today*, June 1944, 10.
20. Payne, *From Prairie to Planes*, 51-54.
21. Ibid., 56-57; *Fort Worth Star-Telegram*, January 11-12, 1942.
22. *Fort Worth Star-Telegram*, March 23, 1943.
23. Ibid.
24. Fouts to TIA, May 30, 1940, Box 41, File 11, AGC Papers, Burnett Library.
25. Carter to Bothwell, Dec. 18, 1941, Box 41, File 11, AGC Papers, Burnett Library.
26. Carter to Carter, Jan. 7, 1942, Box 41, File 13, AGC Papers, Burnett Library. Carter often sent out form letters to numerous local businesses and members of the Fort Worth Chamber of Commerce. He would also send a letter to himself, presumably for his own benefit. Fouts to United States Congress, Feb. 26, 1942, Box 41, File 13, AGC Papers, Burnett Library.
27. David R. Goldfield, *Promised Land: The South since 1945* (Arlington Heights, Ill.: Harlan Davidson, 1976), 5.
28. Kathryn Pinkney, "From Stockyards to Defense Plants, the Transformation of a City: Fort Worth, Texas, and World War II" (PhD diss., University of North Texas, 2003), 78-79; Campbell, *Gone to Texas*, 404.
29. Tindall, *Emergence of the New South*, 687; Dewey Grantham, *The South in Modern America*, (New York: Harper Perennial, 1995), 170; Anthony Gaughan, "Woodrow Wilson and the Rise of Militant Interventionism in the South," *Journal of Southern History* 65 (November 1999): 805.
30. Amon Carter to the *Star-Telegram* Family, Dec. 20, 1940, Box 36, 1940 File, AGC Papers, Burnett Library; Amon Carter to Franklin D. Roosevelt, Dec. 29, 1940, Box 61, 1940 File, AGC Papers, Burnett Library.
31. J'Nell L. Pate, *Arsenal of Defense: Fort Worth's Military Legacy* (Denton: Texas State Historical Association, 2011), 62-63.
32. E. C. Barksdale, *The Genesis of the Aviation Industry in North Texas* (Austin: University of Texas Bureau of Business Research, 1958), 2-3, 8.
33. Fleet to Carter, May 27, 1940, Box 12, File 18, AGC Papers, Burnett Library.
34. Wheatley to Carter, Nov. 22, 1940, Box 12, File 18, AGC Papers, Burnett Library; Edgar Gott to Carter, Nov. 26, 1940, Box 12, File 18, AGC Papers, Burnett Library.
35. Carter to Gott, Dec. 7, 1940, Box 12, File 18, AGC Papers, Burnett Library.
36. Holden to Fleet, Dec. 19, 1940, Box 12, File 18, AGC Papers, Burnett Library.
37. Carter to Sheppard, Dec. 22, 1940, Box 12, File 18, AGC Papers, Burnett Library; Carter to Van Dusen, Dec. 22, 1940, Box 12, File 18, AGC Papers, Burnett Library; Carter to Knudsen, Dec. 22, 1940, Box 12, File 18, AGC Papers, Burnett Library.
38. Pinkney, "From Stockyards to Defense Plants," 87-88; Carter to Van Dusen, Dec. 30, 1940, Box 12, File 18, AGC Papers, Burnett Library.
39. Leon Gross and Raymond Meyer to Carter, Jan. 3, 1941, Box 12, File 18, AGC Papers, Burnett Library; McDaniel to Carter, Jan. 6, 1941, Box 12, File 18, AGC Papers, Burnett Library; Carter to Roosevelt, Jan. 6, 1941, AGC Papers, Burnett Library.

40. William Wagner, *Reuben Fleet and the Story of Consolidated Aircraft* (Fallbrook, Calif.: Aero, 1976), 302.
41. Ibid.; Campbell, *Gone to Texas*, 404.
42. Irving Bernstein, "Americans in Depression and War," in *A History of the American Worker*, ed. Richard B. Morris (Princeton: Princeton University Press, 1983), 176; Byron Fairchild and Jonathan Grossman, *The Army and Industrial Manpower* (Washington, D.C.: Center of Military History, Department of the Army, 1959), 66–67.
43. Kenneth S. Davis, *FDR: The War President, 1940–1943* (New York: Random House, 2000), 327–28; Amon Carter to Tom Connally, Nov. 18, 1941, Box 60, Tom Connally File, AGC Papers, Burnett Library; Tom Connally to Amon Carter, Nov. 18, 1941, Box 36, Tom Connally File, AGC Papers, Burnett Library; Amon Carter to Alben Barkley, Tom Connally, and Sam Rayburn, Feb. 7, 1942, Box 36, 1942 File, AGC Papers, Burnett Library; Amon Carter to Stephen Early, June 5, 1943, Box 61, 1943 File, AGC Papers, Burnett Library.
44. Nenetta Carter to Ruth Carter, Apr. 21, 1941, Box 46, Ruth Carter 1941 File, AGC Papers, Burnett Library.
45. Ibid.; Nenetta Carter to Katrine Deakins, Apr. 26, 1941, Box 46, Ruth Carter 1941 File, AGC Papers, Burnett Library.
46. Nenetta Carter to Ruth Carter, Apr. 26, 1941, Box 46, Ruth Carter 1941 File, AGC Papers, Burnett Library; Ruth Carter to Mrs. Carl Deakins, Apr. 27, 1941, Box 46, Ruth Carter 1941 File, AGC Papers, Burnett Library.
47. Amon Carter to Kent Cooper, Feb. 22, 1943, Box 36, 1943 File, AGC Papers, Burnett Library; *Dallas Morning News*, March 12, 1945.
48. Charles B. MacDonald, *The Mighty Endeavor: The American War in Europe* (New York: Da Capo Press, 1992), 124–28; Amon Carter to Harold Crookes, May 10, 1943, P.O.W. S-Miscellaneous File, Box 148, AGC Papers, Burnett Library; *Dallas Morning News*, May 6, 1945.
49. *Dallas Morning News*, April 15, 1943.
50. Carter to Connally, Aug. 16, 1944, Box 12, File 13, AGC Papers, Burnett Library.
51. Mrs. Burton Carter to Amon Carter, Jan. 7, 1945, Box 36, 1945 File, AGC Papers, Burnett Library; Amon Carter to J. Edgar Hoover, Jan. 12, 1945, Box 36, 1945 File, AGC Papers, Burnett Library.
52. *Dallas Morning News*, February 3, 1945; ibid., May 3, 1945; Deborah E. Lipstadt, *Beyond Belief: The American Press and the Coming of the Holocaust 1933–1945* (New York: The Free Press, 1986), 254–55.
53. Undated Amon Carter memo, Box 37, 1945 File, AGC Papers, Burnett Library.
54. McAdams, "Mudholes, Fairy Godmothers, and Choir Bells," 95.

CHAPTER 8

1. David R. Davies, *The Postwar Decline of American Newspapers, 1945–1965* (Westport, Conn.: Praeger, 2006), 1–5; *Fort Worth Star-Telegram*, September 28, 1949; WBAP Program Schedule, Box 197, WBAP-TV File, AGC Papers, Burnett Library.

2. Kelley, *Foundations of Texan Philanthropy*, 61–64; "Shell Purchases Amon G. Carter Wasson Properties," *The Pecten,* September 1947; Amon G. Carter Foundation, "History of the Foundation," accessed December 15, 2017, http://www.agcf.org/history-of-the-foundation.html. As of December 31, 2016, the foundation had over $647 million in assets, with a majority of grants funding the Amon Carter Museum and educational institutions.
3. Untitled document, n.d., Box 41, File 9, AGC Papers, Burnett Library.
4. "Lena Pope," *The New Handbook of Texas* (Austin: Texas State Historical Association, 1996), 5:269; Letter to Amon Carter, Jan. 12, 1947, Box 138, File 7, AGC Papers, Burnett Library.
5. W. A. Hawkins and Lem Billingsley to Board of Directors, Sept. 12, 1945 Box 138, File 7, AGC Papers, Burnett Library; Amon G. Carter to W. O. Jones, Aug. 20, 1946, Box 138, File 7, AGC Papers, Burnett Library; Amon Carter to Lena Pope, Apr. 16, 1950, Box 138, File 9, AGC Papers, Burnett Library.
6. Lena Pope to Amon Carter, Apr. 29, 1950, Box 138, File 9, AGC Papers, Burnett Library; Katrine Deakins to W. K. Stripling, Dec. 29, 1950, Box 138, File 9, AGC Papers, Burnett Library; Katrine Deakins to Otto Monnig, Dec. 29, 1950, Box 138, File 9, AGC Papers, Burnett Library; Katrine Deakins to Lena Pope, Jan. 3, 1951, Box 138, File 10, AGC Papers, Burnett Library. Mr. Leonard refers to Marvin Leonard, the owner of Leonard's Department Store in downtown Fort Worth. He was a prominent member of the Fort Worth business community and sat on the advisory board of the Lena Pope Home. For more information, see *Texas Merchant* by Victoria and Walter Buenger.
7. *Fort Worth Star Telegram,* May 18, 1949; *Fort Worth Star Telegram,* May 17, 1949.
8. Undated memo, Box 80, File 40, AGC Papers, Burnett Library.
9. C. B. Williams to Amon Carter, May 30, 1949, Box 80, File 40, AGC Papers, Burnett Library; Disbursement of Flood Funds, n.d., Box 80, File 40, AGC Papers, Burnett Library; W. L. Stewart to Amon Carter, Aug. 16, 1949, Box 80, File 40, AGC Papers, Burnett Library; Amon Carter to Fred Florence, June 10, 1949, Box 80, File 40, AGC Papers, Burnett Library.
10. "The Challenge to Fort Worth," n.d., Box 95, File 6, AGC Papers, Burnett Library. St. Joseph Hospital would also be one of the direct recipients of Carter's generosity.
11. "Some Larger Contributions to Date," n.d., Box 95, File 6, AGC Papers, Burnett Library; Amon Carter and Sid Richardson to Fort Worth Greater Hospital Fund, Mar. 5, 1952, Box 95, File 6, AGC Papers, Burnett Library; Amon Carter to G. J. Coffey, Dec. 30, 1953, Box 95, File 7, AGC Papers, Burnett Library.
12. Selcer, *History of Fort Worth,* 149, 175; *Fort Worth Star-Telegram,* October 30, 1952.
13. Kelley, *Foundations of Texan Philanthropy,* 61; W. P. Bomer to Amon Carter, Nov. 18, 1947, Box 89, File 22, AGC Papers, Burnett Library; Amon Carter to Fred Florence, June 10, 1949, Box 80, File 40, AGC Papers, Burnett Library.
14. Octave Proer to Amon Carter, Feb. 14, 1950, Magazine Related Requests File, Box 119, AGC Papers, Burnett Library; Amon Carter to Octave Proer, Apr. 6, 1950, Magazine Related Requests File, Box 119, AGC Papers, Burnett Library; Octave Proer to Amon

Carter, June 19, 1950, Magazine Related Requests File, Box 119, AGC Papers, Burnett Library; Nilada Stara to Amon Carter, Feb. 17, 1950, Magazine Related Requests File, Box 119, AGC Papers, Burnett Library; L. Saysell to Amon Carter, April 22, 1950, Magazine Related Requests File, Box 119, AGC Papers, Burnett Library; Held Mordechai to Amon Carter, Mar. 3, 1952, *Time* Magazine Articles File 2 of 3, Box 206, AGC Papers, Burnett Library; Katrine Deakins to the Garry Moore Show, Mar. 18, 1952, *Time* Magazine Articles File 2 of 3, Box 206, AGC Papers, Burnett Library.

15. *Fort Worth Star-Telegram*, May 11, 1952 and January 15, 1960; Alexander Nemerov, "Projecting the Future: Film and Race in the Art of Charles Russell," *American Art* 8, no. 1 (Winter 1994), 72.
16. Secretary to Amon Carter to Mr. David Findlay, "The Reconnaissance" by Frederic Remington File, Record Group E, Art and Museum Records, Box 2, AGC Papers, Amon Carter Museum; *Fort Worth Star-Telegram*, October 12, 1986.
17. Carter to Knudsen, Feb. 15, 1935, Box 18, File 23, AGC Papers, Burnett Library.
18. Ibid.
19. Ibid.
20. Ibid.
21. Ibid.
22. Carter to R. H. Grant, Apr. 13, 1936, Box 18, File 23a, AGC Papers, Burnett Library.
23. Ibid.
24. Ibid.
25. Grant to Carter, Apr. 23, 1936, Box 18, File 23a, AGC Papers, Burnett Library; Carter to Grant, July 22, 1936, Box 18, File 23a, AGC Papers, Burnett Library; Grant to Carter, July 23, 1936, Box 18, File 23a, AGC Papers, Burnett Library.
26. Carter to Smith, June 26, 1944, Box 18, File 24, AGC Papers, Burnett Library; C. E. Wilson, letter to Carter, Oct. 19, 1944, Box 18, File 24, AGC Papers, Burnett Library.
27. Carter to Garrett, Apr. 15, 1947, Box 18, File 24, AGC Papers, Burnett Library.
28. D. V. Fraser to Carter, Aug. 14, 1950, Box 18, File 26, AGC Papers, Burnett Library; F. G. Gurley to Carter, Sept. 11, 1950, Box 18, File 26, AGC Papers, Burnett Library.
29. Carter to Sloan, Nov. 20, 1950, Box 18, File 26, AGC Papers, Burnett Library. It must be noted here that Carter's definition of the Fort Worth region fluctuated. It varied in size from Tarrant County to all of West Texas. Carter conveniently left out his definition here.
30. Carter to Gurley, Dec. 1, 1950, Box 18, File 26, AGC Papers, Burnett Library; *Fort Worth Star-Telegram*, May 14, 1952.
31. Carter to Garrett, Jan. 4, 1951, Box 18, File 27, AGC Papers, Burnett Library.
32. Thomas Groehn to Carter, Aug. 2, 1951, Box 18, File 27, AGC Papers, Burnett Library.
33. *Fort Worth Star-Telegram*, May 14, 1952; *Fort Worth Star-Telegram*, May 23, 1952.
34. Fouts to Carter, Feb. 12, 1945, Box 41, File 15, AGC Papers, Burnett Library; "For Mr. Carter's Use at Groundbreaking Ceremony," n.d., Box 41, File 15, AGC Papers, Burnett Library.
35. "Remarks of Mr. Amon Carter, Chairman, Executive Committee Trinity Improvement Ass'n on the Occasion of the Groundbreaking Ceremonies at Garza-Little Elm Dam Site November 23, 1948," File 16, Box 41, AGC Papers, Burnett Library.

36. Carter to Glenn Woodson, n.d., File 17, Box 41, AGC Papers, Burnett Library; "Contribution Received from Fort Worth as of March 15, 1950," n.d., File 17, Box 41, AGC Papers, Burnett Library; Carter to Carter, Mar. 26, 1951, File 18, Box 41, AGC Papers, Burnett Library.
37. Carter to Carter, Mar. 3, 1952, File 18, Box 41, AGC Papers, Burnett Library; *Handbook of Texas Online*, Wayne Gard, "Trinity River Navigation Projects," accessed June 10, 2018, http://www.tshaonline.org/handbook/online/articles/ett01.
38. Payne, *From Prairies to Planes*, 62–63; *Fort Worth Star-Telegram*, June 29 and July 11, 1950.
39. *Dallas Morning News*, December 21, 1945; Amon Carter to Harry Truman, Sept. 12, 1945, Box 214, 1945 File, AGC Papers, Burnett Library; Amon Carter to Harry Truman, n.d., Box 214, 1946 File, AGC Papers, Burnett Library; Amon Carter to Harry Truman, Dec. 24, 1945, Box 214, 1945 File, AGC Papers, Burnett Library.
40. *Handbook of Texas Online*, Price Daniel, "Tidelands Controversy," accessed June 10, 2018, http://www.tshaonline.org/handbook/online/articles/mgt02; Campbell, *Gone to Texas*, 414.
41. Campbell, *Gone to Texas*, 416; Amon Carter to Harry Truman, Apr. 17, 1952, Box 205, Tidelands File, AGC Papers, Burnett Library; Amon Carter to Harry Truman, May 6, 1952, Box 205, Tidelands File, AGC Papers, Burnett Library; Harry Truman to Amon Carter, May 19, 1952, Box 205, Tidelands File, AGC Papers, Burnett Library.
42. Flemmons, *Amon*, 296–7, 320; Campbell, *Gone to Texas*, 416–17; Transcript, Claudia "Lady Bird" Johnson Oral History Interview XXI, 8/10–11/81, by Michael L. Gillette, Internet Copy, LBJ Library; Stephen E. Ambrose, *Eisenhower: Soldier, General of the Army, President-Elect, 1890–1952* (Simon and Schuster: New York, 1983), 1:478.
43. James Patterson, *Grand Expectations: The United States, 1945–1974* (New York: Oxford University Press, 1996), 156; Dwight Eisenhower to Amon Carter, June 27, 1949, Box 71, 1949 File, AGC Papers, Burnett Library; Dwight Eisenhower to Amon Carter, Dec. 22, 1949, Box 71, 1949 File, AGC Papers, Burnett Library.
44. *Fort Worth Star-Telegram*, February 10, 1952; Dwight Eisenhower to Amon Carter, Mar. 1, 1952, Box 71, 1952 File, AGC Papers, Burnett Library.
45. Campbell, *Gone to Texas*, 416–17; Estes Kefauver, J. William Fulbright, and Paul Douglas to Amon Carter, Oct. 26, 1952, Box 140, Presidential Campaign File, AGC Papers, Burnett Library.
46. Robert Dallek, *Lone Star Rising: Lyndon Johnson and His Times, 1908–1960* (New York: Oxford University Press: 1991), 208–9, 221–24; Randall B. Woods, *LBJ: Architect of American Ambition* (New York: Free Press, 2006), 150–51; *Fort Worth Star-Telegram*, June 19, 1941; *Fort Worth Star-Telegram*, June 28, 1941; Amon Carter to Lyndon Johnson, June 30, 1941, Box 111, 1941 File, AGC Papers, Burnett Library; Lyndon Johnson to Amon Carter, July 2, 1941, Box 111, 1941 File, AGC Papers, Burnett Library.
47. *Fort Worth Star-Telegram*, July 4, 1948; *Fort Worth Star-Telegram*, July 18, 1948; Lyndon Johnson to Amon Carter, Dec. 28, 1948, Box 111, 1948 File, AGC Papers, Burnett Library.
48. Transcript, Claudia "Lady Bird" Johnson Oral History Interview XXII, 8/23/81, by Michael L. Gillette, Internet Copy, LBJ Library; Transcript, Claudia "Lady Bird"

Johnson Oral History Interview XXX, 3/22/82, by Michael L. Gillette, Internet Copy, LBJ Library.
49. *Fort Worth Star-Telegram,* July 24, 2004; Lucas to Carter, Mar. 20, 1954, Box 24, File 24, AGC Papers, Burnett Library.
50. *Fort Worth Star-Telegram,* July 22, 1954.
51. *Fort Worth Star-Telegram,* July 23, 1954.
52. Ibid.
53. *Fort Worth Star-Telegram,* July 25, 1954.
54. Nenetta Carter to Amon Carter, July 11, 1946, Box 38, Amon Carter Personal File 1946, AGC Papers, Burnett Library; Nenetta Carter to Amon Carter, June 20, 1953, Box 40, Amon Carter Personal File 1953, AGC Papers, Burnett Library.
55. *Fort Worth Star-Telegram,* August 20, 2002.
56. Katrine Deakins to City Hall Secretary, Apr. 13, 1953, Box 40, 1953 File, AGC Papers, Burnett Library; *Dallas Morning News,* March 12, 1953; Clint Murchison to Lyndon Johnson, Mar. 9, 1953, "Carter, Amon G.," LBJA Subject File, Box 106, LBJ Collection; Lyndon Johnson to Amon Carter, Mar. 10, 1953, "Carter, Amon G.," LBJA Subject File, Box 106, LBJ Collection.
57. *Dallas Morning News,* June 23, 1955; *Fort Worth Star-Telegram,* June 24, 1955; Letter, Lyndon Johnson to Amon Carter Jr., June 27, 1955, "Carter, Amon G.," LBJA Subject File, Box 106, LBJ Collection.
58. *Fort Worth Star-Telegram,* June 24, 1955.
59. *Dallas Morning News,* June 25, 1955; *Fort Worth Press,* June 27, 1955.
60. *Fort Worth Star-Telegram,* July 1, 1955.
61. Ibid.
62. *Fort Worth Star-Telegram,* June 25, 1955.

BIBLIOGRAPHY

MANUSCRIPT COLLECTIONS

Amon G. Carter Papers. Amon Carter Museum of American Art Archives, Fort Worth, Texas.
Amon G. Carter Papers. Special Collections, Mary Couts Burnett Library, Texas Christian University, Fort Worth, Texas.
Fort Worth Federal Writers Project, Fort Worth Public Library, Fort Worth, Texas.
Johnson, Lyndon Baines. Papers. Lyndon Baines Johnson Library, Austin, Texas. (Cited as LBJ Collection)
Paddock, Buckley Burton. Papers. Dolph Briscoe Center for American History, University of Texas at Austin, Austin, Texas.
Rayburn, Sam. Papers. Dolph Briscoe Center for American History, University of Texas at Austin, Austin, Texas.
Roosevelt, Franklin D. Papers as President. Franklin D. Roosevelt Library, Hyde Park, New York.
Southwest Collection/Special Collections Library, Texas Tech University, Lubbock, Texas.

GOVERNMENT DOCUMENTS

U.S. Census Bureau, 1870–1940. Washington, D.C. https://www.census.gov/en.html.

PUBLISHED PRIMARY SOURCES

Barnum, P. T. *The Life of P. T. Barnum*. New York: Redfield, 1855.
Ickes, Harold L. *The Secret Diary of Harold L. Ickes*. Vol. 1, *The First Thousand Days*. New York: Simon and Schuster, 1953.
Mencken, H. L. *Thirty-Five Years of Newspaper Work: A Memoir by H. L. Mencken*. Edited by Fred Hobson, Vincent Fitzpatrick, and Bradford Jacobs. Baltimore: Johns Hopkins University Press, 1994.
Rogers, Will. *Will Rogers' Daily Telegrams*. 4 vols. Edited by James M. Smallwood and Steven K. Gragert. Stillwater: Oklahoma State University Press, 1975–79.
———. *Will Rogers' Weekly Articles*. 6 vols. Edited by James M. Smallwood and Steven K. Gragert. Stillwater: Oklahoma State University Press, 1978–82.

NEWSPAPERS AND MAGAZINES

Alpine Avalanche, Alpine, Texas.
American City, New York, New York
Atlanta Journal Constitution
Baltimore Manufacturers' Record
Chicago Daily News
Commercial Appeal, Memphis, Tennessee.
Dallas Dispatch
Dallas Journal
Dallas Morning News
Dearborn Independent
Editor and Publisher, Irvine, California.
Fort Worth Daily Gazette
Fort Worth Press
Fort Worth Record-Telegram
Fort Worth Star-Telegram
Fourth Estate, New York, New York.
Hattiesburg American
Houston Chronicle
Houston Post
Korea Herald, Seoul, South Korea
Lake Como Weekly, Fort Worth, Texas
Miami Tribune
Nashville Tennessean
The Nation
New York Herald Tribune
New York Times
The Pecten, Shell Oil Company, Houston, Texas
Pittsburgh Post
Providence Journal
Saturday Evening Post

Temple Telegram
Time
Urbana Evening Courier
Waterloo Courier
West Texas Today, Abilene, Texas
Wichita Falls Record News

BOOKS

Abbott, Carl. *How Cities Won the West: Four Centuries of Urban Change in Western North America*. Albuquerque: University of New Mexico Press, 2008.

———. *The Metropolitan Frontier: Cities in the Modern American West*. Tucson: University of Arizona Press, 1995.

Alperin, Lynn M. *History of the Gulf Intracoastal Waterway*. Washington, D.C.: Institute for Water Resources, 1983.

Ambrose, Stephen E. *Eisenhower: Soldier, General of the Army, President-Elect, 1890–1952*. 2 vols. New York: Simon and Schuster, 1983.

Andersen, Gary Clayton. *Will Rogers and "His" America*. Boston: Prentice Hall, 2011.

Badger, Anthony J. *The New Deal: The Depression Years, 1933–1940*. New York: The Noonday Press, 1989.

Barksdale, E. C. *The Genesis of the Aviation Industry in North Texas*. Austin: University of Texas Bureau of Business Research, 1958.

Benton, Joe. *100 Years in Montague County, Texas*. Saint Jo, Tex.: IPTA Printers, 1958.

Bernstein, Irving. "Americans in Depression and War." In *A History of the American Worker*, ed. Richard B. Morris, 151–86. Princeton: Princeton University Press, 1983.

———. *Turbulent Years: A History of the American Worker, 1933–1941*. Boston: Houghton Mifflin, 1971.

Brady, Tim. "U.S. Airlines from 1930 to World War II." In *The American Aviation Experience: A History*, ed. Tim Brady, 171–84. Carbondale: Southern Illinois University Press, 2000.

Bremner, Robert H. *American Philanthropy*. 2nd ed. Chicago: University of Chicago Press, 1988.

———. *Giving: Charity and Philanthropy in History*. London: Transaction Press, 2000.

Brown, Norman D. *Hood, Bonnet, and Little Brown Jug: Texas Politics, 1921–1928*. College Station: Texas A&M University Press, 1984.

Brownell, Blaine A. *The Urban Ethos in the South, 1920–1930*. Baton Rouge: Louisiana State University Press, 1975.

Buenger, Victoria, and Walter L. Buenger. *Texas Merchant: Marvin Leonard and Fort Worth*. College Station: Texas A&M University Press, 1998.

Burrough, Bryan. *The Big Rich: The Rise and Fall of the Greatest Texas Oil Fortunes*. New York: Penguin Press, 2009.

Campbell, Randolph B. *Gone to Texas: A History of the Lone Star State*. New York: Oxford University Press, 2003.

———. "History and Collective Memory in Texas: The Entangled Stories of the Lone Star State." In *Lone Star Pasts: Memory and History in Texas*, ed. Gregg Cantrell and Elizabeth Hayes Turner, 270–82. College Station: Texas A&M University Press, 2007.

Carlson, Paul H., and Bruce A. Glasrud, eds. *West Texas: A History of the Giant Side of the State*. Norman: University of Oklahoma Press, 2014.

Cashion, Ty. *The New Frontier: A Contemporary History of Fort Worth and Tarrant County*. San Antonio: Historical Publishing Network, 2006.

Cates, Cliff Donahue. *Pioneer History of Wise County: From Red Men to Railroads—Twenty Years of Intrepid History*. St. Louis, Mo.: Nixon-Jones, 1907.

Conkin, Paul K. *The New Deal*. New York: Thomas Crowell, 1967.

Cox, Patrick. *The First Texas News Barons*. Austin: University of Texas Press, 2005.

———. "John Nance Garner." In *Profiles in Power: Twentieth-Century Texans in Washington*, ed. Kenneth Hendrickson Jr., Michael L. Collins, and Patrick Cox, 42–65. Austin: University of Texas Press, 2004.

Dallek, Robert. *Lone Star Rising*. Vol. 1, *Lyndon Johnson and His Times, 1908–1960*. New York: Oxford University Press, 1991.

Davidson, Rondel V. "La Reunion." *Handbook of Texas Online*. http://www.tshaonline.org/handbook/online/articles/uel01.

Davies, David R. *The Postwar Decline of American Newspapers, 1945–1965*. Westport, Conn.: Praeger, 2006.

Davis, Harold. *Henry Grady's New South: Atlanta, a Brave and Beautiful City*. Tuscaloosa: University of Alabama Press, 1990.

Davis, Kenneth S. *FDR: The War President, 1940–1943*. New York: Random House, 2000.

Edsforth, Ronald. *The New Deal: America's Response to the Great Depression*. Malden, Mass.: Blackwell, 2000.

Ely, Glen Sample. *Where the West Begins: Debating Texas Identity*. Lubbock: Texas Tech University Press, 2011.

England, B. Jane. "Wise County." *Handbook of Texas Online*. accessed December 4, 2016, http://www.tshaonline.org/handbook/online/articles/hcw14.

Fairchild, Byron, and Jonathan Grossman. *The Army and Industrial Manpower*. Washington, D.C.: Center of Military History, Department of the Army, 1959.

Fairclough, Adam. *Better Day Coming: Blacks and Equality, 1890–2000*. New York: Penguin Books, 2001.

Farman, Irvin. *The Fort Worth Club: A Centennial Story*. Fort Worth: The Fort Worth Club, 1985.

Fenberg, Steven. *Unprecedented Power: Jesse Jones, Capitalism, and the Common Good*. College Station: Texas A&M University Press, 2011.

Fenoglio, Melvin E., ed. *Story of Montague County, Texas: Its Past and Present*. Montague County, Tex.: Curtis Media, 1989.

Flemmons, Jerry. *Amon: The Life of Amon Carter, Sr., of Texas*. Austin, Tex.: Jenkins, 1978.

———. *Amon: The Texan Who Played Cowboy for America*. Lubbock: Texas Tech University Press, 1998.

Fort Worth Petroleum Club. *Oil Legends of Fort Worth*. Fort Worth: Taylor, 1993.

Freidel, Frank. *Franklin D. Roosevelt: A Rendezvous with Destiny*. Boston: Little, Brown, 1990.
Goldfield, David R. *Cotton Fields and Skyscrapers: Southern City and Region, 1607–1980*. Baton Rouge: Louisiana State University Press, 1982.
———. *Promised Land: The South since 1945*. Arlington Heights, Ill.: Harlan Davidson, 1976.
Graham, Don. *State Fare: An Irreverent Guide to Texas Movies*. Fort Worth: Texas Christian University Press, 2008.
Grantham, Dewey W. *The South in Modern America: A Region at Odds*. New York: Harper Perennial, 1995.
Green, George N. *The Establishment in Texas Politics: The Primitive Years, 1938–1957*. Norman: University of Oklahoma Press, 1984.
Gregg, Rosalie. *Wise County History: A Link With the Past*. Decatur, Tex.: Wise County Historical Survey Committee, 1975.
Hankins, Barry. *God's Rascal: J. Frank Norris and the Beginnings of Southern Fundamentalism*. Lexington: University of Kentucky Press, 1996.
Hart, Brian. "George Lewis Rickard." In *Handbook of Texas Online*. http://www.tshaonline.org/handbook/online/articles/fri15.
Hinton, Diana Davids, and Roger M. Olien. *Oil in Texas: The Gusher Age, 1895–1945*. Austin: University of Texas Press, 2002.
Jameson, John R. *The Story of Big Bend National Park*. Austin: University of Texas Press, 1996.
Jones, Jan. *Billy Rose Presents . . . Casa Mañana*. Fort Worth: Texas Christian University Press, 1999.
Kelley, Mary L. *The Foundations of Texan Philanthropy*. College Station: Texas A&M University Press, 2004.
Kennedy, David M. *Freedom from Fear: The American People in Depression and War, 1929–1945*. New York: Oxford University Press, 2001.
Knight, Oliver. *Fort Worth: Outpost on the Trinity*. Norman: University of Oklahoma Press, 1953.
Lipstadt, Deborah E. *Beyond Belief: The American Press and the Coming of the Holocaust, 1933–1945*. New York: Free Press, 1986.
MacDonald, Charles B. *The Mighty Endeavor: The American War in Europe*. New York: Da Capo Press, 1992.
Mason, Paul. *The First: The Story of Fort Worth's Oldest National Bank*. New York: Newcomen Society in North America, 1977.
McAdams, Ruth. "Mudholes, Fairy Godmothers, and Choir Bells." In *Grace and Gumption: Stories of Fort Worth Women*, ed. Katie Sherrod, 87–102. Fort Worth: Texas Christian University Press, 2007.
McComb, David. *The City in Texas: A History*. Austin: University of Texas Press, 2015.
Meek, Philip. *Fort Worth Star-Telegram: "Where the West Begins."* New York: Newcomen Society in North America, 1981.

Miller, Char, and Heywood T. Sanders. *Urban Texas: Politics and Development.* College Station: Texas A&M University Press, 1990.
Minor, David. "Crafton, TX." *Handbook of Texas Online.* Accessed December 4, 2016, http://www.tshaonline.org/handbook/online/articles/hncah.
Moore, Jerome. *Texas Christian University: A Hundred Years of History.* Fort Worth: Texas Christian University Press, 1974.
Nasaw, David. *The Chief: The Life of William Randolph Hearst.* Boston: Houghton Mifflin, 2000.
Neal, Steve. *Happy Days Are Here Again: The 1932 Democratic Convention, the Emergence of FDR—and How America Was Changed Forever.* New York: Harper Perennial, 2005.
Ohl, John Kennedy. *Hugh S. Johnson and the New Deal.* DeKalb: Northern Illinois University Press, 1985.
Olien, Roger M., and Diana Davids Hinton. *Wildcatters: Texas Independent Oilmen.* College Station: Texas A&M University Press, 2007.
Pate, J'Nell L. *Arsenal of Defense: Fort Worth's Military Legacy.* Denton: Texas State Historical Association. 2011.
———. *Livestock Legacy: The Fort Worth Stockyards, 1887–1987.* College Station: Texas A&M University Press, 1988.
Patenaude, Lionel V. *Texans, Politics, and the New Deal.* New York: Garland, 1983.
Patterson, James T. *Grand Expectations: The United States, 1945–1974.* New York: Oxford University Press, 1996.
Payne, Darwin, and Kathy Fitzpatrick. *From Prairie to Planes: How Dallas and Fort Worth Overcame Politics and Personalities to Build One of the World's Biggest and Busiest Airports.* Dallas: Three Forks Press, 1999.
Phillips, Michael. *White Metropolis: Race, Ethnicity, and Religion in Dallas, 1841–2001.* Austin: University of Texas Press, 2006.
Ragsdale, Kenneth. *The Year America Discovered Texas: Centennial '36.* College Station: Texas A&M University Press, 1987.
Reynolds, Clay. *A Hundred Years of Heroes: A History of the Southwestern Exposition and Livestock Show.* Fort Worth: Texas Christian University Press, 1995.
Rich, Harold. *Fort Worth: Outpost, Cowtown, Boomtown.* Norman: University of Oklahoma Press, 2014.
Rogers, Betty. *Will Rogers.* Norman: University of Oklahoma Press, 1979. Originally published 1941.
Rudel, Anthony J. *Hello, Everybody! The Dawn of American Radio.* Orlando, Fla.: Harcourt, 2008.
Sanders, Leonard. *How Fort Worth Became the Texasmost City.* Fort Worth: Texas Christian University Press, 1986.
Schlesinger, Arthur M. *The Politics of Upheaval.* Boston: Houghton Mifflin, 1960.
Selcer, Richard F. *Fort Worth: A Texas Original.* Austin: Texas State Historical Association, 2004.
———. *A History of Fort Worth in Black and White: 165 Years of African-American Life.* Denton: University of North Texas Press, 2015.

Serling, Robert J. *Eagle: The Story of American Airlines.* New York: St. Martin's Press, 1985.
Shapiro, Herbert. *White Violence and Black Response: From Reconstruction to Montgomery.* Amherst: University of Massachusetts Press, 1988.
Stickle, Arthur Waldo. *The State of Texas Book: One Hundred Years of Progress.* Austin: Bureau of Research and Publicity, 1937.
Terrell, Joseph. C. *Reminiscences of the Early Days of Fort Worth.* Fort Worth: Texas Christian University Press in cooperation with Texas Wesleyan University, 1999.
Tindall, George Brown. *The Emergence of the New South, 1913–1945.* Baton Rouge: Louisiana State University Press, 1967.
Tyler, Ron, Douglas E. Barnett, and Roy R. Barkley, eds. *The New Handbook of Texas.* 6 vols. Austin: Texas State Historical Association, 1996.
Van Zandt, K. M. *Force without Fanfare: The Autobiography of K. M. Van Zandt.* Fort Worth: Texas Christian University Press, 1968.
Wagner, William. *Reuben Fleet and the Story of Consolidated Aircraft.* Fallbrook, Calif.: Aero, 1976.
Welsh, Michael. *Landscape of Ghosts, River of Dreams: An Administrative History of Big Bend National Park.* Washington, D.C.: National Park Service, U.S. Dept. of the Interior, 2002.
Woods, Randall B. *LBJ: Architect of American Ambition.* New York: Free Press, 2006.
Woodward, C. Vann. *Origins of the New South, 1877–1913.* Baton Rouge: Louisiana State University Press, 1951.
Yagoda, Ben. *Will Rogers: A Biography.* New York: Knopf, 1993.

JOURNAL ARTICLES

Anderson, Paul Y. "Johnson and the Freedom of the Press." *The Nation,* August 30, 1933, 234–35.
Biles, Roger. "The Urban South in the Great Depression." *Journal of Southern History* 56, no. 1 (February 1990): 71–100.
Brown, Norman D. "Garnering Votes for 'Cactus Jack': John Nance Garner, Franklin D. Roosevelt, and the 1932 Democratic Nomination for President." *Southwestern Historical Quarterly* 104 (October 2000): 149–88.
Dollar, Charles M. "The South and the Fordney-McCumber Tariff of 1922: A Study in Regional Politics." *Journal of Southern History* 39, no. 1 (February 1973): 45–66.
Felt, Jeremy P. "The Child Labor Provisions of the Fair Labor Standards Act." *Labor History* 11, no. 4 (Fall 1970): 467–81.
Fischer, Claude S. "Changes in Leisure Activity, 1890–1940." *Journal of Social History* 27, no. 3 (1994): 453–75.
Gaughan, Anthony. "Woodrow Wilson and the Rise of Militant Interventionism in the South." *Journal of Southern History* 65, no. 4 (1999): 771–808.
Haas, Edward F. Review of *New Men, New Cities, New South: Atlanta, Nashville, Charleston, Mobile, 1860–1910,* by Don H. Doyle. *Journal of American History* 77, no. 4 (March 1991): 1370–71.
Henderson, Amy. "Media and the Rise of Celebrity Culture." *Organization of American Historians Magazine of History* 6, no. 4 (1992): 49–54.

Karnes, David. "The Glamorous Crowd: Hollywood Movie Premieres between the Wars." *American Quarterly* 38, no. 4 (1986): 553–72.

Lifset, Robert, and Brian C. Black. "Imaging the 'Devil's Excrement': Big Oil in Petroleum Cinema, 1940–2007." *Journal of American History* 99, no. 1 (June 2012): 135–44.

Lucko, Paul. "A Missed Opportunity: Texas Prison Reform during the Dan Moody Administration, 1927–1931." *Southwestern Historical Quarterly* 96, no. 1 (1992): 27–52.

Nemerov, Alexander. "Projecting the Future: Film and Race in the Art of Charles Russell." *American Art* 8, no. 1 (Winter 1994): 70–89.

Patenaude, Lionel V. "The Garner Vote Switch to Roosevelt: 1932 Democratic Convention." *Southwestern Historical Quarterly* 79, no. 2 (October 1975): 189–204.

Porter, David. "Representative Lindsay Warren, the Water Bloc, and the Transportation Act of 1940." *North Carolina Historical Review* 50, no. 3 (1973): 273–88.

Posner, Russell M. "California's Role in the Nomination of Franklin D. Roosevelt." *California Historical Society Quarterly* 39, no. 2 (June 1960): 121–39.

Rae, John B. "Financial Problems of the American Aircraft Industry, 1906–1940." *Business History Review* 39, no. 1 (Spring 1965): 99–114.

Rubin, Louis D., Jr. Review of *The Texas League: A Century of Baseball, 1887–1987*, by Bill O'Neal. *Southwestern Historical Quarterly* 92, no. 2 (October 1988): 383–84.

Rutland, Robert. "The Beginnings of Texas Technological College." *Southwestern Historical Quarterly* 55, no. 2 (October 1951): 231–39.

Schwarz, Jordan A. "John Nance Garner and the Sales Tax Rebellion of 1932." *Journal of Southern History* 30, no. 2 (May 1964): 162–80.

Stamm, Michael. "Newspapers, Radio, and the Business of Media in the United States." *Organization of American Historians Magazine of History* 24, no. 1 (January 2010): 25–28.

Whitman, James Q. "Of Corporatism, Fascism, and the First New Deal." *American Journal of Comparative Law* 39, no. 4 (October 1991): 747–78.

THESES AND DISSERTATIONS

Hooks, Michael Q. "The Struggle for Dominance: Urban Rivalry in North Texas, 1870–1910." PhD diss., Texas Tech University, 1979.

Ide, Yoshimitsu. "The Significance of Richard Hathaway Edmonds and his *Manufacturers' Record* in the New South." PhD diss., University of Florida, 1959.

Kinch, Samuel, Jr. "Amon Carter: Publisher-Salesman." Master's thesis, University of Texas at Austin, 1965.

Pinkney, Kathryn. "From Stockyards to Defense Plants, the Transformation of a City: Fort Worth, Texas, and World War II." PhD diss., University of North Texas, 2003.

INDEX

References to illustrations appear in italic type.

Allred, James, 151–53
American Airlines, 4, 119, 159–60, 187, 193, 195; Carter on board, 128–29, 131; founding, 67–68
American Airways. *See* American Airlines
American Copying Company (ACC), 17–19
American Newspaper Publishers Association (ANPA), 107, 178
Amon G. Carter Foundation, 5, 9, 42, 133, 205, 229n2; art purchases through, 185–86; donations, 179, 208; establishment, 176, 178–79
Arlington, Texas, 23, 25, 50, 53, 190–91
Armour and Company, 21–22, 33, 82
Atlanta Journal-Constitution, 6

Austin, Texas, 58, 66, 95–96, 124, 153
AVCO (Aviation Corporation), 67–68, 129–30
aviation. *See* American Airlines; Carter, Amon

Baltimore Manufacturers' Record, 6
Barnhart and Swasey Advertising Company, 19
Barron Collier, 25
Baugh, Sammy, 139
Bell Helicopter, 4
Big Bend National Park, *90*; creation of, 149–59
Big Bend Park Association, 153, 155, 157–59
Bowie, Texas., 4; Carter childhood in, 15–17, 19, 48–50, 113

Brooks, Addie Carter, 14, 50, *80*
Buchenwald, 175
Buck, Ray, 199–200
Budd, Ralph, 140–43
Burlington Railroad controversy, 139–43, 225n37
Burton, Willard, 24, 46
business progressivism, 8; Carter as business progressive, 6, 91–92, 99, 112, 128; philosophy, 27–29, 109; prominence in Texas, 55–56, 65

Carpenter, John, 122, 125, 152, 194, 207
Carter, Amon, 5, 6; and American Airlines, 67–68, 129–31; as art collector, 4, 132–34, 185, 208–9; aviation interests, 4, 44–45, 67–68, 119, 128–32, 159, 193–94; and baseball, 50–52; birth, 12; childhood and adolescence, 13–15; death, 207–8; Democratic Party, 55, 76–77, 91–92, 99–100, 101–3, 105, 107, 112, 115, 118, 195–98; early ventures, 15–17; founding of the *Star*, 23–24; legacy, 3–5, 208–9; literature, 9–10; marriage to Minnie Meacham Smith, 177, 204; marriage to Nenetta Burton, 46–47, 78, *83*, 144–46; marriage to Zetta Thomas, 19–20, 45–46; move to Fort Worth, 20, 23; oil, 5, 45–46, 119, 132–34; personal wealth, 53, 78, 132–33, 177; philanthropy, 41–43, 178–84, 208; purchase of the *Telegram*, 25–26; racial attitudes, 32, 70–71, 97, 181, 183; rivalry with Dallas, 7, 10, 41, 110–11, 129–30, 194, 207; Stetson "Shady Oak" hats, 72, 74, 101, 136; "Texas myth," 5, 133; as traveling salesman, 17–19; urban boosterism, 4–9, 27, 29, 92, 105–6, 118, 123, 128, 177, 209
Carter, Amon, Jr., 11, 144–46, 207; birth, 46; education, 147–48; heir to Carter Publishing, 48, 145, 205; POW status; 172–75; service in World War II, 172
Carter, Bertice, 19, 46–48, 77–78; career, 205; death, 206
Carter, Ella Patterson, 14, 49, *80*
Carter, Giles, 12, 13
Carter, Josephine Ream, 12–14, 212n2
Carter, Minnie Meacham, 177; marriage to Amon, 204; reaction to Amon's art, 18
Carter, Nenetta Burton, 13; and Amon Carter Foundation, 176, 178; marriage to Amon, 46–47, 78, *83*, 144–46; post-marriage life, 170–71, 174, 205
Carter, Ruth, 11, 134, 185, 205–6; birth, 78; relationship with Amon, 144–46, 170–71
Carter, William, 12, *80*; background, 13; death, 49; relationship with Amon, 48–49; vocation, 13–14, 48
Carter, Zetta Thomas, 11, 47, 50, 77–78; marriage to Amon, 19–20, 45–46, 78
Carter, Roy, 49
Chicago White Sox, 51–52
Civil Aeronautics Authority (CAA), 160–61, 193
Colorado and Southern Railroad, 139–41, 143
Connally, Tom, 100, 102, 106, 121, 169–70, 174, 194
Consolidated Aircraft, 5, 8, 149, 159; Carter's efforts to land, 165–69
Cooper, Gary, 136–37
Cox, Patrick, 6, 9, 28
Crafton, Texas, 12–14
Crafton Oil, 133
Culver Military Academy, 147–48, 172

Dachau (German concentration camp), 175
Dallas, Texas, 6, 17; and aviation, 159–61, 194; Big Bend National Park efforts, 152–54, 156; General Motors plant,

186–90; lynching of Allan Brooks, 32; rivalry with Carter, 7, 10, 41, 110–11, 129–30, 186, 194, 207; rivalry with Fort Worth, 7–8, 10, 21–22, 28, 41; Trinity Canal efforts, 120–23, 125–26, 128, 193
Dallas Herald, 24
Dallas Morning News, 10, 33, 37, 92, 125, 137, 205
Deakins, Katrine, 90, 146, 171, 179, 184, 186
Dealey, George, 8
Democratic National Convention (1928), 72–73, 76
Democratic National Convention (1932), 101–3
Dempsey-Tunney Fight, 77

Earhart, Amelia, 67
Editor and Publisher, 34, 39
Edmonds, Richard Hathaway, 6
Eisenhower, Dwight D., 3, 90, 150, 175, 177, 194; friendship with Carter 196–99, 204, 207–8
El Paso, Texas, 67, 186, 199
Evans, Silliman, 58, 60, 66, 124, 129

Farley, James, 77, 102, 105–6, 110, 115, 117
Ferguson, James "Pa," 56, 57, 59–65, 66, 93–94, 104
Ferguson, Miriam "Ma," 56, 59–65, 66, 93–94, 103–4, 151, 157
First Armored Division, 172
First National Bank, 48, 94
Fleet, Ruben, 165–68
Flemmons, Jerry, 9, 196
Fouts, John, 122–24, 162, 191
Fort Worth, Texas, 3–8; and aviation, 44–45, 67, 129–30, 159–61, 193–94; early growth and development, 20–22; early newspapers, 23–24; founding, 21; and General Motors, 186–91; and Great Depression, 92, 94–97, 99; identity of, 6, 20, 28, 164; and New Deal, 109–12; oil industry in, 28–30, 33, 45, 94; progressive era, 29–31; race riots in , 31; rivalry with Dallas, 7–8, 10, 21–22, 28, 41; segregation in, 22–23, 28, 30–31, 183; and Trinity Canal, 120–26, 162, 191–93; and World War I, 29–30; World War II, 164–69
Fort Worth and Denver Railroad, 16, 21, 49, 113; and Burlington controversy, 139–43
Fort Worth Board of Trade, 21, 27, 29, 43
Fort Worth Cats, 40, 52, 137
Fort Worth Chamber of Commerce, 31, 45, 167, 186, 191, 197, 227n26
Fort Worth Chief, 23
Fort Worth Club, 8, 23, 27, 97; founding, 43–44; Carter presidency, 44; Carter suite in, 69, 72–75, 185, 200
Fort Worth Democrat, 23–24
Fort Worth flood (1949), 180–82
Fort Worth Gazette, 24, 37, 43
Fort Worth Item, 22
Fort Worth National Bank, 8, 25
Fort Worth Press, 86, 110
Fort Worth Record, 28, 37–38
Fort Worth Star, 23–26
Fort Worth Star-Telegram, 4, 9, 39, 53, 95, 147–48; boosting tool, 41, 44; expansion and growth, 28, 32–35, 37–40, 78, 178; founding, 25–26; political influence, 55, 60–61, 64–66, 76, 92–93, 98, 101, 104, 112, 114, 115, 124, 141–43, 152–53, 153, 182, 194–95, 198, 199–201, 203–4; and West Texas, 7, 33, 40, 152
Fort Worth Telegram, 22–26
Foulois, Benjamin "Bennie," 128, 130
Fourth Estate (trade newspaper), 10, 34, 43
Free Milk and Ice Fund, 41–42
Frontier Centennial, 4; concept of, 109–10; funding, 111, 187–88

Garner, John Nance, 3, 106, 109, 194, 207; and New Deal, 91, 113–15; 1928 Democratic National Convention, 74; 1932 Democratic National Convention, 100–103; Roosevelt third term, 115–17
General Motors, 4, 8, 162, 177, 195; Carter's wooing, 186–91
Goldwyn, Samuel, 136–37
Goodfellows Fund, 41–42
Grady, Henry, 6
Great Depression, 92; Carter's response, 98–99; in Fort Worth, 94–95; in Texas, 93–94, 96–97
Greater Fort Worth International Airport (Amon Carter Field), 193–94, 206

Harriman, Averell, 129, 195
Hawks, Frank, 130–32
Hearst, William Randolph, 44, battle with Carter, 35–39; support of John Nance Garner candidacy, 100
Hobby, William P., 7, 57
Holden, William, 167, 169, 190–91
Hoover, Herbert, 73, 76; and Great Depression, 94, 98–99; and RFC creation, 111; WBAP, role in naming, 40
Hoover, J. Edgar, 173–74
Hoover, Lou, 17–18
Hopkins, Harry, 125
Houston, Texas, 7–8, 33, 56, 72–76, 96, 135, 154, 156, 162, 192
Houston Chronicle, 7
Houston Post, 37, 57, 93

Ickes, Harold, 173; and Big Bend National Park, 151, 158–59; clash with Carter, 116–17; PWA funding for Fort Worth, 109–10; Trinity Canal funding, 125
Interstate Commerce Commission (ICC), 140–43

Johnson, Hugh, and NRA newspaper code, 107–8
Johnson, Lady Bird, 196
Johnson, Lyndon B., 10, 206; break with Carter, 202; Carter support, 194, 199–202; eulogy for Carter, 1, 207
Johnston, Alva, 38; biographical sketch of Carter, 25, 135
Jones, Jesse, 7, 8, 73, 117, 156; Carter's death, 207; relationship with Carter, 105, 106, 152; and RFC, 91, 110–11, 166; as secretary of commerce, 161

Kay, Harry, 78
Kelley, Mary L., 9, 179
Kichai Indians, 12
Kinch, Samuel, 9, 38
Knight, Oliver, 9
Knudsen, William, 167–68, 186–87
Ku Klux Klan, 65; 116; Carter attitude toward, 64–65; and Fergusons, 60, 64; 1928 Democratic National Convention, 74–75

labor, 55, 98; Carter attitude toward, 106–7, 108–9, 112–14, 169–70, 195; and New Deal, 112–13
Lake Como, 183
Lake Como Weekly, 183
Lanham, Fritz, 121–22
La Reunion, 13, 212n
Lena Pope Home, 179–80
Leonard, Marvin, 229n6
Lindsay, Miriam, 96
Love Field, 159, 193
Lucas, Wingate, 202–4

McAdoo, William, 102–3
McCaleb, D. C., 23
McIntyre, O. O., 69–72
McNary-Watres Act, 129
Meacham Field, 68, 159, 165

Mencken, H. L.: at 1928 Democratic National Convention, 72–76; at 1932 National Democratic Convention, 103
Miller, Roy, 120–22
Montague County, Texas, 14, 15
Moody, Dan, 56; battle with Fergusons, 60–64; as governor, 65–66; and Great Depression, 93
Moody, Mildred, 66
Monnig, William, 121, 123
Mosig, Carl, 125
Mt. Gilead Baptist Church, 97

National Industrial Recovery Act, 109, 197
National Recovery Administration (NRA), 221n31; creation, 107; newspaper code, 107–8
Neff, Pat, 56, 64, 65; and creation of Texas Tech, 57–58
New Deal, 4, 56, 78, 103, 117–18; Carter's attitude toward, 91–92, 99, 106–7, 109, 112–15
New South, 20, 91, 211–12n6; movement/philosophy, 6, 128; race in, 181, 183
Nocona, Texas, 14, 50
Norris, J. Frank, 34, 51, 214n11

O'Brien, Davey, 84, 137, 139
O'Daniel, Wilbert Lee "Pappy," 154; Senate race (1941), 199–200; Big Bend National Park efforts, 155–58
oil. See Carter, Amon; oil industry; oil interests and Fort Worth
Ousely, Clarence, 37

Paddock, B. B., 23–24
presidential election (1928), 76–77
presidential election (1932), 101–3, 105
Public Works Administration (PWA), 107; funding for Will Rogers Memorial, 109

racial segregation, 20, 22–23, 31; Carter's attitude toward, 28, 97, 181–83
Rayburn, Sam, 10, 170, 173; 1932 Democratic National Convention, 102; and Trinity Canal, 122, 127
Reconstruction Finance Corporation (RFC), 91, 100, 106, 110–12, 166
Record, A. G., 23
Red Cross, 96, 99, 175, 180–81
Remington, Frederic, 4, 133–34, 185
Richardson, Sid, 8, 90, 132, 182, 196–97, 199, 201
Rivercrest Country Club, 32, 53, 78, 83, 145, 183, 185, 207
Rodgers, Cal, 44, 82, 216n31
Rodgers, Woodall, 160–61
Rogers, Will, 10, 40, 134, 137; charity efforts, 96–99; columns about Carter, 69, 72, 100–101, 104–5; death, 132; friendship with Carter, 73–74, 77, 209
Roosevelt, Eleanor, 173
Roosevelt, Elliott, 106, 111–12, 126, 130, 167
Roosevelt, Franklin D., 4, 16, 91–92, 173, 194; Big Bend National Park creation, 150–51, 155–59; New Deal, 108–18; 1932 Democratic nomination, 100–105; Trinity Canal efforts, 126–27; World War II, 164–70
Rose, Billy, 3, 111, 188, 208
Russell, Charles, 4, 133–34

San Antonio, Texas, 8, 33, 96
San Antonio Express, 92
Seventh Street Gang, 8
Shady Oak Farm, 67, 69, 72, 74, 88–89, 101, 106, 122, 135, 137, 181
Sheppard, Morris, 100, 106, 121–22, 158, 167, 169, 194, 199
Shivers, Allan, 207
Sloan, Alfred P., 189
Small, Clint, 93
Smith, C. R., 131
Southern Air Transport, 67–68

Southwestern Exposition and Fat Stock Show, 109, 111
Speck, Hugh, 205
Sterling, Ross, 56, 93–94, 99; Great Depression, 103–5
Stevenson, Adlai, 198, 202
Stevenson, Coke, 154–55, 158–59; 1948 Senate campaign, 200
St. Joseph Hospital, 147, 179, 182, 206, 229n10
Stripling, W. C., 52
Stripling, W. K., 8, 25, 52
Swasey, Edgar, 19, 35
Swift and Company, 21–22, 33, 123

Texas Air Transport (TAT), 67–68
Texas and Pacific Railroad, 21, 52, 190
Texas Centennial, 109–11
Texas Christian University, 10, 52, 179, 207; Carter's support of football team, 137, 139; stadium funding, 138–39
Texas Federation of Women's Clubs, 96, 157
Texas Technological College, 4, 6; establishment of, 57–59; Carter on board, 64–65
Tidelands controversy, 195–96, 198
Time, 6, 10, 13, 106, 145
Trinity Improvement Association (TIA), 120, 162, 192–93
Trinity River Canal Association (TRCA), 120–27
Trinity River canalization, 9, 119–28, 161–63, 191–93, 197, 202, 223n4
Trinity River Navigation Association (TRNA), 120–22, 125
Truman, Harry S, 90, 177–78, 194, 197, 200–202; Tidelands controversy, 195–96

United Auto Workers (UAW), 112, 195

Van Zandt, Khleber, 23

Walker, Jimmy, 69, 135
Waggoner, W. T. "Pappy," 30, 94–95, 138, 225n35
Waples, Paul, 24–26, 31–33
Wasson Field, 133–34, 137
Watson, Edwin, 167
WBAP Radio, 4, 27, 39–41, 65, 98, 122, 154, 158
WBAP-TV, 4, 178
West Texas, 29, 38, 58–59, 132–33; Carter and, 4, 7, 27, 33, 40–41, 45, 54, 101, 117, 122, 150–53, 179, 209, 230n29; Fort Worth's relationship with, 20, 22, 28, 30, 143, 186
Wise County, Texas, 12, 13
Westerner, The, 136–37
West Texas Chamber of Commerce (WTCC), 58, 142
Wheeler-Lea Transportation Act, 127–28, 161
Whiteman, Paul, 111, 135, 207
Will Rogers Memorial Complex, 4, 109–11, 137, 209
World War I, 29–30, 45
World War II, 149; and Amon Carter Jr., 172–76; impact on Big Bend National Park efforts, 156–58; mobilization for, 163–65
Wortham, Louis, 32, 34–35, 41
Wright, Jim, 177; 1954 campaign, 202–4

YMCA, 42–43

www.ingramcontent.com/pod-product-compliance
Lightning Source LLC
Chambersburg PA
CBHW020932180426
43192CB00036B/648